S0-BXX-424

A WOMAN'S GUIDE TO SPECTATOR SPORTS

KATHRYN LANCE

A & W Visual Library
New York

Other books by Kathryn Lance

GETTING STRONG

RUNNING FOR HEALTH AND BEAUTY

Copyright © 1980 by Kathryn Lance

All rights reserved. No part of this work may be reproduced or transmitted in any form or by any means, electronic or mechanical, including photocopying, recording, or any information storage and retrieval system, without permission in writing from the publisher.

Published by
A & W Publishers, Inc.
95 Madison Avenue
New York, New York 10016

Text design by Ronald F. Shey

Art by Richard Sheinaus

Library of Congress Cataloging in Publication Data

Lance, Kathryn.
    A woman's guide to spectator sports.

    Bibliography: p.
    Includes index.
    1. Sports. 2. Sports for women. I. Title.
GV704.L36   1980   796   79-23448
ISBN 0-89104-182-6 (paper)   0-89104-183-4 (cloth)

Printed in the United States of America

To the memory of my sister Margaret Jane and my grandmother Agnes Beach Haisley, who both loved baseball truly, deeply, and with a sense of fun.

CONTENTS

FOREWORD

When friends and colleagues learned that I was working on a book about spectator sports, their most common reaction was along these lines: "What are you, a traitor? You've been writing about physical fitness for years. Why are you suddenly encouraging people to sit in front of the tube and get flabby?"

I was surprised and dismayed by this reaction, because, of course, that was not my intention at all. In fact, I became interested in spectator sports myself largely as a result of my own participation in sports, which began only in my late twenties and early thirties. But I found that understanding spectator sports was often as difficult for a novice as beginning a program of physical fitness: both topics are often made obscure by the jargon of experts who have forgotten that they, too, were once beginners. It was and is my intention to clear up this confusion, to break through the mystique surrounding spectator sports.

Still, I admit there is a danger in urging women (or men) to become informed spectators. Not only are a growing variety of pro and semipro sports available in most American cities, but there are more sports shows on TV than any other category of programming. If you tried to catch everything that is available, you would never leave the TV set for more than a few minutes at a time. Therefore I urge all readers, whatever their interest in watching sports, to participate in sports first. In fact, playing a sport is one of the best ways of learning about it (which is one reason men generally know so much more about sports than women). Go out and jog, swim, play tennis, even shoot a few baskets, and then, tired and exhilarated from the joy of physical effort, shower off, open a can of beer or soda, and settle down to watch your favorite team in action.

ACKNOWLEDGMENTS

This book would not have been possible without the help of a great many people. I want first of all to thank my consultants, who patiently answered my many questions and went over the manuscript for accuracy. (Any errors are, of course, my responsibility.) These generous people are: Steve Goldstein, of the *New York Daily News;* Ray Siegener, of Sports Productions, Inc.; Robert Cenedella, writer and baseball lover; John Sposato, artist and basketball lover; Jack Feuer, soccer writer; and Shirley Walton, hockey writer and radio personality.

In addition I want to thank the following for their special help: Elizabeth Phillips of the National Football League; Arthur Richmond of the New York Mets; Lindsey Nelson, formerly of the Mets; Paul Blocker of the Sun Bowl; Louise Maxon Rae of the *El Paso Times;* Beverly Eckman of the *Detroit News;* Jim Bouton of WCBS News; the publicity departments of the New York Knicks, the New York Rangers, and the Baseball Hall of Fame; and the Office of the Commissioner of Baseball.

For their helpful suggestions and additions to the manuscript I want to thank also David Grambs and Bert Sugar.

Many friends and acquaintances shared with me their own knowledge of and love of sports. I particularly want to thank Carson Rutherford, Bob Abel, Peter Bradley, Jon Fried, John Filcea, Dale Fuller, George Nuttycombe, Jack Shanahan, Serge Dusolliet, and my running buddies Bernie Schneider, Jean Bonhomme, Bob Scalice, and Phil Eder.

For their patience and support during all those months when I did nothing but talk about, read about, and watch sports, I want to thank my parents, John F. and Kathryn H. Lance; my brother and sister-in-law, John and Daphna Levit-Lance; Betsy Cenedella; Connie Graham; M. Kathleen Erie; Dave McKay; Valerie Andrews; Gene Busnar; Ana Pacheco; Ed Gilbert; Joe Ambrosino; and Alan Harbater. Thanks also to everyone at the Allstate, including John Rogers, Peter Christianson, George Mwangosi, George Burns, Diane Greenfield, Irv Elias, Richard Goldberg, Mark Gordon, Herb Rippe, Tom Keating, Mike Slater, Chris Humphrey, and especially Mike Roberts, for his imitations of Howard Cosell.

I am very fortunate in having as a friend and editor Diane Giddis, who continues to help me grow as a writer. I want to thank her for her good judgment, thoughtfulness, and the long hours of hard work she has given to this project.

Finally, I want to thank Terry Wolf and Nan Schubel for their help in preparing the manuscript, as well as for their friendship and moral support; and very special thanks to Nina Kimenker, without whose dedication, intelligence, and cheerfulness I could never have finished the book.

PART 1
MEN, WOMEN,
AND SPORTS —
AN INTRODUCTION

CHAPTER 1
WHY SHOULD A WOMAN WATCH MEN'S SPORTS?

If you're already a fan of one or more spectator sports, I don't need to tell you about the lure of sports. It is a gut level attraction, something like falling in love. The more you care for the person or the sport, the harder it is to explain. "Well, yes, I know Harvey's funny-looking, but he's so *sweet*" is not very different from, "All right, so the Giants haven't had a winning season in ten years, but wait till next year." To the nonfan, the idea of millions of Americans watching thousands of hours of sports programming each year is as incomprehensible as Harvey's sex appeal may be to your mother.

Although there are thousands of women who love sports just as much as men do, a far greater number are turned off by the very idea of sports. There is probably not an American woman alive who has come through our public or private school systems without at least being exposed to football, baseball, and basketball. But most women don't know very much about what is going on in these games because we haven't played them. And even the most knowledgeable female fan is seldom a devotee of many sports to the extent that a majority of men are. Following sports seems to require a knowledge of complex terminology and statistics, and for many sports the love of violence and bloodshed as well. Furthermore, there are so many different sports that just keeping them straight requires an effort. Finally, with the new cultural emphasis on participating in sports for fun and fitness, organized spectator sports may appear old-fashioned and outmoded, doomed to a slow extinction by attrition.

Yet this is not so. On the contrary, pro sports is one of America's biggest and fastest growing industries. A recent poll in *TV Guide* indicated that 90 percent of all men and 76 percent of all women watch at least some sports programming each year. And gate attendance for all major sports continues to rise each year, even though the price of tickets is rising too.

Why are so many people watching so many sports?

Well, for one thing, because sports are there. Watching a game passes the time. And if it's in the company of other people, it passes the time in an agreeable way. Go into any bar in this country on a Sunday afternoon in the fall and you will find a sizable knot of spectators (mostly if not entirely men) gathered around the TV set watching football games and exchanging comments and predictions ("Those turkeys don't have a chance." "Look at Wackenhut run!"). The game provides otherwise separate lonely people, who have little in common, with a chance to come together for a few hours and interact without the responsibility of real relationship. These shared games may lead to arguments, of course, but this is yet another purpose of spectator sports: to allow pent-up aggressions a harmless outlet. (It is also true that sports arguments can lead to serious fights and even murders, usually when the participants have been drinking). One reason arguing about sports is such a good way to let off steam is that most disputes are easily resolved. They center on statistics, for example, which can be looked up (the score of a close game in 1971, or the exact rule about some obscure point in hockey); or they are matters of opinion that unlike opinions on politics and religion, don't really challenge or threaten anyone. (Is artificial grass ruining the game of baseball? Who was the greatest quarterback of all time?)

Another reason people watch sports is to be part of a historic event. In any given year, for any given sport, some important record or other will be broken, and there is something extremely satisfying about witnessing such an occurrence. This sort of drama was played out in the summer of 1978 when Pete Rose, the third baseman for the Cincinnati Reds baseball team, was on a hitting streak. For a period of several weeks Rose broke record after record. As he began to approach the all-time record, prime-time television was interrupted whenever he came up to bat, so that no one would miss the dramatic moment when Pete either set another record or ended his streak. The same year, the Muhammad Ali–Leon Spinks boxing rematch, in which Ali was attempting to win the World Championship title for an unprecedented third time, was likewise considered a major event. Spectators paid as much as fifty dollars for seats over a quarter mile from the boxing ring, while the broadcast of that show had one of the largest audiences in television history. In both cases, the majority of spectators probably knew little about the sport involved, but simply wanted to be present during a magical moment.

To most spectators, these record-breaking happenings are more than just sporting achievements: they are in a sense a link with the past. Cities and major corporations may fail, the atmosphere and oceans may grow ever more polluted, the climate may even change, but one thing is eternal: the sports records books. All new records are at once a bettering of and an affirmation of the old records, of the history of sport and of ourselves.

Finally, and perhaps most importantly, people watch sports to have fun. Whether you're cheering yourself hoarse at the ball park or stadium, or simply relaxing with snacks in your own living room while ten men play basketball on your TV screen, sports gives you a chance to unwind, relax, smile, and have an old-fashioned good time. Even casual spectators get caught up in the fun and excitement of a game, and for true fans a good sporting event beats any other form of entertainment.

Most of the reasons I have discussed for watching sports apply to both men and women. But for women there are two further reasons to watch sports. One of these is that you may have no choice. The most familiar example of a captive sports-watcher is the so-called football widow, who is depicted as spending all her weekends abandoned and resentful while her husband or boyfriend sits glued to the tube. It needn't be a boyfriend or lover, of course; when I was a teen-ager my younger sister was a baseball fan to the exclusion of almost all else. Occasionally I would go to games with her and sit there mystified while she cheered and kept score. Because I enjoyed her company I kept attending games and watching them with her on television, but it was years before baseball was more to me than an ordeal to be gotten through.

If you are some version of a football widow you can, of course, simply ignore the sports fanatics around you, but that isn't easy to do in a country where ignorance of sports is tantamount to ignorance of society itself. Furthermore, if you are a businesswoman, your ignorance of sports may be hindering your career.

In *Men in Groups,* writer Lionel Tiger discusses the place of sports in society. Speculating on the purpose of spectator sports, he quotes the sociologist Rolf Meyersohn, who maintains that spectators don't get anything "useful" from sports. Rather, "What they get is this: a common interest is developed and perpetuated which enables virtually any American male to carry on intense conversations with any other."

This communicative aspect of sports is one of the foundations of the American business community. The common language, sports, serves not only as an icebreaker to begin business dealings, but also as a kind of badge of identity. As Pearl Meyer, a woman executive, says in *Money* magazine, "They're not really talking about baseball. They're really saying, 'Hello. How are you? We have a lot in common.'"

A woman who can't speak that language starts any business interaction with a built-in disadvantage. This is not to say that women executives must be able to spout baseball statistics or compare the defensive capabilities of all NBA teams, but rather that any woman with some knowledge of these things will find it easier to relax with her male colleagues; sport is, as we have seen, the perfect nonthreatening way to make small talk.

There is a further practical advantage for a businesswoman to be familiar with sports: just as growing numbers of female executives are taking male clients to dinner, so many of them are now attending sporting events in the box seats reserved by many corporations for business entertainment. A woman who finds herself hosting or being invited to such a function will find it helpful to have at least some idea of what is going on during the game.

With all these good reasons to join the majority of sports-watchers in this country, it is still difficult for a female would-be fan to become better informed about any sport. In fact, the more of a sport illiterate you are, the harder it is to learn about any sport you are interested in. This is so for a variety of reasons. One is that most traditional guides to watching sports are filled with the same jargon and double-talk used by sportscasters. Since most sportswriters and sportscasters are men who are speaking to other men, the assumption is that their audience has at least a working knowledge of the major team sports, having played them. But if you don't already know a running back from a cornerback, the infield from the outfield, a pick from a rebound, you will only be further confused.

Asking a friend or loved one usually doesn't help much either because many fans tend to overexplain, answering your questions in such detail that you are left more befuddled than ever; others, while wanting to be helpful, may justifiably resent being interrupted in the middle of a game. Besides, if you're like most people, you may find it embarrassing to ask a question that seems extremely basic, reasoning that you should already know.

The purpose of this book is to answer those questions about sports you were embarrassed to ask. It is a basic guide to the five most important team sports in America. I make no assumptions about your level of knowledge of the game, although each section is organized in such a way that you can skip the fundamentals of any sport you're already familiar with.

Beyond an outline of each sport, this book defines sports terminology and provides a guide to following sports in person and through the media. While it won't make you an expert, it will enable you to knowledgeably talk and read about sports, and to know what questions to ask when something puzzling comes up.

Whether you want to learn more about sports for business reasons, for your own pleasure, or simply to find out more about a game you already like, this guide should help you to understand the world of men's professional sports. Which brings us to the title of this chapter: Why should a woman watch *men's* sports?

The answer is simple: on the professional level—that is, on the level at which games are televised, written about, and discussed in the media—men's sports is all there is. We'll take a look at some of the reasons for this in the next chapter.

CHAPTER

2 THE JOCK MYSTIQUE

In *Annie Hall*, the Oscar-winning comedy of 1977, there was a scene that summed up typical American assumptions about men and sports. The hero, played by Woody Allen, is seen hiding out from the crush of a boring cocktail party in his host's bedroom, glued to a televised Knicks basketball game. After a while his wife comes in and tries to persuade him to return to the party. She is presented as a pretentious nag who doesn't understand that Woody needs to be alone, away from her superficial world, in communion with his sport.

Another movie from the same year, *House Calls*, makes much the same point. In this movie Walter Matthau wants to watch a basketball game, which had been played earlier but is to be televised on a tape replay. Glenda Jackson, with whom he is spending the evening, offhandedly tells him the final score of the game just as he is about to start watching it. The ensuing tantrum thrown by Mr. Matthau shows us how deeply important sports is to the average male, and how insensitive to it all is the lovely and otherwise intelligent Ms. Jackson.

Unfortunately, there is more than a germ of truth in this view of sports as essentially a male domain. In spite of the fact that more women are participating in and watching sports than ever before, on almost every level of spectator sports there is widespread if largely unrecognized discrimination against women. This discrimination is perhaps most obvious in large sports complexes, where bathroom facilities for women are less adequate than those for men, as well as in the growing use of sexy, half-naked cheerleaders on the sidelines of football games. Somewhat less obvious is the systematic exclusion of women from the sports establishment. For example, a few hours of watching televised sports will demonstrate that nearly all announcers for any sport are men. Only for women's events, such as women's tennis or gymnastics, is there a token female expert, usually an ex-player. Even when you do see a woman sports announcer or commentator, she is more likely to have been chosen for her beauty than for her knowledge of sports.

Women sportswriters fare no better. Although more women are being allowed to do a little writing about sports for various magazines and newspapers, they are almost always assigned mainly to cover women's events, or unisex contests such as equestrian events. The women who cover other sports equally with men make up a small fraction of one percent of sportswriters in the country.

Even those few women who have managed to land jobs as sports reporters are at a disadvantage, because with few exceptions they are excluded from male athletes' locker rooms. Now I have to admit that this explosive question seems at first to be a tempest in a teapot. To the average fan, all that is important is that the game be reported, and it doesn't really matter who does the reporting or from where. Still, the very idea of a woman in a man's locker room—which is, after all, where almost all postgame interviewing takes place—provokes violent reactions, usually on the order of: "Not till they let men in women's dressing rooms!" This seems to be a valid point, but in fact it avoids the real issue, which is that women's sports are not televised and written about to the same extent as men's sports—in fact, they are barely covered at all. Therefore, any woman who wishes to write about or broadcast a sport that is considered important and that will help her get exposure as a writer is being denied access to the same information as her male colleagues.

There are no women officials in any men's sports. The one would-be exception was Bernice Gera, whose heartbreaking story is related by Nora Ephron in *Crazy Salad*. Gera had grown up a baseball fanatic and wanted nothing more in the world than to participate somehow in the game. Ignoring all advice, she paid her own way through umpires' school, where she put up with insults and abuse to learn how to officiate her favorite sport. Upon graduation, she found that no jobs were open to her. Finally, after years of self-sacrifice and dedication, Gera was hired to work in a minor-league game, only to discover that her co-umpire refused even to communicate with her. The strain led her to commit one mistake during the game, and the predictable if unfair scorn and derision that followed proved too much for her: she resigned from baseball.

But it is as players that woman are most seriously discriminated against, and that is why this book is a guide to men's sports. For although women play all sports that men play, women fans seldom get a chance to hear about them, much less to see them. Unless you live in a college town in New England, for example, you probably don't know that ice hockey is one of the fastest-growing intercollegiate sports for women. If you don't scan the fine print on the sports pages of a large metropolitan newspaper, you are probably unaware of the existence of women's pro softball and basketball leagues. There are many such leagues, both in schools and on a pro and semipro level. But they are very difficult for most women fans to find out about because they are not covered by the media, especially television. (In the summer of 1978, the men's open golf tournament received three days of continuous coverage for over ten hours of programming. The comparable women's tournament was scheduled for two hours of coverage on two consecutive days—this despite the fact that one of the participants was the exciting young player Nancy Lopez, who had already won more tour money her first year than any other player, woman *or* man.)

The sad fact is that those who schedule prime-time sports simply won't give women athletes a chance. It is a self-fulfilling prophecy: there is very little women's sports available; therefore nobody wants to see women's sports. To this many men add that women's sports are much less interesting than men's sports. (Of course, most of these men have probably never even seen women's sports.) Yet, if women's sports are so uninteresting, why did the Women's Basketball League draw relatively large crowds in its first year, despite the fact that most of the teams have to play in such facilities as remote high school gymnasiums? And how can men who avidly watch sexy cheerleaders going through jumping routines claim that it's deathly boring to watch women athletes with beautifully conditioned bodies being active and skillful?

It is this seeming contradiction that is, I believe, at the root of all the discrimination against women in sports, both as participants and as spectators: the institutionalizing of sports as an all-male activity comparable in solemnity to ancient lodge rituals.

These rituals, characteristic of primitive societies, served the purpose of defining roles for men and women and of training youngsters in the sex-specific skills they would need as adults. Division of labor along sexual lines was probably important to the survival of the creatures who became modern humans, and I'm by no means the first to propose that organized sports are a throwback to those days. In *Men in Groups* Lionel Tiger suggests that "sports behavior is functionally equivalent to the hunting pattern with which the human male has been endowed by evolution." In other words, Tiger, who believes that hunting behavior is instinctive, feels that participation in team sports fulfills an inborn need for group male activity that is not available to modern men in other ways. And certainly the fact that most teams consist of nine to eleven players, which according to Robert Ardrey is the optimal size for a hunting band, is suggestive. It may also help to explain, in part, the hostility of men when it comes to women in sports: as Ardrey points out in *The Social Contract,* any men who allowed women into their hunting band would be at a disadvantage in terms of survival because the women would be somewhat slower, less strong, and handicapped by pregnancy much of the time.

In most primitive societies, there were separate lifelong ritualistic activities for the two sexes, with clearly marked rites of passage between childhood and adulthood. On the men's side, such rituals might include sacred dances, secret signs, and even a secret language, all of which must be strictly kept from the women. Males were trained to belong to the men's group from the time they were little boys, and usually joined only after a painful initiation rite designed to show bravery and the ability to bear pain. If the women were allowed to participate in these activities at all, it was generally as passive spectators of special shows or dances, with the true meaning of the ritual remaining sacred and inviolate.

Let's compare primitive rituals to commercial spectator sports in America today. First, little boys start to train for the "lodge" from early childhood. Although some little girls are very interested in sports, it's mostly little boys who memorize baseball statistics, collect sports cards, and follow their teams from a very young age. It's also little boys who begin to play sports and then stick with it; most girls, even those who are so-called tomboys, generally stop playing active sports by their teens. Not only does societal pressure encourage them to engage in more "feminine" pursuits, but girls have far fewer athletic role models to follow.

Like the lodge, sports has its rites of passage: in place of the transition from childhood to manhood, players move from sandlot or college ball to professional sports, and an important part of membership in the club seems to be how much pain a player can or is willing to take. If you doubt this, pick up any sports magazine and read about football players. It is not only common but expected for an injured player to stay in the game unless he is actually disabled. Many football and basketball players end their careers virtual cripples. But it is a point of pride to be able to "take the pain," to prove you are a man, and to be able to return that pain by deliberately injuring other players. Much of the language of sports reflects this attitude: football players speak of giving and receiving "punishment." "Hitting" is one of the main features of both hockey and football, and far from being an exaggeration, the term is usually an understatement. Intimidation and fear are a major part of the relationship between the pitcher and the batter in baseball. The idea of playing with pain, of giving everything, including the integrity of one's body, to the team/club/lodge is so extreme that injured players will enter a game anesthetized to the point where they can bear the pain of possibly severe injuries. The danger of playing in such a state is obvious, as Bob Gross, a basketball player for the Portland Trail Blazers, reported after a game in which he was seriously hurt: "I didn't even feel it when my ankle broke—just heard the snap."

This is not to say that great female athletes never play while they are injured or in discomfort, but in women's sports pain is not glorified as an end in itself the way it is in men's sports. Men can no longer undergo painful puberty rites or prove themselves by going one-on-one with a saber-toothed tiger, so they do it through suffering in sports, and by combating other athletes in continuing mock battles.

Just as primitive women were excluded both from participation in the hunt and watching of the male rituals, so today we are excluded from participating in and appreciating men's sports. We are allowed along for the ride if we wish, but only as cheerleaders. Women are not announcers because we are not supposed to know the meaning of the sacred words. Letting a woman into a locker room contaminates the purity of the sport just as letting her into the lodge would jeopardize the sanctity of the men's rituals.

This view is reflected in the following report of a football game (as quoted in *Leftfield*), which appeared in the *Cleveland Plain Dealer* on February 26, 1978: "After their halftime stint, the girls [the Cleveland Cavalettes] return to their seats, neatly lined up like obedient wives tending to women's business while the menfolk retire to the den for cigars and rank talk, the ancient tribal rite's solemn stateliness being broken only when some of the more excitable girls yell, stamp, or raise triumphant fists at a well-executed play."

Even James Michener, who bends over backward to be fair to women throughout his book, *Sports in America*, draws the line at co-ed sports. His argument seems to be that women of any age or any level of ability should not be permitted to compete on an equal basis with men because a woman who wins humiliates a man. He admits that this is not fair, but points out that this is how things are, and how they *should* be is irrelevant.

As women win more and more gains in the drive for equality and as the traditional roles begin to blur and fuse, the exclusivity of men's sports seems to become even more entrenched. In fact, in many ways sports seem to be a kind of last bastion of male supremacy. I do not mean to imply that there is a conscious conspiracy to keep women ignorant of sports, but rather that discrimination against women is perhaps more pervasive throughout the world of sports than in any other (primarily) masculine endeavor.

Although these are some of the reasons I believe spectator sports have traditionally been inaccessible to women, in the rest of this book I hope to show that sports are not nearly so arcane as they appear. I know that I may be accused, in writing this book, of further slowing the acceptance of women's sports by giving even more emphasis to men's sports. However, I believe that only when more women become informed spectators as well as athletes, only when we learn the "lodge secrets" and show that we are indeed as sophisticated about sports as men, will doors begin to open to us. As growing numbers of women demonstrate their interest in spectator sports, the policy makers—those men who control the funding of sports and sports programming—will have to take notice. A nation of women spectators will not tolerate exclusively male coverage of exclusively male sports, nor will we continue to pay directly (through ticket prices) and indirectly (through taxes) for sports arenas that provide few if any women's sporting events. When enough of us demand equal rights in all areas of sports, it will become a matter of economic necessity for the sports establishment to admit women—as announcers, commentators, writers, and ultimately on a business level. Only when we ourselves have become policy makers will women's sports attract the financial backing and media attention accorded to men's sports today.

In the meantime, there is much in men's sports that is enjoyable by both sexes, and the more knowledgeable you are about these sports, the better you will be able to follow women's sports when and where they become available.

CHAPTER 3 THE WORLD OF SPORTS

THE OWNERS

In moments of wild fantasy I sometimes think that if I ever got rich I would buy a baseball team. Imagine the fun: following my personal team throughout the season, participating in strategic decisions about the game and personnel, and, best of all, always having the best seats in the house.

This fantasy shows precisely why I would be a failure as a sports owner. In the early days of pro sports, many owners were wealthy individuals who loved a sport, but such owners are becoming rare these days. Now corporations and consortiums own teams, and those few individuals who are owners are usually more interested in tax shelters than the joy of sport. The tax benefits of sports ownership are substantial and complex, and involve such tricky maneuvers as depreciating players over a period of time, as if they were tractors or drill presses.

Apart from the tax benefits, team ownership is lucrative in other ways as well, and this is because the sports leagues in this country are in effect legal monopolies. The way they work is this: each professional league offers a limited number of "franchises" for that sport, and only those who pay for a franchise can operate teams

16

in that league. Furthermore, with a few exceptions, the franchises are exclusive for a given geographical area. Anyone who wants to be an owner of a team must thus wait for a given franchise to be sold, as new ones are created only rarely (through merger or the creation of new teams, called expansion teams).

Now since the leagues have exclusive rights to operate a given sport in a given geographical area, and since the money-making potential of pro sports is incalculable, rivals to the established leagues have arisen from time to time in all of the sports. In fact, the pro sports teams that are seen on network TV are largely the survivors of competition among rival leagues, who have struggled like dinosaurs till only the fittest remain.

In the case of baseball, there are two separate leagues, the American and the National, which have coexisted peacefully for most of this century and which operate in effect as one league. In football, basketball, and hockey the situation is a little more complicated. The present leagues, the National Football League, the National Basketball Association, and the National Hockey League are all the result of the merger of two rival leagues. In football, the distinction still appears in the league's division into two rival conferences—the American and the National—which reflect the structure of the old leagues. In basketball and hockey, the number of teams that were absorbed into the NBA and NHL were few; the leagues are simply subdivided along geographical lines. After merger, the teams that infringed on the geographically exclusive area of an existing team had to pay heavy indemnities to the original teams.

Soccer is still in the dinosaur stage; that is, it has two professional leagues both of which are fighting for supremacy in the sport. The most prominent league, the North American Soccer League, is itself the result of consolidation of competing leagues; its rival, the American Soccer League, also emerged from that early rivalry. The important point about soccer is that it is the only truly international game with international rules, and it may be that the league that most closely conforms to international standards will ultimately emerge the victor.

In addition to major sports leagues there are also "minor-league" teams in many cities, as well as semipro leagues, which are often supported by local industries. Rules can vary from league to league and from level to level within each sport; to avoid confusion, therefore, I am confining my discussions to the rules for the most widely recognized professional leagues for each sport. In the case of soccer this means the NASL, simply because their games are the ones most often televised. If you go to see a team in one of the lesser known leagues, the rules will not be greatly different from those presented in this book.

There is an interesting contradiction inherent in the setup of pro sports leagues, and that is the fact that all of the owners have a common interest as co-holders in a monopolistic and profitable enterprise; on the other hand, they are each rivals with distinctly different interests because of the competition among their teams. In an effort to preserve tranquillity, each sport has a commissioner, who is chosen and paid by the owners to oversee the sport and settle all disputes. Ultimately, of course, as an employee of the owners, the commissioner's most important duty is to protect their interests, particularly in conflicts between players and owners. To give you an idea of the seriousness with which all this is taken, the commissioner of basketball is none other than the former chairman of the Democratic National Committee.

THE MEDIA

It is largely due to lucrative television contracts that sports has become such a big business. The networks in their turn are delighted with most sports contests, including the so-called junk sports, because sports programming is a reliable money-maker. (I include as "junk sports" events that are created primarily for television. Those I have seen range from such interesting and unusual events as arm-wrestling and tiddlywinks championships to dubious contests in established sports between celebrity nonathletes.) Advertising time for the 1979 pro football Superbowl, one of the year's big events in sports, sold for nearly two hundred thousand dollars for thirty seconds.

Those expensive commercials do more than sell beer and cars, of course: in many cases they have changed the nature of some of the games they make available. These changes are not generally visible to the TV viewer, because the commercial itself fills a gap, but commercial time can be quite noticeable at games attended in person. In football, for example, many plays are obviously delayed during commercial breaks, and fans often become fidgety while waiting for the invisible commercial to end.

Sometimes the delays themselves can alter the momentum of a game. In the fast-moving team sports, especially hockey and basketball, one team can suddenly seem to come alive, to appear virtually unstoppable. Anything that breaks that momentum, such as a deliberate time-out by the opposition or a break for a commercial, can disorient the team and thwart its attack.

In both hockey and soccer the problems presented by the demand for commercial time are almost insurmountable, and this is an important reason why neither sport is more widely telecast. I will go into the specifics in the sections on each sport, but the key point is that the nature of both sports, particularly soccer, is essentially nonstop action. In the case of hockey, commercial breaks merely slow the game; in soccer they take place *during* the action, because there are no natural breaks in the game. Certain rules changes have been initiated in hockey to make it more amenable to commercial breaks (as some changes have been made in the past in football and basketball), but similar changes in soccer would completely transform the sport as most of the world knows it.

Whatever sport you watch, then, be prepared for many commercial breaks, and if you want to get a head start for the kitchen, listen for these telltale words by the announcer: "And now a break in the action . . ." Ninety-nine times out of a hundred they will be followed by a beer commercial.

Which brings us to the announcers themselves. The ability and personality of these men are enormously varied. Some, like Lindsey Nelson, who worked for years for the New York Mets baseball team, see their jobs primarily as popularizers of the sport. Nelson tries to strike a fine balance between in-depth commentary, so as not to alienate the longtime viewer, and explanation of basic points of the game for the benefit of new viewers and especially children, who he feels are extremely important to the future of sports. Nelson succeeds admirably, managing to combine useful information with interesting and sometimes thrilling accounts of the sports he obviously loves. At the other extreme are the announcers who see themselves primarily as "experts," and who go out of their way to show off their own in-depth knowledge of sport by using obscure insider terms. Still others have a showmanlike approach, often inventing colorful and unintelligible phrases to describe what is going on. Of course these men are reporting essentially the same things over and over, and I understand their desire not to keep using the same old words, but this sort of commentary can be very confusing to new viewers of a sport.

As a rule, soccer and hockey announcers include the most information in their commentary, since these sports are still relatively new in the United States and have a presumably uninformed and growing audience; the least informative announcers are those for football, simply because that game is so loaded with terminology and has so many players that it's almost impossible to follow the fine points without a sports dictionary in your lap.

Announcers for local teams are paid by, or at the very least approved by, the team they cover. They are therefore partisan, and for many fans listening to an obviously biased announcer is part of the fun. Some local announcers go so far as to criticize officials' calls on the air, though this is generally frowned on by the leagues.

National announcers are paid by the networks and are often accompanied in their duties by an ex-athlete from the sport to provide "color," explaining the ins and outs of the game. Many of these players give excellent insights, particularly on confusing or difficult plays.

All announcers and sportswriters, local and national, like to use vivid images to describe what they are seeing, and so hyperbole is common: "crushed" or "mugged" instead of "defeated," for example. I've also noticed that most commentators tend to hype the importance of many plays during a game. You will often hear announcers refer to "a really big play," or state, "This could be the most important play of the game . . ." Don't bet on it. Chances are the announcer will refer to a later play in the same breathless tones.

A final note on sportscasters: Howard Cosell has done for TV journalism much what Tom Wolfe did for print journalism in the sixties, by projecting his own personality into the game coverage. Many young sportscasters are beginning to follow his lead, though none is as skillful as the master himself. Not only does he explain at great length what is actually going on in the game, particularly where strategy is concerned, but Cosell also personalizes his analysis, attempting to put himself and the audience in the position of the hapless player: "And so, with twenty-two stitches in his chin . . ." Cosell once began a description of the Dodger catcher, Steve Yeager, who had been injured before the All-Star game. Cosell and his imitators are worth listening to, at least once in a while. I've found that people who watch him tend to talk right back to the tube; "Shut up, Howard!" seems to be the most common comment. But there is no question that Howard Cosell has struck a deep chord with many people: in a poll in *TV Guide,* he was rated the best-liked sportscaster in America; in the same poll, the man who drew most votes for *least*-liked sportscaster was also Howard Cosell.

If you miss seeing a game in person or on TV, you can always read about it the next day in the papers. Sports news, in fact, is considered one of the most salable features of a newspaper, and many local dailies devote an entire section to it.

The task of a sports reporter is somewhat more complicated than that of a news reporter. First, of course, the reporter must describe the game(s) he is covering, using language as fresh as possible to write about something he has written about many times before. Second, he must provide more detailed information for the box score, or statistical summary of the game. Finally, the reporter is expected to provide "color," in the form of interviews with participants in the game, and whenever possible to include inside or background information. Because there is usually so much space in a newspaper devoted to sports, there is pressure to produce a great deal of this sort of material. Furthermore, sports reporters who are touring with a team on a road trip often find themselves with a story deadline but no game to report. For example, an East Coast reporter who is covering a night game in California will be unable, because of the time difference, to send a summary of the game in time for the morning edition. Since the hometown folks are hungry for news of their local team, the poor reporter must try to dig up some kind of story that will not be too repetitive of all the similar stories he's written in the past.

Because so much sports news is produced, then, the local fan is assured of a constant stream of information on the games, personalities, trials, tribulations, and triumphs of her favorite teams. However, she should also be aware that a lot of what she reads in the paper is "noninformation"—stories that would not be printed if there weren't such a need to fill up space. An example of this sort of nonstory is the interview with players in which they discuss their team's chances for the season (or end of the season, or play-offs, or whatever). Such stories tend to sound pretty much alike, and the players usually all agree that if the team continues to play well (or, alternatively, breaks out of the slump) things look pretty good.

A more pernicious form of empty sports journalism is the endless speculation and gossip that often centers around controversial players or teams. This sort of reporting often serves to further inflame already existing feuds, or in some instances to create them. Perhaps the most vivid recent example of this occurred in the summer of 1978, when the New York Yankees, who had won the World Series the previous year, were pushed into the national headlines by some especially vicious internecine warfare (which some critics felt was actually caused or at least exacerbated by those very headlines). What happened, briefly, was this. Billy Martin, the manager of the Yankees, a man known for his quick temper and lack of tact, was displeased with the performance of his superstar right fielder, Reggie Jackson. The owner of the team, George Steinbrenner, not only considered Jackson a prodigy deserving of special treatment, but also had difficulty getting along with Martin. These and other squabbles had been reported routinely by the press for nearly two years, but when the Yankees began to go into a serious midseason slump, New York reporters jumped on the team and began speculating that the reason the Yankees were losing was because they couldn't stop feuding long enough to concentrate on baseball.

As the seasonal slump continued, Martin removed Jackson from the starting lineup, and the situation was brought to a head when Jackson, playing as designated hitter (a kind of substitute; see page 67), flagrantly disobeyed Martin's instructions at a critical point in a game. Infuriated, Martin suspended Jackson for a number of days. The angry comments of both men were reported in great detail in the press, as was Steinbrenner's criticism of the way Martin had handled the situation. Martin, still furious, apparently had too much to drink in the company of a sports reporter one evening. The reporter then called Steinbrenner to tell him what Martin had said, and printed the statement in his column the next day: referring to Jackson and Steinbrenner, Martin had supposedly said, "One's a born liar, the other's convicted." (This latter designation referred to the fact that Steinbrenner had once been convicted of conspiracy in the mishandling of campaign contributions.) In the meantime (and coincidental with Jackson's suspension), the Yankees pulled out of the slump and began winning games, but after his remarks had appeared in print Martin's days were numbered—no one was surprised when he tearfully announced his resignation several days later.

The new manager, a noncontroversial veteran named Bob Lemon, took command of the Yankees, who continued to win games, eventually going on to capture the World Series for the second year in a row. What is interesting about the Yankees' turnaround is that it coincided not only with Lemon's stewardship of the team but also with a newspaper strike in New York. Many fans felt that the Martin-Jackson-Steinbrenner incident would never have occurred if it had not been for inflammatory reporting, and further, that the Yankees were able to function far better in the absence of scrutiny by the press.

It is true that any celebrity, including a professional athlete, must give up some privacy as part of the price of fame, but in no other field are rivalries and feuds as closely monitored and even magnified as they are in the world of sports.

Sports magazines, too, tend to indulge in this sort of gossip, but because the sports periodicals come out weekly or monthly instead of daily, there is much less speculation and more of an emphasis on straight sports reporting and profiles of players and teams.

There is an additional caveat for women fans who want to read about sports: because the vast majority of sports reporters, both those for newspapers and for periodicals, are men writing for men, women's sports receive minimal if any attention in the press, and the language of most sports reporting is as a rule more sexist than that found elsewhere in a newspaper or in other periodicals.

THE ATHLETES

Where do they come from, all these men who make a living playing sports? In most cases they come straight from the American dream: just as it used to be common for a little boy to dream of growing up to become president, now many youngsters aspire to the life of a famous pro athlete. For each sport there is a somewhat different period of training required before professional status is achieved, and of course for every boy who makes it there are thousands who fail along the way. Briefly, here is how the majority of athletes are recruited for each sport:

BASEBALL   These days many baseball stars are emerging from a very few colleges that specialize in baseball (mostly on the West Coast and in Florida), but traditionally, baseball players have come up through the "farm" system, which is much what it sounds like. In essence, it is a way to grow new crops of well-trained baseball players by taking young inexperienced men with talent and putting them on minor-league teams where they play with others of equal ability, all the while being coached by professionals. They move up through a series of increasingly better teams, all owned or supported financially by the parent team, until ultimately they are good enough to play on the parent team itself.

FOOTBALL   The majority of pro football players are recruited straight out of college, where they have been playing on football scholarships. There is a growing controversy about the fact that
many of these players attend classes only nominally and leave college unprepared for anything but football, which can be a terrible
hardship for those whose careers are cut short by injury, or who are
not good enough to make it in the pros. The college players in turn
come from the high schools. Because football is such an important
revenue source for schools with good teams, high school superstars
are recruited as vigorously by college coaches as good college players
are by the pro teams.

BASKETBALL   Pro basketball players are also trained in the
colleges. Perhaps because less time is spent in training than in football, basketball players seem to have less trouble obtaining an education while they play their sport.

HOCKEY   The majority of hockey players come from Canada,
where they have been playing in various leagues since they were very
young children. Hockey teams also make limited use of a farm system similar to that of baseball, and recruit directly from colleges as
well.

SOCCER   Soccer players too are mostly trained foreigners, because this sport is still new in America and there supposedly aren't
professional-caliber natives available. This situation is beginning to
change with the growing popularity of soccer on college campuses,
and according to the U.S. star player Shep Messing, the superstar
goaltenders of the future may be Americans.

To make sure that they are aware of all the available young
talent in their sports, pro teams make use of scouting systems, either
employing trained scouts of their own or hiring a scouting service.
These sports scouts are men who travel around the country—to
colleges, minor leagues, and even high schools—to look for raw
talent that may be useful to their teams. In many cases boys teen-
aged and even younger are evaluated, not only for talent and skill,

but for projected growth patterns (will he grow tall enough to play in the pros?).

To prevent exploitation of very young men, there are strict rules about when an athlete is eligible to enter the pros. In football, for example, a boy may not join a pro team until the year his college class graduates (he may have dropped out in the meantime, but he is still bound to wait until his classmates receive their sheepskins). Thus each year there is a fresh pool of young talent that the teams divide among themselves by means of a "draft," a system whereby teams choose one at a time the cream of the new crop of players. The teams choose in the reverse order of their finish the preceding season, with the worst team picking first, the second worst picking second, and so on. When all teams have chosen, another round begins, and this system continues until all the players have been claimed. Because the draft is so important for stocking or strengthening a team, "future draft choices"—or the picks a team may be entitled to in the future—are often used as bargaining chips in negotiations between teams.

Once a player has signed with a pro team he is still not guaranteed a job (unless his contract is for so much money that the team has no choice but to play him). Final personnel decisions are made during training camp, a period preceding the regular season for each sport when the veterans from the previous year as well as the new, untried players from college or farm, or simply off the street, work out and compete for the openings available on the team. The purpose of training is twofold: to get regular players in shape for the coming season, and to look over the new players, a lucky few of whom may prove good enough to make the team.

It is in training camp that the professional athlete is first treated as the extended adolescent he will be for the rest of his playing career: he is given strict rules about what to eat, what to wear, how to exercise, how much sleep to get—even, in some cases, how long he may wear his hair. In many ways, a pro athlete becomes a nonperson; he may be traded or "dealt"—usually without his permission and often against his wishes—to another team; he may be "sent down to the minors" or even released outright ("cut"). (However, very valuable players often negotiate a contract with their team by insisting on a "no-cut" clause in the contract, which means that they may not be cut from the club until the contract has run out. Some players are even able to negotiate "no-trade" clauses as well.) A player who is not performing up to expectations is sometimes "put on waivers," which is a preliminary step to being released by the club. When a player is "waived," any club interested in him can buy him for a specified (usually very low) "waiver price." If no team expresses an interest in him after a certain period of time, the player is said to have "cleared waivers" and may now be disposed of (cut, traded, or sold) by his team. Sometimes a player is put on waivers as a warning for bad play, or simply on speculation to see if other teams want him. His team retains the option of withdrawing him from waivers.

The players who make it are well compensated for all the insecurity, of course: They make a lot of money and have a chance at fame, and also in many cases become spokesmen for commercial products or set themselves up in businesses they can pursue when their playing careers are over. Not only do star athletes get to hang out with actors and politicians, but sometimes they actually become actors and politicians (O.J. Simpson and Bill Bradley are perhaps the two best-known examples). In recent years, the very best of the superathletes can even become instant millionaires simply by signing with a team.

BEHIND THE MILLION-DOLLAR HEADLINES

Until very recently in the world of sports, professional athletes not only had few rights, but they were poorly paid, the joy of playing being considered compensation enough for the lucky few who made it to the pros.

Collective bargaining and court challenges to standard sports contracts began to change this old "plantation" concept, however, and today many athletes are represented by agents who help them to get the best possible contracts as well as the most money the market will bear. In fact, a whole new area of law, which deals with the negotiation of professional sports contracts, is attracting growing numbers of lawyers and spawning courses in law schools.

Only a tiny minority of pro athletes reach actual millionaire status, of course, but almost all players are now aware of the ins and outs of the fine print in sports contracts. So complex is this issue, and so far reaching in terms of how it affects or may affect the sports we see, that stories about contract negotiations and lucrative deals sometimes take up as much space on the sports pages as do reports of the games themselves.

Probably the largest amount of this news space goes to the stories about free agents and potential free agents. In legal terms, a free agent is a player who is not under contract to any club and can therefore sell himself to the highest bidder. A man may become a free agent by simply being dropped from his club. If he is a valuable player (or considers himself one) he may become a free agent by "playing out his option." This usually occurs if the player and his team cannot come to an agreement on a new contract. Instead of signing, the player invokes the "option clause" in his contract, which means he elects to play one more year for the team at a cut in pay. The following year he is automatically released from the team as a free agent and may negotiate with any team, including his former team.

The details vary somewhat from sport to sport (there are as yet no free agents in hockey, for example), but free agents are becoming increasingly common. Perhaps the biggest recent headlines concern the free agents in baseball. At the end of the 1977 season, Pete Rose, who throughout his long career with the Cincinnati Reds was one of the best hitters and fielders in baseball, failed to reach agreement with his club. Rose played out his option in 1978, then set out in pursuit of a dream to become the highest-paid player in the history of the game of baseball. He briefly achieved that dream by signing with the Philadelphia Phillies for $800,000 a year for four years. Alas for Pete, shortly thereafter another superplayer, slugger Jim Rice of the Boston Red Sox, re-signed with his team for a long-term 5.4 *million*-dollar contract, thus making Rose the second-highest paid player in baseball.

There is a great deal of concern among the owners, fans, and even some players over escalating supersalaries. A very good player will attract a significant number of fans to a game, of course, but as payrolls for a team rise so do ticket prices, and the fear is that these prices will have to be raised to the point where fans will no longer be able or willing to come to games. That point has not yet been reached, but most observers feel that a downward trend in this wage spiral is necessary and overdue.

Of course most athletes never make anywhere near the amount of money made by the superstars, but most of them are paid far better than they would be for entry-level jobs in almost any other business or profession.

Still, in spite of all the material gain and glory, there is a dark side to the life of a professional athelete. For one thing, these men are undeniably risking their future health, and many leave their sport (particularly football and basketball) essentially crippled. Furthermore, not all young men have the foresight to sensibly invest the unprecedented amounts of money they are suddenly receiving and, like many adolescents, live only for the present. Bill Bradley speaks movingly in his book *Life on the Run* about the sad retirement from professional sports of men who somehow thought that the pro life would never end.

The lucky ones, those who do not make a career in another field or simply spend their days dreaming about past glory, sometimes stay in their sport with "front-office" jobs (in the business end of a team they have played for) or as coaches.

THE OTHER MEN ON THE TEAM

The man most visible among the nonplayers on a team is generally the coach (in baseball, the manager). It is he who makes the strategic and tactical decisions that can mean the difference between a winning and losing season—and often mean the difference between his keeping or losing his job. Coach of a pro sports team must rank in the top five of jobs with highest turnover. The coach's very visibility works against him. There may be many reasons for a team to have a losing season—poor players, a string of injuries, bad coaching decisions, personality conflicts, even simple bad luck. Whatever the reasons, it is usually the coach who is fired. In addition to a head coach each team has a general manager who handles the financial and business dealings of the team, and usually is in charge of buying and trading players as well as negotiating salaries (a few coaches serve both functions).

Each team also has assistant coaches, sometimes with specialized functions (in football, separate offensive and defensive coaches; in baseball, special coaches for batting and pitching), and one or more trainers. Trainers have always seemed to me to be the most overworked men in sports. Not only are they responsible for seeing that uniforms are clean and ready, with towels and other supplies kept stocked in the locker room, but they also are responsible for packing everything that will be needed for road trips, and on top of all that they also administer minor first aid (anything very serious is, of course, taken care of by a team doctor) and rubdowns for any players who need them.

With the exception of some managers, few of the men behind the scenes receive any of the glory or wealth enjoyed by their athletes; their main reward is participating in a sport that they love.

OFFICIALS

In *Smithsonian* magazine, writer Michael Olmert comments on the development of modern sports by pointing out that in medieval sporting events no officials were required: the honor of the contestants was presumably enough to stop cheating, fighting, and illegal maneuvers. Or perhaps the sports were just simpler in those days.

All of the sports described in this book require officials to control the games. In the last two years alone a new official has been added for both football and basketball, and there is talk of adding a new official to baseball as well (for scoring purposes). In both football and basketball the new official was needed, it was felt, to curb illegal injurious actions by the players. Only time will tell if this maneuver will work.

The officials are called by various names: referee, umpire, linesman. The specifics of each and their major duties will be explained in the sections on each sport. All the officials are paid by the leagues, and some are full-time professionals, others part-time. In each sport the officials share the road life of the athletes, but make far less money, and all are exposed to a great deal of abuse from fans, managers, players, and sometimes sportswriters.

CHAPTER 4

SPORTS TALK

While each sport has a specialized vocabulary of its own, there are many terms that apply to most or all the major sports. In addition, there is a large body of slang that commonly appears in newspaper and magazine articles and on the air. Following are brief definitions for those sports terms and slang words you are most likely to see or hear.

ASTROTURF   Also referred to as "rug" and "carpet," this is a synthetic lawn that was first developed for the Astrodome, an enclosed stadium in Houston, when it was noticed that the dome prevented sunlight from reaching the natural grass far below. Astroturf, which is used by many but not all teams in baseball, football, and soccer, is the focus of several controversies in the sports world. Some claim that it increases player injuries, while others say that the opposite is true. In baseball the ball seems to bounce higher and faster on Astroturf than on grass, which creates problems for players who are used to natural grass. There is no question that the substance changes the nature of any sport played on it—for the better or worse, depending on who you are talking to. Also at controversy is the matter of cost: there are published figures showing both that it is more costly and less costly than natural grass. Some teams have been experimenting with yet a third sort of playing surface, called Prescription Athletic Turf, or PAT, which consists of real grass grown in an artificial soil system. Whatever you may say about artificial playing surfaces, one thing is sure: they are here to stay.

BENCH   The bench is where all the players of a team sit before games and between plays. It is also where you find any player who is not playing—whether because of an injury or infraction, or simply because he doesn't play often. Such a player is said to be on the bench, sidelined, or, simply, "benched."

CELLAR   A team is in the cellar if it is the last team in the rankings compared to other teams in its division.

CHOKE   A player is said to choke if he fails to perform as expected in a crucial game situation because of fear or nervousness.

CLUTCH   In common American slang, "clutching"—panicking—suggests a crisis, and that is what it means in sports as well. You will often hear sports announcers speak of a clutch situation or a clutch player. A clutch situation is a critical moment in the game, usually requiring exceptional performance from the players involved; a clutch player is one who plays extremely well under pressure and can usually be counted on to help get his teammates out of a jam.

DEFENSE   The five sports described in the chapters that follow are all team sports. While the number of players on a team varies from sport to sport, and while their methods of trying to win are different, each team is always playing either *offense* or *defense*. This division may be formal, as in baseball, where there is an orderly alternation between offense and defense, or it may be a fluid, rapidly changing situation as with hockey, basketball, and soccer (football lies somewhere between; usually there is an orderly alternation between offense and defense, but sometimes the situation changes rapidly and dramatically). However, when the transition is made between offense and defense, these things are always true: First, only one team at a time is on offense while the other defends; second, the offensive team is always the one that is "on the attack," the one that is trying to score goals, baskets, or runs. Third, the defensive team is mainly occupied in trying to prevent the attacking team from scoring, while at the same time looking for opportunities to reverse the situation and go on the attack itself. Throughout the book I use the term "attacking" synonymously with "offensive."

In most team sports, the players on a team normally alternate between playing offense and defense; however, in some circumstances there may be special players or even separate teams for offense and defense. This is most important in football and will be discussed in that section.

DYNASTY   See *Teams.*

EXPANSION TEAM   See *Teams.*

FLAKE   See *Player types.*

FRANCHISE   See *Player types.*

GAME PLAN   See *Strategy.*

GAMES   There are a number of slang terms used to refer to games and special game situations. One of the most common is a "must game." This usually refers to a game that is considered crucial for a team; for example, a game that they must win in order to get into the play-offs. A game that is very close or tied in the waning moments is often said to be "anybody's game," while a game in which one team is hopelessly behind is often called "out of reach" for that team.

HOT DOG   See *Player types.*

INJURED LIST   See *Roster.*

LINE, MORNING LINE, POINT SPREAD Many newspapers publish a daily guide for bettors, knowing full well that the majority of those bettors will place bets illegally with bookies (although bets among friends often make use of the line). The line is determined by a number of sports experts in Las Vegas before a series of big games, and this is how it works. Let us say that the line on a mythical game is the Kennibunkport Klams by ten over the Walla Walla Wallflowers. This means that the Klams are favored to beat the Wallflowers by *at least ten points*. If you are "betting the line," then, and you pick Kennibunkport to win, they must win by at least eleven points; if you bet on Walla Walla, all the Wallflowers have to do is lose by fewer than ten points—they have thus "beat the spread."

MATCHUP This term usually refers to two players from different teams who play opposite each other during a game. If it is a "good" matchup, the players are considered to have equal or offsetting capabilities.

MONEY PLAYER See *Player types.*

MOMENTUM A team that has momentum during a game is playing extremely well and often seems to score easily. In some sports, especially basketball, a team that is behind will deliberately call time-out or commit a violation in order to try to stop that momentum. A team can sometimes be said to have momentum through a series of games, if they consistently win these games and beat all or most opponents.

OFFENSE See *Defense.*

PLAY A specific action or series of actions within a game. Each of the sports has set plays that are practiced by the team members and then put into action during a game situation. A "textbook" play is a standard, well-rehearsed play that works to perfection in a given situation.

PLAYER TYPES   One of the most delightful things about sports is the many slang terms used to describe players. Among the more colorful are the following:

Flake   A flake is a player who seems to march to the beat of a different drummer. His strangeness may take the form of unruliness, such as a player who consistently refuses to take orders or constantly fights; or it may consist of merely oddball actions. One of the best modern examples of a flake is the Philadelphia relief pitcher Tug McGraw, who describes himself as the "Kellogg of flakes." Not only has McGraw been known to send out for pizza *during* a game, but he once protested poor play on the part of his teammates by throwing into the air first his cap, then his glove. He had nearly finished unbuttoning his shirt when the team manager removed him from the game for "immaturity."

Franchise   A franchise, as explained in the preceding chapter, is the legal right to operate a team in a given area. Occasionally one player for a team is so valuable that he comes to be known as "The Franchise"—in other words, the team would be worthless without him.

Hot dog   A player who, through flamboyant, attention-getting techniques, "plays to the crowd." The term is usually used in a derogatory way, with the common complaint that the player is not getting media attention through excellent performance but through his antics. Some hot dogs are, however, extremely good (though sometimes erratic) players. A recent example is Reggie Jackson of the New York Yankees, who has achieved widespread attention through his often spectacular hits as well as through his many ill-considered remarks to the press. It has been said of Jackson that "there's not enough mustard in the world to cover him."

Money player   This is a player who can always be counted upon to play well, particularly in important games or game situations.

Streak player   A player who alternates spurts of excellence with periods of mediocrity. (See also *choke, clutch, rookie, starter.*)

PLAY-OFFS   At the end of any sports season further competition is arranged among the better teams to determine who is best overall. For details, see the sections on individual sports.

POSSESSION The rules determining possession are lengthy and complicated in the official rulebooks for each sport. In general, the person or team in possession of the ball or puck is the one who is physically in control of the object at a given moment in time. (A common synonym for possession is control.) In some situations, a team or player may be penalized by losing possession. This is very important, because only the team actually in possession can score points.

REBUILDING See *Teams.*

ROOKIE Short for recruit, this term refers to any player who is playing his first full year with the parent team. Rookies are seldom the most outstanding members of a team, because no matter how good they may have been in college or in the minor leagues, they have not had experience playing under the pressure of pro games. When a rookie is exceptionally good, or even becomes one of the leaders of his team, he excites widespread interest and becomes a candidate for Rookie of the Year in that sport.

A player's second year with a team is often referred to as his "sophomore year," and it is not uncommon for a player who has had an outstanding rookie year to then suffer from "sophomore slump," or fail to live up to the promise of that first year. Mark Fidrych, a colorful and outstanding pitcher in his rookie year, was injured early in the second year; this case of sophomore slump was a severe disappointment to his team, the Detroit Tigers, which had sold a large number of season tickets to people whose main interest in the team was largely the chance to see Fidrych play. On the other hand, another star rookie, Mike Bossy of the New York Islanders hockey team, beat the sophomore jinx predicted for him by scoring more goals than any other player in the league during his second year.

ROSTER This is the number of men that a team is legally allowed to "carry" (pay, have uniforms for, take to all the games) and is larger than the number of men who play at any given time. The number of men allowed on the roster varies not only from sport to sport, but from one part of the season to the next, and even from year to year, as interseason rules changes are sometimes made. The most important thing to know about the roster is that the limit placed on the number of players allowed can often have important strategic consequences, because some positions in each sport are so important that the coach must be certain of having at least one healthy backup player to fill that position. If a key player is injured and won't be able to play for some time, he may be put on the "injured list" and another player from a farm team put on the roster in his place. A player who is on the injured list continues to receive pay, but may not rejoin his team until a set period of time has passed, even if he has recovered before then.

SERIES   A series is a set of two or more games played between the same two teams. A home-and-away series is a two-game series played alternately on each team's home field or court.

STARTER   A starting player is one who physically plays from the outset of a given game. The term also refers to the players on a team who usually start games (but may be substituted for later). Starters are usually those players who are most experienced and reliable; sometimes an inexperienced player will show so much ability that he becomes a starter.

STRATEGY   A feature all sports have in common is the use of strategy and tactics. Strategy is the overall idea for a game, or so-called *game plan,* which is usually determined by the head coach (in baseball, the manager). While a team might use the same general strategy throughout the season, it may be modified for a particular game because of a player's injury, or to exploit known weaknesses in the opposing team.

Tactics   are simply maneuvers used to carry out overall strategy, and are often determined by the individual players themselves. For example, an overall strategy might be to play a very fast game without allowing the opposition, which is known to be slow, a chance to regroup; a tactic for achieving this end might be for one player to constantly make a certain move that disorganizes the defense.

STREAK PLAYER   See *Player types.*

SUBSTITUTE   This is any player who comes in to play instead of a starter during the course of a game. The rules for substitutions vary greatly; see sections on the individual sports for details.

SUDDEN DEATH   This is a method of breaking ties used in some sports, in which the game goes into overtime and the team scoring first wins immediately.

TACTICS   See *Strategy.*

TEAMS   Just as players may be characterized as to expected performance, so sometimes are teams. A team is said to be a *dynasty* if it has been very good for a number of years, winning a significant number of championships. An *expansion* team is a new franchise, formed from a pool of usually inferior players, whenever a league decides to expand. As a rule, expansion teams do very poorly for a number of years. A team is said to be *rebuilding* if it has lost a number of good players through retirement or trades, and is now making use of young, inexperienced players in the hope that they will one day form a good veteran team.

TEMPO   The tempo refers to the pace of the game.

WILD CARD   Play-off series are supposed to be played among the best teams in a league. In some sports, weaker teams called wild-card entries are allowed into the play-offs in order to increase the size of the viewing audience.

HOW TO USE
THIS BOOK

We are now ready to go on to the individual sports. But before we do, I'd like to explain how the book is organized.

For each sport, there is first a fact sheet giving such information as the number of men on a team, where it is played, length of a game, and a listing of pro teams.

The fact sheet is followed by a short introductory section and then a chapter on the basics, intended for those who have little or no knowledge of the sport. The next chapter, How the Game Is Played, goes into more detail, both for the benefit of beginners and those fans who may have questions about certain aspects of the game. The fourth part, Behind the Action, covers the basics of strategy and tactics, showing what to look for in a game. Finally, in Following the Game, there is material on reading about the sport; what to look for in televised and live games; play-offs and awards.

Throughout the book I have given examples of "announcer-ese" and explained the terminology you will encounter in reading about and listening to sports. I hope that this book will make sports more enjoyable for seasoned sports fans, and a happy new experience for those who have just started.

PART 2
BASEBALL

BASEBALL FACT SHEET

Where played: baseball diamond, marked off on large grassy field.

Game divisions: nine innings, each divided into two half innings. No time limit.

Average duration: approximately two and one-half hours.

Offense/defense consideration: Visitors bat first; home team in last half of the inning.

Governing bodies: American League and National League.

Number of players: two teams of nine men each.

Number of players on the roster: 25 maximum; 24 minimum.

Equipment: bat and ball; uniforms; leather gloves; a mask for the catcher; hard plastic batting helmets; spiked shoes.

Regular season: April to September (followed by play-offs).

TEAMS

AMERICAN LEAGUE

East	West
Toronto Blue Jays	Oakland A's
Milwaukee Brewers	California Angels
Cleveland Indians	Seattle Mariners
Baltimore Orioles	Texas Rangers
Boston Red Sox	Kansas City Royals
Detroit Tigers	Minnesota Twins
New York Yankees	Chicago White Sox

NATIONAL LEAGUE

East	West
St. Louis Cardinals	Houston Astros
Chicago Cubs	Atlanta Braves
Montreal Expos	Los Angeles Dodgers
New York Mets	San Francisco Giants
Philadelphia Phillies	San Diego Padres
Pittsburgh Pirates	Cincinnati Reds

CHAPTER
5 THE ALL-AMERICAN SPORT

Whoever wants to know the heart and
mind of America had better learn baseball.

—JACQUES BARZUN

There is a widespread notion that baseball is a slow, even boring game. If you have ever played the similar game of softball, you know that isn't so. On the contrary, the excitement in baseball builds from play to play, from minute to minute, in a way and with an intensity different from that in all the other team sports.

Rather than slowness, there is a majesty in baseball, which results from its existence, as Gilbert Sorrentino says, "outside of time." The other team sports are played within definite boundaries in a strict time limit set by a clock. Even when a game goes into overtime in these sports, the duration of that overtime is prescribed.

Not so with baseball. Although the average baseball game lasts about two and one-half hours, some individual games have lasted upward of six hours, and theoretically, a game could go on forever, although in very unusual circumstances a game may end in a tie.

In the other sports, furthermore, there is always a theoretical moment when the game is decided—that is, when, because of time restrictions, it becomes mathematically or physically impossible for the score to alter radically. Even in basketball, with its breathtakingly close final moments, there is a point at which the team that is ahead can "run down the clock" and prevent the opponents from winning, if not tying.

But in baseball, not until the very last man is put out at the end of the last inning can you be certain that a team that is hopelessly behind will not, in fact, go on to win the game. Baseball great Yogi Berra's statement that "the game isn't over till it's over" is illustrated each season with startling last-minute comebacks—some of them even determining championships. One of the most dramatic such turnarounds occurred in the 1929 World Series, when the Philadelphia A's overcame an 8-0 lead and went on to win 10-8 in the ninth inning. In this way baseball is a reflection of the American dream: the old idea that anyone, no matter how down on his luck, can somehow, through diligence and hard work, prevail.

In the words of Chicago White Sox owner Bill Veeck, baseball is "a game to savor, not to gulp," a cerebral game that nevertheless seems more complicated than it really is. In fact, even if you know absolutely nothing about baseball, you will probably enjoy the first game you attend in person. A large part of baseball's appeal, after all, is the pleasure of just being there in the ball park, surrounded by other cheering fans in the warm summer air, while on the grass below grown men are playing a child's game for their pleasure and ours.

CHAPTER 6
THE BASICS

Perhaps the best place to begin with the game of baseball is the stadium (or "park") in which it's played, usually a green oasis situated somewhere in the middle of a cement jungle. The green, whether it is natural grass or Astroturf, is marked by a 90-foot-square configuration in the middle, called the "diamond." This diamond-shaped area is anchored by a base at each of its corners. These are first, second, and third bases, and at the bottom, home plate. Home plate, which is flat and has five sides, can easily be distinguished from the three other bases (or "bags"), which are canvas and filled with kapok, a soft cottonlike material. Each base is a station on the way to a one-point score, called a "run." Runs are made by players who have earned the right to advance in order around the bases; only a complete counterclockwise circuit, starting with home plate and ending there, earns a run.

The immediate area of the diamond itself is called the "infield," while everything beyond it is the "outfield." In addition, the back edges of home plate form a right angle with two "foul lines" that extend the length of the field to the outfield fence. Everything between the foul lines is known as "fair" territory, while the area outside those lines is considered out-of-bounds, or "foul."

The size of the diamond is identical in every baseball field, but the size and shape of the outfield, as well as the height of the fence surrounding it, vary from park to park. Some baseball teams, for example, must share their facilities with a football team, while still others play in parks designed at the turn of the century. Thus, each park has special rules that apply only to that park, called "ground rules"; usually these have to do with unlikely situations, such as a ball striking the dome of a covered stadium.

Below is a diagram of a baseball field.

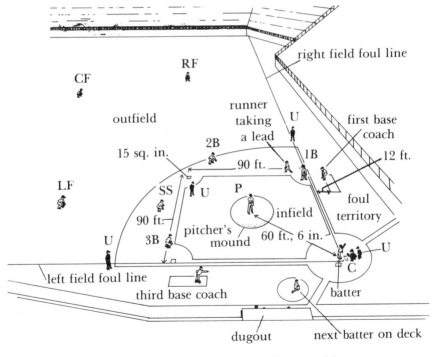

CF

RF

right field foul line

outfield

runner taking a lead   U

first base coach

15 sq. in.   2B   1B   12 ft.

90 ft.

LF

SS   U   P

infield   foul territory

90 ft.   pitcher's mound   60 ft., 6 in.

U   3B

C   U

left field foul line   batter

third base coach

dugout   next batter on deck

P: pitcher, C: catcher , 1B: first baseman, 2B: second baseman, 3B: third baseman, SS: shortstop, LF: left fielder, CF: center fielder RF: right fielder, U: umpire

When a team is on defense, its nine members take their positions "in the field." In the middle of the diamond stands the pitcher, who works from the "pitcher's mound," a mound of dirt located 60 feet 6 inches from home plate. The pitcher's job is to "pitch" or hurl the baseball from a small white slab, known as the pitcher's rubber, atop the mound. A member of the team on offense, known as the "batter," stands in either of two batter's boxes to the side of home plate and tries to hit the ball with his bat.

Behind home plate is yet another box, called the "catcher's box." There the catcher squats, ready to catch the pitcher's "deliveries," or pitches, with a large leather glove, and directing the pitcher's actions by the means of secret signals given by wiggles of the fingers of his ungloved hand.

In positions around the base path—the dirt area that circumscribes the three bases—stand the four infielders: the first baseman, the second baseman, the third baseman, and the shortstop, who plays between second and third bases. The three outfielders, who stand in the area beyond the infield and between the foul lines, are known as the left fielder, right fielder, and center fielder. The primary aim of each of these seven men, who are categorically called "fielders," is to catch any balls hit by the batter and otherwise prevent members of the opposite team from scoring runs.

In addition to the players, there are four men dressed in red or black jackets, one stationed near each base. These are the umpires, whose job it is to arbitrate the game.

The classic confrontation in baseball is the one between pitcher and batter. The pitcher tries to get the batter either to swing at the ball and miss, or to hit it so that it can be converted to an "out." An out is a term referring to the temporary removal of a player on offense from the game.

A batter is out when:

1. He hits a "fly ball" that one of the four infielders, the three outfielders, the pitcher, or the catcher catches before it touches the ground. This includes any foul balls (those hit outside the foul lines) that are caught in the air.

2. He hits a ball that one of the fielders—usually an infielder— picks up off the ground and throws to the first baseman, who catches

it and touches the base—or the batter himself—before the batter reaches it. This is known as "grounding out" or being "thrown out."

3. He "strikes out." A batter may swing at and miss the ball, for a swinging strike, or he may fail to swing at a pitch that passes through the "strike zone," for a called strike. The strike zone is defined as that area directly above home plate between the batter's knees and armpits (in the National League) or his knees and shoulders (in the American League). The umpire, stationed behind the plate, judges whether or not the ball has passed through the strike zone if the batter doesn't swing at it. (Not swinging at the ball is known as "taking the pitch.") If it is a strike of either kind, the umpire raises his right arm. When the umpire has called three strikes, the batter is out.

If the batter hits a foul ball that is not caught on the fly, this too counts as a strike for the first two strikes. Once a batter has two strikes of any kind against him, however, a foul ball does not count as a strike, and he can "foul off" pitches indefinitely. (This is also known as "staying alive." Luke Appling, a former shortstop for the Chicago White Sox, once fouled off seventeen straight pitches to protest the stinginess of his team's owner, who wouldn't give him free passes for his family. The balls, which were hit into the stands and kept as souvenirs by fans, ended up costing the owner far more than the price of the tickets.)

While the nine members of the defending team are concentrating their efforts on getting the batter out, his aim is to "get on base." The most common way of getting on base is to get a hit—to hit the ball thrown by the pitcher and race to first base before the ball is retrieved and thrown by a fielder to the first baseman. If the batter reaches the base before the ball, he is declared "safe" by the umpire. A hit can take the form of a ball hit to the outfield, a "grounder" (a ball hit to the ground), or even a "bunt" (a ball intentionally hit softly in the area of the plate, where it may be hard for any fielders to reach).

Every pitch that isn't a hit is either a strike or a "ball." A ball is a pitch that does not pass through the strike zone (and is not swung at). The umpire indicates that the pitch is a ball by straightening up from his crouch and making no further gesture. The pitcher is allowed only three balls; on the fourth ball, the batter goes automatically to first base, and is said to have "walked" or received a "base on balls." (The number of balls and strikes is known as the "count." A count of three balls and two strikes is a "full count.")

Finally, a batter is "granted" first base when he is hit by a pitched ball anywhere on his body.

Summing up, then, one of two things happens to a batter whenever he is up. He can be put out—by flying out, grounding out, or striking out. Or he can get on base—by getting a hit; by getting a base on balls; or by getting hit with a pitch.

If he is out, he must return to his team's dugout, the protected bunkerlike area where team members who are not playing sit on a long bench. If he gets on base, he becomes a "base runner" or, simply, "runner." In either case the next batter, who has been waiting "on deck" (in a circle marked off for that purpose) comes to the plate.

RUNNING THE BASES

Once a batter has reached base, his object is to advance to the next base without being put out and, ultimately, to score a run. Normally, a runner can move to the next base only when the batter is proceeding to first; that is, when a fair ball has been hit or the batter has been walked. A runner may not go to the next base if the batter hits a foul ball or a fly ball that is caught. (However, *after* a fly ball has been caught he may run at his own risk, provided he remains on or touches the original base before doing so. Touching the base after the fly is caught is known as "tagging up.")

A runner may also move to the next base by "stealing" it—running for a base when the batter has not hit the ball into play, but at great risk of being put out. We'll take a closer look at stealing in Chapter Eight.

A base runner can ordinarily be put out one of four ways. The two most common are for a fielder to tag him with the ball when he is not touching a base (the runner is thus "tagged out"); or for him to be "forced out." A runner is "forced" when another runner is moving to the base he is on, thus literally forcing him to go on to the next base. If the ball is caught by a fielder who touches that base before the runner reaches it, he is out.

(Frequently a runner, in order to avoid being tagged out, will "slide" into a base—that is, skid along the ground, usually feet first but sometimes head first, and touch the base with his foot or hand.)

A base runner can also be put out, more rarely, if he runs outside the base paths to avoid being tagged, or if he is hit by a batted ball while not on base.

There are certain situations in which the ball is considered "dead" and runners are not free to run (or, of course, to be put out). The most common reasons for a dead ball include a foul; a balk by the pitcher (see page 77); "time" being called by the umpire at the request of the manager or player; a batter being hit by a pitch; or a fan touching the ball. There are a variety of other reasons, most of them very unusual, such as a pitched ball's lodging in the umpire's face mask.

SCORING

Sometimes a batter will hit a fair ball that the opposition fielders cannot reach in time to prevent him from running beyond first base. This kind of hit is called an "extra base hit," specifically a "double" if it enables him to reach second, and a "triple" if he reaches third. (A hit that allows him to reach first is called a "single.") Occasionally a ball will be hit over the outfield walls for what is called a "home run" or "homer." The batter then runs or trots around the bases to home, being careful to touch each one. When this happens not only does the batter score but so does every other man who may be on base.

Far less frequently, a ball is hit into the far corners of the outfield and the batter, an extremely fast runner, manages to reach home plate before the ball is thrown there. This kind of hit is known as an "inside the park" home run, and it is very exciting to watch.

An equally thrilling moment is when there are three men on base ("the bases are loaded") and a batter "drives them in" on a home run. Called a "grand slam," this is one of the most dramatic occurrences in baseball.

Less exciting but still dramatic is the situation in which the bases are loaded and the pitcher walks the batter. Each of the runners is forced to move up a base, including the man on third, who goes to home. In this case the pitcher is said to have "walked in a run."

No matter how many men on a team bat and/or reach base, as soon as three batters are out, the entire side is out ("retired"). The defensive players trot off the field, and after a short interval, the nine members of the other team station themselves in the positions abandoned by the members of the previous team. One of the players formerly on the field now comes up to home plate and faces the pitcher for the opposing team.

This orderly progression, in which the teams take turns facing each other's pitchers, is known as an "inning." (Each team's turn at bat is called a half inning.) The first half is called the "top"; the second half the "bottom." A standard baseball game has nine innings, unless there is a tie at the end of the ninth inning, or unless the home team is leading at the end of the first half of the ninth—in which case there would be no need for them to come to bat again.

Because baseball games never (theoretically) end tied, and because there's no "sudden death" overtime or special tie breaker, a game tied after nine innings proceeds by adding new innings, on an inning-by-inning basis, until the tie is broken (with the home team batting last). It's thus possible, and not uncommon, for a baseball game to last a very long time—as many as twenty or more innings. In the bottom of the last inning, the home team needs to bat only until they have scored the winning run, at which point the game is over.

Unlike the other major team sports, which are always played as scheduled regardless of weather or anything short of major disaster, a baseball game can be delayed, interrupted, or even postponed ("called") because of weather conditions, usually rain. When a game is postponed because of rain, the owners of the team call it before the first pitch; after the game has started the umpires decide whether or not to postpone. It was said of the owner of the St. Louis Cardinals in the thirties, Sam Breadon, that he would often call a game if someone so much as "spit," so that he could reschedule it as part of a weekend doubleheader (two games in one day) to attract more fans. Whenever a game is delayed or interrupted by rain, the infield is covered with a tarpaulin by a ground crew while everyone waits for the rain to stop.

If five innings have been played before postponement—four and a half if the home team is ahead—the game is considered a complete, regulation game. If the game is tied in the fifth inning or later, then it must be finished at a future time when the teams meet again. If fewer than five innings have been played, the umpire declares "no game," and the game must be replayed in its entirety, perhaps as part of a doubleheader later in the season.

The concept of a doubleheader, by the way, is unique to baseball; with very few exceptions a regular ticket to such an event entitles you to see two full ball games for the price of one. A doubleheader in which the first game is played in the late afternoon and the other at night is known as a "twi-night" doubleheader.

CHAPTER 7
HOW THE GAME IS PLAYED

As we have seen, the aim of each team in a baseball game is quite simple, depending on whether it is "up" (batting) or in the field: to score runs, and to prevent the other team from scoring. In this chapter we'll take a closer look at the individual players and how they achieve these goals.

THE FIELDERS

The first, second, and third basemen are responsible for catching any balls hit in their direction, as well as for "covering" their respective bases. A man does not stand directly on his base (except when he wants to be in contact with the base to get a runner out), but rather in its general vicinity—how far and in what direction he stands away from it depends on the strategic situation.

Possibly the most important member of the infield is the shortstop, who, as we have seen, stands between second and third base (to help plug up the "hole" there, where many batted balls escape the infield). In addition, the shortstop helps the second baseman to cover second, and usually relays or "cuts off"—catches and holds—throws from the outfield. The shortstop is often the best fielder on the team, renowned more for his skill with the glove than with the bat.

Since the shortstop and second baseman have functions that often overlap, they may decide between them their field position on given plays. Sometimes the shortstop will cover second, for example, while the second baseman plays near the hole between second and first. They may alternate as relay or cutoff men, again depending on the situation at the moment.

Outfielders are each responsible for approximately one third of the outfield. Left field is on the batter's left as he faces the pitcher; right field is on his right. All three men are responsible for catching, retrieving, and returning any balls that are hit beyond the infield. The most important man here is the center fielder, because he covers the widest territory and is usually the fleetest.

A good outfielder needs an excellent "arm," which means that he should be able to throw long distances accurately to help put out runners in the infield, or to stop a run from scoring. Outfielders must also be able to run quickly (to get to a well-hit ball) and have a highly developed sense of timing. A good outfielder must be able to "get the jump on the ball": sometimes a well-timed catch against the outfield wall can prevent a ball from going over the wall, turning a sure home run into a caught fly ball for an out. If was said of Joe DiMaggio, the great Yankee outfielder, that he was "off at the crack of the bat," knowing just where to go and how to play the ball.

A cardinal rule for all fielders is "Don't make errors." The whole point of professional sports is, after all, that men who have reached the pro level are supposed to be beyond making mistakes. All professional athletes have occasional lapses, of course, but only in baseball is the concept of a player's mistake carried to almost Calvinistic extremes. If a fielder fails to make what is considered a routine play (routine by professional standards) and this mistake results in a man getting on or advancing a base, the fielder is charged with an error. The error, like all other official notice of player performance, goes in the record books forever.

THE CATCHER

The catcher, obviously, must catch any ball that is not hit by the batter, as well as put out any player who is running to home plate. If he misses a ball that should have been a routine catch, he is charged with an error known as a "passed ball," and runners advance at their own risk. The catcher also helps the pitcher decide how to pitch to any given batter and, because he is the only defensive member facing all the other members of his team, often directs their actions on the field. Finally, the catcher assists the pitcher in several important fielding plays, which we will examine in the next chapter.

THE PITCHER

Although some players in other positions might dispute this, it is generally agreed that the pitcher is the most important player on a baseball team. He is, after all, the first line of defense for his team: if he pitches well, few opposing batters will get on base and there will be little need for tricky fielding plays to prevent them from scoring. Moreover, the pitcher controls the pace of the game, and a really good pitcher can almost single-handedly make a difference between a loss and a win by his team.

Ron Guidry, the best pitcher in the American League in 1978, was considered so good that opposing teams virtually conceded any game he would be pitching. His pitches were so difficult to hit that a catchphrase began to circulate to reassure players who had to bat against him: "Ron Guidry is *not* God."

Because pitching is such a strenuous activity, the pitcher is the only regular member of his team who does not start every game. Most starting pitchers play every fourth or fifth day to allow their pitching arm time to recover, and a team without at least four or five sound starters has little hope of a winning season. These usually include at least one left-handed pitcher—called a "southpaw" because his left hand supposedly faces "south" (ball parks were originally designed with home plate to the west and center field to the east to avoid glare from the setting sun).

The pitcher's major function, as we have seen, is to pitch the ball to the batter in such a way that he will miss it; misjudge it and let it go by for a called strike; or hit it so that it can easily be fielded. To do this the pitcher uses two psychological weapons: intimidation and deception.

Although baseball has the lowest serious injury rate of the major sports, it still has its hazards, and at no time is this more apparent than when a batter, protected only by a plastic batting helmet, stands to one side of the plate and faces a pitcher who is about to throw a very hard ball at speeds of up to one hundred miles an hour. Few batters in the major leagues have been seriously injured by a thrown ball, yet the potential is always there, and every batter is aware of it. So is every pitcher, and exploitation of this awareness is a basic tool of pitching. Former Yankee pitcher Ryne Duren intimidated batters *before* he faced them. After coming into the game Duren would throw his first "warm-up" pitch against the backstop (the screen that keeps foul balls from hitting spectators behind home plate). Since he wore glasses that looked as if they were made of the ends of Coke bottles, this ploy was very effective in making the batters wonder if he was going to hit them as well.

Sometimes a pitcher uses a "brush-back" pitch in order to intimidate a batter. The purpose of this pitch is to stop a batter from "crowding the plate" (standing very close to home plate), which not only makes it easier for him to hit any balls thrown to the outside of the plate but also blocks the catcher's view of base runners. In order to "brush" such a player back, a pitcher will occasionally throw "high and inside"—above the strike zone and close to the batter—as a warning to move away from the plate. Such a pitch, if well-controlled, generally has the desired effect. However, unless the pitcher has pinpoint control the brush-back can be dangerous, for the pitch could hit the batter in the head.

To the average spectator, especially those viewing on TV, every pitch may look alike. To a batter, however, every variation in the pitcher's motion, in the speed of the ball, in the way it moves, and in the exact position it takes over the plate are important. Every batter has a certain area of the strike zone that he "likes," or hits best in, and he will be "looking for" a pitch within that area. This area is called his "power zone." For some batters, this might be "inside" (toward him), while others may prefer to hit high or low within the strike zone. As a rule of thumb, the lower a pitcher can throw consistently (within the strike zone) the better he is likely to do, because low balls are more likely to be hit to the ground, while higher balls are more likely to be hit in the air.

And this is where the deception comes in. Until the very last second, a pitcher tries to make all of his pitches look alike. Thus, the batter cannot make a decision about whether to hit, or how, until the ball has left the pitcher's hand. A split second later the ball is over the plate. Although pitchers usually have one standard pitch that they specialize in, most have at least one variant as well that is thrown with the same motion, the better to fool the batter. (Pitchers are generally characterized by their most effective pitch—you may hear a man referred to as a "knuckleballer," for example.)

The extent to which some pitchers go to disguise their pitches is legendary. Satchel Paige delivered his from behind his "satchellike" feet; Dazzy Vance tore the sleeve of his shirt so that it waved distractingly behind the ball; and Luis Tiant has a herky-jerky motion that makes him look as if he is alternately counting the house, disco-ing, or having seizures.

Unless you are actually at a game and have a good vantage point, it will be difficult to tell what sort of pitch has been thrown. When watching a pitcher you should bear in mind that the ball generally does not follow a straight trajectory, a fact that makes life difficult for batters. Through various ways of gripping the ball and moving his wrist and arm, the pitcher is able to get the ball to behave in ways that make sense only to an expert in aerodynamics and that are barely detectable to the naked eye, but that make quite a difference in the ability of the batter to respond and hit accurately.

Following is a brief look at some of the pitches you are likely to see or hear about.

FASTBALL This is perhaps the basic pitch in baseball. Some of the greatest fastball pitchers have been clocked as throwing at up to and over one hundred miles per hour. When a fastball pitcher has his "stuff," meaning that his pitch is "on" and accurate, most batters give up in despair. However, on days when the speed or accuracy is off, fastballs are not that difficult to hit, which is one reason some fastball pitchers have a high number of both strikeouts and home runs on their record.

Although it may change direction at the last minute, a fastball is generally fairly straight in its trajectory. A fastball pitcher is exciting to watch, and announcers often use vivid language in describing him: "He's throwing smoke now."

Closely related to the fastball is the *change-up*. Also called a "change of pace," or an "offspeed pitch," the change-up is designed entirely to deceive. It looks like a fastball but does not reach the plate with the same velocity, causing the batter to swing too soon. When a change has been thrown, the announcer may say something like, "He took something off the ball . . . strike two!" What he took off the ball was a little speed.

BREAKING PITCHES This term describes a variety of pitches that are not straight in their trajectory but curve or drop when they reach the plate. The principal breaking pitches are:

Curveball Also called simply a "curve," this has a spin that tails away from the batter. It curves down and away from a right-handed batter if the pitcher is also right-handed. A curveball thrown by a left-handed pitcher will curve down and away from a left-handed hitter, but down and *toward* a right-handed hitter. It is considered very difficult for a right-handed hitter to hit a good curve thrown by a left-handed pitcher. The chief disadvantage to a curve is that it is a somewhat slower ball, and therefore the batter has a longer time to judge and hit it (time in this case being measured in split seconds).

Slider A slider, or "nickel-curve," is very much like a curve—it curves down and away from a right-handed hitter when thrown by a right-handed pitcher, but the "break" on the ball is noticeably less than that on a curve. It is delivered in a manner similar to a fastball. A good slider is such an effective pitch that one pitcher, Sparky Lyle, throws virtually no other type.

Screwball A screwball is a "reverse curveball," delivered in such a way that if a right-hander throws it it breaks down and *toward* a right-handed hitter, while a left-handed pitcher throws it to break down and toward a left-handed hitter.

Sinker Also called a "sinking ball," this pitch is similar to a curveball, except that it does not curve laterally but drops abruptly over the plate.

When watching a pitcher throw any of these breaking pitches, you may be astonished to see the umpire call a strike when the catcher has had to reach far to the side of home plate to catch an especially hard-breaking (strongly curving) ball. That, of course, is the purpose of these pitches: to pass over the plate in such a way that the batter will swing where they were, but now aren't. As Phil Rizzuto, announcer for the Yankees, points out: "It's not where the catcher catches it, it's where it went over home plate."

SPECIALTY PITCHES Specialty pitches are used most often by pitchers who have "lost something" from their fastball due to age or injury, although some pitchers have made a career of specialty pitching. The two pitches you are most likely to hear about are the *fork ball*, which behaves like a sinker but is thrown with the fingers in a "forked" position, and the *knuckle ball*.

The knuckle ball, also called "knuckler," is the most exciting pitch to watch next to a really superb fastball, because when it is "on," it is extremely unpredictable—hard to hit and hard to catch.

Before explaining why this is so, this might be a good time to mention that a pitcher can be charged with an error known as a "wild pitch." This is a pitch that goes so far from the strike zone that the catcher is unable to catch it. The ball is still in play during a wild pitch, however, and any men who are on base are free to advance (at their own risk) while the catcher tries frantically to get to the ball. (If the ball gets by the catcher through his own fault, he is charged with a passed ball.)

A knuckle ball derives its name from the fact that the pitcher grips it with the tips of his fingers, leaving his knuckles visible around the edge of the ball. The ball is then thrown straight. And by straight, I mean absolutely straight, for the knuckle ball if thrown properly has no spin on it, which makes it subject to the whims of any air currents that may be around. The result is that the ball, when it reaches the plate, takes completely unpredictable little hops, dips, and flutters. According to Charley Lau, former major-league catcher and highly respected batting coach, "There are two theories on hitting the knuckle ball. Unfortunately, neither of them works."

Catching the knuckler is not much easier than hitting it. Many catchers wear a special oversized mitt for this pitch, but it is rare when his knuckle ball is on for a pitcher not to commit at least a couple of wild pitches. This is also why many managers often remove a knuckleballer from a close game in the late innings, to prevent him from inadvertently walking anyone home, even though he may be striking out a lot of batters.

Although some pitchers have been knuckleballers throughout their career, others take it up only later, like the great, courageous Jim Bouton, who, though retired from baseball for ten years, made a brief comeback to the major leagues at the age of thirty-nine by developing a dependable knuckler. (To obtain greater control of the ball, Bouton reportedly serrated his fingernails with a file.)

ILLEGAL PITCHES   Illegal pitches come in two varieties: the *spitball* (also "spitter" or "mudball") and the *beanball*.

The spitball's name comes from the fact that in the early days of baseball some pitchers literally spit on the ball before throwing, to make it easier to put spin on the ball. This pitch was outlawed in the twenties, because a "loaded" ball behaves differently in the air from one that has not in any way been doctored. A pitcher caught delivering a loaded or defaced ball today is penalized by having that pitch called a ball; the second time he is ejected from the game. The same penalties apply to a pitcher who puts the ball or his fingers to his mouth before delivering a pitch (although it is all right for a pitcher to rub his hands with rosin, from a rosin bag kept at the back of the pitcher's mound).

Some pitchers consider it part of the fun of the game to throw an occasional spitter and get away with it. The popularity of the pitch as well as the variety of ways it has been delivered are reflected in the official rules of baseball, which prohibit "rubbing the ball" with a variety of foreign substances, among them licorice!

More dangerous is the descriptively named beanball, also known as a "knockdown pitch," which is deliberately aimed toward the batter's head. Although such pitches have always been illegal, before 1978 the rule was seldom enforced if the pitcher was not too obvious about it. As a result, so-called beanball wars occasionally erupted, with one pitcher throwing at a particularly troublesome hitter (perhaps in retaliation for something the man did earlier in the game), only to find one of his own men or himself targets of the other side's pitcher in the next half inning. One player, Jake Powell of the Yankees, took on the whole Red Sox bench during a game in the thirties in which he was hit by a beanball. In order to stop such exchanges the umpires began enforcing the rule against beanballs at the start of the 1978 season. Now the first pitcher throwing a beanball is warned; the next such pitch by any pitcher results in automatic ejection from the game for the pitcher and his manager. Surprisingly, many batters as well as pitchers have objected to this new ruling, and it seems to have had little effect on the continuing popularity of the pitch.

A beanball, of course, must be distinguished from a pitch that accidentally hits a batter (and results in a walk). If a pitcher begins to lose control and hits more than one or two batters, his manager usually removes him.

A pitcher who is known to throw an occasional beanball definitely has a psychological advantage over the batter. Al Hrabosky, the colorful pitcher known as the "Mad Hungarian," cultivates the image of a pitcher who will knock you down as soon as look at you. In an interview on the tricks of his trade, he told *New Times* magazine that "I want them to think I'm so crazy, so sick, I just might stick it in their ear."

THE BATTER

Most ballplayers are either right-handed or left-handed. Whether a player is one or the other is important to his position (a fielder should be stationed so that he can most easily catch and throw those balls that are likely to come to him), but even more important in batting. Most hitters "pull" the ball (and are called "pull" hitters); this means that they tend to hit best to the side of the ball park that corresponds to where they stand at the plate. Since right-handers stand to the left of home plate, they tend to hit toward left field; left-handers toward right. A ball that is not pulled, but hit to the unexpected side, is called an "opposite field" hit, which for a right-handed hitter is to right field, for a left-handed hitter to the left. A ball is usually hit to the opposite field for strategic reasons. A player who can hit the ball effectively to all fields is called a "spray hitter."

The issue of whether a hitter bats left- or right-handed—if he does both, he is a "switch hitter"—is particularly important in relation to the pitcher. For example, a right-handed batter against a left-handed pitcher—and vice versa—is better able to judge a curveball, since it's easier to see a pitch breaking toward you than one breaking away. And a left-handed batter against a right-handed pitcher has an advantage in that he has a step-and-a-half "jump" to first base. Some players who are naturally right-handed bat left-handed for a further reason: the batter's right—or dominant—hand pulls the bat through while the left hand guides. Thus Ted Williams, Ty Cobb, and many other power hitters "threw right, batted left."

A batter's "handedness" also affects his ability to hit in different ball parks. Extra-base hits and home runs may be easier for different handed players depending on the relative size and depth of the left and right fields in a given ball park. A right-handed batter with little power might hit home runs in a park with a fairly shallow left field, for example; but the same batter could have trouble in a larger park, where hits that would have gone over the wall elsewhere are easily caught by an outfielder. So important is the configuration of a ball park that at one point the Yankees and the Red Sox considered trading Joe DiMaggio and Ted Williams, because each hitter was better adapted to the other's park. And Yankee Stadium—called the "House That Ruth Built"—was built to conform to his hitting power: because he was a left-handed batter, they erected a short right-field wall to accommodate him.

Just as important as where a ball is hit is how it comes off the bat. That is, some balls are easier or more difficult to field depending on whether they are hit high, low, hard, or softly. The most common terms for certain types of hits are:

FLY BALL, FLY A fly ball, as we have seen, is any ball hit high into the air. Most flies are caught, usually by an outfielder. When a fly is hit into the infield, the umpire will sometimes call an "infield fly." An infield fly is called if there are runners at first and second, or the bases are loaded, with no more than one man out. When an infield fly is called, the batter is automatically out, whether it is caught or not. This rule was established out of fairness to the runners, who would be forced to run if a fielder deliberately missed or dropped a fly ball in hopes of getting a double play (see page 77).

As we have seen, players cannot run on a fly ball until after it is caught, and if they are off base when this happens, they must tag up (retouch the base) before running. If an infield fly is not caught, however, batters may run without retouching base.

POP FLY, POP-UP This is simply a fly that is hit very high, usually a short distance into the infield. When it is hit foul near home plate, it is usually caught by the catcher.

BOUNCER A ground ball that bounces noticeably. A *chopper* is a ball that bounces high, usually in the infield. If it hits the ground just in front of home plate, then bounces out of the range of the infielders, it is called a "Baltimore chop."

DRIBBLER A ball that rolls or bounces weakly in the infield.

Normally harder to field are:

LINE DRIVE A ball hit very hard and straight but not high off the ground. Sometimes a line drive is hit directly at a fielder and caught before it hits the ground, but more commonly it is hit into the outfield for a base hit.

BLOOPER, BLOOP (also called "Texas Leaguer") A short fly ball that is hit just beyond the infield, outside the infielders' range but too far in for the outfielders to catch.

BUNT As mentioned before, a bunt is a soft hit, designed to roll only a few yards from home plate but placed in such a way that neither the pitcher, catcher, nor other infielder can easily field it. The batter "squares to bunt" at the last minute, ideally after the pitch has left the pitcher's hand. To do this he turns and faces the pitcher, the bat thrust out in front of him, and simply lets the ball hit the bat, trying to direct its motion. In a well-executed bunt, the batter can often reach first base before any fielder can throw the ball to first.

If a man has two strikes against him and bunts foul on the third strike, he is out.

Occasionally, a batter will hit a ball so hard that his bat breaks (though the ball may still travel quite a distance—even over the wall). This sort of hit is known as a "broken bat hit." In a freak accident, Dodger catcher Steve Yeager was nearly killed when part of a broken bat pierced his throat.

SUBSTITUTIONS

Substitutions may be made at any time, but once a player has been removed from the game he may not reenter it later.

Almost all substitutions are made while the team is up, unless a fielder is injured while fielding. The principal exception to this is a pitcher. A substitute pitcher is called a "relief pitcher," or reliever, and he may be brought in for many reasons, the most common of which is that the starting pitcher is tiring or simply having a bad day. (See Chapter Eight for more about relief pitching.)

PINCH HITTER A pinch hitter is a batter who has not yet played and who is called in to take a teammate's turn at bat. He is usually used in special situations—to replace a weaker hitter or one who bats from the opposite side of the plate. Normally the pinch hitter bats only once. If he remains in the game and assumes the position in the field of the man he has replaced, he is no longer a pinch hitter but a regular substitute.

PINCH RUNNER This player, who is usually very fast, is sometimes put in for a man who is already on base but who is injured or who simply can't run as fast. A pinch runner is often brought in in the later innings when a team is losing and desperately needs a run, in the hope that his speed (in the event of a subsequent hit) or base-stealing ability will lead to an ultimate score. Like the pinch hitter, the pinch runner is used only once; if he remains in the game he is considered a regular substitute.

DESIGNATED HITTER The two major leagues of organized baseball, the National and the American, have mostly identical rules except for the size of the strike zone and the use of the player called the designated hitter, or DH. The DH is used only in the American League, and isn't really a substitute but is, in effect, a tenth member of the offense. The DH does not play a position on the field but rather takes a turn at bat *instead* of the pitcher, because pitchers are usually poor hitters and to spare the pitcher extra effort. (In the National League, a pinch hitter may hit for the pitcher, but that automatically removes the pitcher from the game, requiring the use of a relief pitcher in the next inning.)

COACHES

Helping the members of the team to play effectively are a number of coaches for each team. From a white-ruled rectangle adjacent to first base, the first-base coach helps the runner to decide whether or not to break for second. From a similar rectangle the third-base coach signals runners on base when to run or steal, usually relaying the decision of the manager of the team. He also sometimes signals the batter whether or not to swing at the next pitch.

A pitching coach works with pitchers to develop their skills, and sometimes there is an infield coach who advises infielders. Every team has a coach who works with the players on their batting.

OFFICIALS

The four umpires in baseball are more of a visible presence in the game than officials in other team sports, particularly the umpire behind home plate, also called umpire in chief or plate umpire.

It is generally conceded that baseball officiating is the best, in the sense of being most fair and balanced, of all the team sports. When you consider that almost all of the umpires' decisions are judgment calls, it is remarkable to see how video replays of close calls at a base repeatedly prove the umpires right. One reason for their accuracy is that most plays in baseball involve only two or at most three men, and so are easier to sort out than plays in hockey or football, where a tangle of flailing bodies may obscure what is actually happening. In an extreme of objectivity unique to baseball, an umpire who sees something illegal, such as a player scoring a run without touching one of the bases, does not mention it unless the other team "appeals" to him for a decision.

Although baseball does not have any system of fouls and penalties like the other team sports, the umpire has clear authority to eject players (and managers) from the game for a variety of offenses, ranging from unsportsmanlike conduct to excessive arguing. This doesn't stop players and managers alike from strenuously protesting calls, of course. Yet umpires seldom give in. Occasionally an umpire will ask for a confirmation of his call from one of the other umpires, but the ultimate decision is his, and woe be unto the player or manager who will not accept it. The legendary umpire Bill Klem once warned Yankee player Jake Powell, who had thrown his bat in the air in disgust: "If that bat comes down, you're out of the game." (The colorful Klem also reportedly said, pointing to his heart: "I've never made a mistake in here.")

From time to time there is talk of replacing umpires with videotape replay machines, but this is unlikely to happen. As Al Clark, an American League umpire, put it, "If you took the human element out of our game it wouldn't be the same. Can you see [a manager] kicking dirt at a machine?"

Ultimately, then, it is the human element in baseball that makes it so accessible. In the next two chapters we will examine the basic offensive and defensive plays. But the essence of baseball could not be more simply stated than it was by the great Willie Mays: "When the other guy throws it I hit it; when the other guy hits it I catch it."

CHAPTER
8 BEHIND THE ACTION

THE MANAGER

After a contested play during a game I was listening to one day, I heard the following exchange between the announcers:

ANNOUNCER 1: Let's see if he throws his hat on the ground and kicks it.

ANNOUNCER 2: He only does that when he's losing.

ANNOUNCER 1: That's right. Aha, look there! He just kicked the dirt!

The man they were referring to was Ralph Houk, colorful manager of the Detroit Tigers, and although I was not there I could well imagine the scene, one of my favorite in baseball: a good old nose-to-nose argument between manager and umpire.

The uninitiated baseball fan can easily get the impression that the manager's major duty is to argue with umpires as hotly and dramatically as possible. While this is a function most managers serve gladly, the manager's primary job is one of the most demanding in baseball, and perhaps of all sports.

Not only must he plan offensive and defensive strategy for each game, but he must also balance present needs against those of the future, in a long season with games scheduled almost daily. He is responsible during the game for planning play-by-play tactics as well as overall game strategy, and for observing how his players— and those on the other team—are performing in this particular game. If someone is obviously having an off-day, for example, the manager may want to substitute for him, but only at the most strategic moment. He must also be able to second-guess his opposing managers and know a great deal about most of the players his team will be meeting throughout the year.

In short, the manager must be a virtual computer of information, a master planner, and on top of that should possess the human qualities necessary to keep his team members as happy as possible during the long season.

This seemingly thankless job is nevertheless one of the most sought-after occupations in sports. Many managers began as ballplayers, and most of them love the game of baseball with an intensity epitomized by Tom LaSorda, manager of the Los Angeles Dodgers, who insists that he bleeds "Dodger Blue" and refers to "that great Dodger up in the sky."

THE LINEUP

The first decision any manager makes for a given game is which pitcher to use, and that decision is almost automatic, since he will usually tend to go with the "rotation," or start the pitcher who is supposed to pitch on that day. Some exceptions can be made, of course, depending on who the opposing pitcher is, injuries to the staff, and this particular pitcher's record against the opposition.

Next, the manager chooses his lineup, which is recorded and presented to the chief umpire before the game. The lineup is the listing of the starting players, along with the positions each will fill, in the order that they will bat. This batting order is extremely important for reasons strategic and tactical, and there can be no deviation from it. If a substitute comes in for any player, he must bat in that player's position in the lineup.

Since the object of the game is to get more runs than the other team and since the only way to score runs is to get men on base, the batting order is set up to maximize the chances of getting men on base.

The first batter is called the "lead-off man" (announcer: "And Pond is leading off, followed by Herrera and Marx . . ."). This batter is a player who can be relied on to get on base a high percentage of the time he is up. Ideally, he is also a very fast runner and/or a good base-stealer.

A prime duty of the men who follow the lead-off batter is to help advance him around the bases and ultimately home. The second and third batters are thus among the team's most reliable hitters. The fourth and fifth batters, who are usually the best power hitters on the team, are supposed to hit a long ball (or even a home run) to "drive" anyone on base home. (The fourth man is said to bat "cleanup.")

Generally, the remaining four hitters are less able in descending order, although sometimes a good player will be found here, and on some teams with a lot of power—which means that they have a lot of good hitters—even the last men will be good. In the American League the DH, who hits for the pitcher, may be found anywhere in the batting order, depending on his skill as a hitter. In the National League, however, the pitcher must bat for himself, almost always in ninth position.

You will often hear announcers speak of the "top" or "bottom" of the order—these terms merely refer to where in the batting order the team is in a given inning. In general, if the bottom of the order is up you can't expect much hitting, while the top of the order promises excitement. (Of course there are exceptions to every rule. It was the bottom of the Yankees' batting order that produced the largest number of hits and runs to enable the team to win the 1978 World Series.)

Occasionally, in a poorly pitched game, a team will "bat around," which means that the entire order comes to bat during the same inning. Although this generally makes for a one-sided game, it can be a lot of fun to watch your own team pile up runs this way.

Although it is the manager's duty to plan the overall strategy for a game, it is up to the players to carry out that strategy. To see how they do it, let's take a look at the basics of offensive strategy.

OFFENSIVE STRATEGY

In *All About Baseball*, Leonard Koppett states that the three main duties of a batter are, in order:

1. Avoid striking out;
2. Advance any base runners;
3. If no one is on base, get on base in any way you can.

At first glance, rule number one may seem too obvious to mention—no batter wants to strike out. But there is more than one way for a batter to make an out, and in many cases batters will deliberately risk being put out in pursuit of goal two, to advance base runners. To understand how this works, let's take a look at what Lindsey Nelson terms the "essential" play of baseball, the "hit and run."

The hit-and-run play is designed to advance a runner from first to second base, because a good runner can often get from second to home plate on a single. (Second base is considered "scoring position.")

The hit and run usually occurs when there are fewer than two men out and a man is on first (and no one on second). A given pitch will be prechosen by the manager for the hit and run, and this will be conveyed to batter and runner by means of signals. The instant the pitch chosen—say the second pitch—leaves the pitcher's hand, the runner, who has a few steps' lead off base, breaks for second as fast as he can. The batter, on his part, swings at the ball, no matter what kind of pitch is thrown. He tries to hit through the hole vacated by the infielder, who has rushed over to second base to protect it against the runner from first. If the second baseman has moved toward second, the batter will try to hit the ball between first and second base; if the shortstop is covering, he will aim for the left side of the infield. Even if the batter is thrown out he will probably succeed in advancing the runner, and if he hits the ball safely there are now two men on base.

Another way for the batter to advance the runner in this sort of situation is to hit a sacrifice bunt. If the bunt is well-executed, it is generally too late for a fielder to throw to second by the time he retrieves the ball, and all he can hope for is to throw the batter out at first.

Similar to the hit and run is the "squeeze play." The theory is the same—that is, the batter's purpose is to advance the runner—but in this case the runner is at third and the idea is to get him home to score.

There are two types of squeeze play you will hear announcers mention: the safety squeeze and the suicide squeeze. The principle is the same in either case, the main difference being that in a safety squeeze the runner does not start running for home *on* the pitch, but rather waits until he sees that the batter has bunted safely to the ground. This is to protect against the possibility of the batter missing the pitch, or hitting a pop-up—which, if caught, makes any man caught off base liable to be put out, and unable to continue running without first returning to the base to tag up. (Since the ball will presumably be in the infield, this presents a real danger to the runner at third.)

A suicide squeeze is a squeeze play in which the runner throws caution to the winds and, as with a hit and run, begins to run on the pitch. On a suicide squeeze the runner is trusting the batter not to pop up and is prepared to slide into home before anyone can retrieve the ball and tag him out.

Sometimes runners will begin to run on the pitch when to the uninitiated there does not seem to be any obvious play. This always occurs when two men are out and the count is full on the batter (meaning that three balls and two strikes have been called). In this situation there is no real danger to the runners: the batter will get a hit, in which case the runners can and must advance; or he will foul, in which case they can't be put out anyway; or he will strike out or hit a fly that is caught for the third out.

A final way in which a batter helps runners to advance is by hitting a "sacrifice fly." This play usually occurs when there are runners at second and/or third, and fewer than two men out. The batter hits a long, fly ball deep to the outfield. Unless the ball goes over the wall, the outfielder will probably catch it, putting the batter out. However, if the ball is hit far enough runners at third and sometimes even at second should be able to tag up and score.

In each of the situations I have described the logical play is usually clearly indicated, meaning that any player or manager would know, say, that a hit and run is called for, or that a bunt is likely. Of course, the team in the field will be prepared for the play, too, and will modify what it does accordingly. For example, if expecting a bunt, the infield will play "in," or closer to the plate. In response, the opposing manager may decide to "take the play off" and have the batter do something altogether different. A lot of baseball strategy thus consists of second-guessing between the two managers.

Generally, a manager wants to "go with the percentages"—to use plays that have worked in a certain situation a majority of times—but he also wants to keep the opposition off balance with the element of surprise. So, although it may seem prudent to have the batter attempt a sacrifice bunt toward third base, the manager may change his mind when he sees that the defensive manager has anticipated his move. Or, instead of having the sacrifice attempt take place on the second pitch, he may decide to do it on the third pitch, and so on.

Since all of these plays require the cooperation of two or more players, the managers constantly signal their intentions. In the case of the team at bat, the manager sends messages to the batter in the form of prearranged signals through the third-base coach, and this is why you will see most batters glancing toward third base regularly for odd hand motions, removal of a cap, or other body language. They want to find out if a play is "on," or if there are other instructions. The opposition, meanwhile, tries to "steal" the signals.

If the batter is confused about a play coming up, or doesn't understand the signals, he may ask the umpire to signal time-out, and confer with the coach on one of the base lines.

DEFENSIVE STRATEGY

Beyond his pitching duties, the pitcher is responsible for fielding balls hit toward the mound and covering first base and home when the regular fielders are drawn away. In addition, and perhaps as important as the pitching, he is responsible for "holding" runners on base and preventing offensive plays. He does this, of course, with the cooperation of the catcher and infielders, all of whom are aware of the other team's strategy and are ready to counter with their own.

You will most often see the pitcher "holding the runner on" when there is a man on first and fewer than two men out, because this is a situation favorable for a steal. Most runners will take as long a lead off first base as they think they can get away with, while the pitcher counters by quickly throwing (before the pitch) to the first baseman. If the runner does not return to the bag quickly enough, he can thus be tagged out or "picked off." Usually the man retreats in time, but the threat of a pick-off generally limits the lead a runner can safely take. Sometimes the runner is caught in the middle of a steal, and when this happens the first and second basemen (or occasionally the pitcher) engage in a "run down," closing in on the hapless runner who tries desperately but seldom with success to avoid the tag. A rundown can occur any time a batter is caught off base, and between any two bases, but is most common on a steal attempt.

Any pick-off throw must be quick and unexpected in order to catch the runner off-guard, but there are strict rules governing the manner in which it can be thrown. To begin with, on every pitch the pitcher must keep one foot on the rubber—the 24-inch-wide slab atop the pitcher's mound—until he releases the ball. If no men are on base he will usually use the "full windup," moving his arms up and then behind him before delivering the pitch. If there is a man on base, he will pitch from a "set position," standing sideways on the mound—so that he can see the runner on base—with his hands at his chest or waist. He may go into a "stretch" motion first, extending both hands over his head, but he must return to the set position before throwing. While in this position he can throw either to the plate or to a base. Once he goes into his windup or has started to deliver the pitch, however, he must follow through, or he will have committed a "balk." If he steps toward a base as if to throw there and fails to complete the throw, he will also be charged with a balk. If the umpire decides that the pitcher has committed a balk (and this is one of those tricky areas that is often protested), all runners move up a base. If no one is on base when a balk occurs, it simply counts as a ball.

Thus, the pick-off is a deceptive play that cannot be *too* deceptive, and a pitcher with a good pick-off move, one that cannot be detected till the last minute, has a real advantage over the runners.

When there is a man on first and a hit-and-run play is expected, the pitcher, catcher, and second baseman may participate in a defensive ploy known as a "pitchout," which, if they've guessed right, will take place on the same pitch the opposing team has chosen for the hit and run. On a pitchout, the pitcher goes into his usual pre-pitch moves, but then, instead of trying to pick off the runner—who by now usually has a large lead—and instead of throwing a normal pitch, he throws the ball fast and wide of the plate. The catcher is there ready to catch and throw it immediately to second, where the second baseman is waiting to tag out the runner.

The pitch, of course, is registered as a ball, but since the fielders, who have received the signal from the catcher, are anticipating the throw, their chances of getting the runner out at second are excellent, not only because of the speed of the throw but because the catcher has a clear, unobstructed view of the base.

Another exciting and frequent defensive combination is the "double play," where two men are put out on the same play. The most common one occurs at second and first bases, and this is how it usually works:

A man is on first. The batter hits an infield grounder, but the ball is fielded and quickly relayed to the man covering second. This fielder quickly steps on the bag before the runner reaches second, putting him out—remember, he is forced to run—and then throws to the first baseman, who waits for the throw with his foot on the bag to get the runner out. In some cases the batter may be thrown or tagged out first, but this is less desirable, since once the batter is out there is no longer a force at second, and the man running to second would have to be tagged to be put out.

A double play can also occur if a batter hits a high fly that is caught and the runner is then tagged out before he returns to base; or if the batter strikes out and the runner is thrown out stealing a base.

In order to prevent double plays, it has been a time-honored practice for the runner at first base to slide into second in such a way as to interfere with the second baseman, thus preventing him from throwing to first for the second out. Extreme interference maneuvers have always been illegal, but were seldom enforced until 1978, when umpires began "calling" them. A runner who tries to be too much of a juggernaut these days is charged with interference and the batter is automatically out.

A very rare event, which I myself have never seen, is a "triple play," in which *three* offensive men are put out on the same play. A triple play is extremely exciting, not only because it is so uncommon but because it is only possible when there are two or three men on base, and no men are out. Writer Robert Cenedella describes a triple play he saw in a game between the Mets and the Giants in the early sixties: "It was the second game of a doubleheader that had gone into extra innings. With the score still tied the Giants had the bases loaded and Orlando Cepeda came up. He hit a short line drive to the hole between shortstop and second and Roy McMillan, the shortstop, leaped and caught it for the first out. Then in one stride he stepped on second before the runner to third could tag up. Meanwhile, the runner from first to second skidded and turned back to first, but McMillan threw to the first baseman in time for the third out." Cenedella goes on to point out that if McMillan had tagged the last runner before he could turn around, this would have been an *unassisted* triple play, one of the rarest events in baseball.

Double and triple plays are normally possible only if a force situation exists, because there simply isn't enough time to tag more than one runner out on a play. Therefore, the team in the field will sometimes create force situations by deliberately putting men on base. This is most likely to occur if there is one man out; a double play will then retire the side. The usual way to put a man on base is to issue an intentional walk. When an intentional walk is planned, the catcher and pitcher cooperate in an almost balletic exercise in batter frustration: slowly the pitcher delivers a ball far to the side of the plate, where the catcher is waiting. He returns the ball, and the process is repeated until four balls have been thrown, at which time the batter walks to first.

Sometimes an intentional walk will be given not only to create a force but also to avoid a power hitter. The theory is that it is worth the risk of allowing another man on base in order to pitch to a poorer hitter, or one who has problems with this particular pitcher.

Related to the intentional walk is the tactic known as "pitching around" the batter, in which the pitcher throws a lot of very canny pitches at the "corners" (of the strike zone), which may or may not be called balls but which are placed where the batter is unlikely to be able to hit them. This often results in a base on balls, but again, the risk of putting an extra man on base is deemed less than the risk of the same man hitting a long ball or even (shudder) a home run.

The one thing a pitcher does *not* want to do is to give up a walk unintentionally, because any man on any base is a potential run. As soon as the pitcher has thrown more balls than strikes, he is said to be "behind the hitter" or "in the hole." Conversely, a batter with two strikes against him before three balls have been thrown is in the hole.

It is usual for a pitcher to "give up" a few unintentional walks and perhaps a home run or two during a game. When he walks batter after batter, however, or begins throwing wild pitches, hitting batters, or giving up a string of hits, he and the team are in trouble, and the manager must do something about it.

PULLING THE PITCHER

The question of when, or if, to take out the starting pitcher is a traditional headache for baseball managers, and it is almost guaranteed to lead to arguments in bars and in the stands. ("I tell ya we would of won if he'd only left the Catfish in." "Are you nuts? He shoulda took him out in the first inning.")

In order to decide what to do about a pitcher who is having difficulties, the manager has to be thoroughly familiar with this pitcher. Many pitchers, for example, are "wild" in the first inning or two, meaning that they tend to throw a lot of balls and perhaps give up a hit or two or even a run. But then they often "settle down" and pitch extremely well for the rest of the game. If a pitcher remains wild beyond two or so innings, giving up several runs, almost any manager would pull him. But the decision is usually not so clear-cut.

At the first sign of trouble for a pitcher, someone will usually go over and talk to him. Often this is the catcher, but sometimes it is the pitching coach or manager. If the manager makes a second "trip to the mound" during the same inning, the pitcher is automatically removed from the game.

A pitcher may be removed at any time, even in the middle of pitching to a particular batter, if he is having a great deal of trouble. Many pitchers resent being taken out and will sometimes argue about it, but most accept it with good grace. On the other hand, some pitchers will request to be taken out, perhaps because of a sore arm or for other reasons—like Ron Guidry, the New York Yankees pitcher who asked to leave a game because he had accidentally swallowed his plug of chewing tobacco and was afraid that he was going to throw up on the mound.

Once the starting pitcher is gone for whatever reason, he is replaced by a man from the "bullpen," a small fenced area usually beyond the outfield fence where the relief pitchers wait during the game. (It is so named because at the turn of the century the reserve players—including the pitchers—rested in the outfield underneath the omnipresent Bull Durham Tobacco signs.) If the manager thinks that he may need to bring in a reliever, he telephones to the bullpen for one or more pitchers (right- and left-handed) to begin "warming up"—throwing pitches to a catcher—to loosen their arm. Sometimes a reliever will warm up several times only to sit down again when the original pitcher has managed to get himself out of a jam.

Although relief pitchers have always been a part of the game of baseball, it is only in the last few years that relieving has become a specialty in itself. Today's relief pitcher must be ready to come into the game at any moment—a left-handed reliever may be called in to pitch to a powerful left-handed hitter, for example—but usually he is called in in the late innings to take over for a pitcher who is already in trouble. Relievers are sometimes called firemen, because they're expected to come in and "put out the fire." Since a relief pitcher usually plays only in crisis situations, the job requires a man with nerves of steel and utter reliability.

A reliever who pitches poorly may, of course, be relieved himself.

The decision of when to remove a pitcher on the mound is handled the same way in both the American and National leagues. But his removal as a batter is completely different in the two leagues because of the DH rule.

The DH (designated hitter), you recall, is a player whose sole responsibility is to take the pitcher's turn at bat. In the National League the pitcher takes his turn at bat the same as any other player, and this often leads to thorny strategic problems, particularly in the late innings.

Imagine that you are a National League manager. Your best ("ace") pitcher, Gesundheit, has been pitching, but the opposition is leading anyway, 2-0, in the top of the eighth inning. Your team comes up, and somehow two men get on base, although there are two outs. The next batter up is Gesundheit.

What do you do? It's quite possible that none of your men will get on base in the ninth inning, even though the top of the batting order is coming up. On the other hand, the top of the opposition's order is coming up too, and Gesundheit is the best pitcher you have.

You certainly can't count on him to get a hit. Your choices are these: you can leave Gesundheit in for the almost certain out (thus "stranding" two men on base); or you can take him out for a pinch hitter who may drive in a run or two. This means that you will have to go with a new pitcher in the next inning, who may very well give up more runs, but you'll still have another half inning to try to come back. In this situation, most managers would pull the pitcher for a pinch hitter.

PLAYING THE FIELD

Fielders have quite a bit of freedom about where they actually stand and will position themselves according to tactical needs of the game at a given moment. I mentioned before that on a bunt the infield will play close to the base lines (known as "playing shallow"); conversely, a known long-ball hitter will be met by an outfield moving back from its usual positioning (known as "playing deep").

Another decision fielders are often presented with is which runner to put out: if the choice is between the throw to first to get the batter or a throw elsewhere to get a more advanced runner, the fielder will usually throw the runner out. This sort of play is called a "fielder's choice."

There are many other types of decisions and playing combinations in baseball, and part of the thrill of the game is watching an outfielder make a brilliant jumping catch, then a throw to the infield; or seeing a fleet-footed base runner stealing a base when it is least expected. Another part of the fun of baseball, perhaps more important here than in any other sport, is keeping track of all these plays, and that's what we'll do in the next chapter.

CHAPTER 9 FOLLOWING THE GAME

THE STATS

Statistics are kept in all sports, and such important determinations as team rankings, championship berths, and player awards are influenced by them. But in no other sport are statistics so revered as in baseball, where they approach a kind of religious status.

One reason for this is that professional baseball has been played in the United States longer than the other sports, and so the records go back a very long way. Furthermore, the teams and leagues in baseball have been comparatively stable, as has the game itself, with very few important rules changes. In his short story "The Institute for the Foul Ball," author Spencer Holst, whose father was a baseball writer, describes the Official Baseball Records as "the most sacred" of all statistical compilations. And if not the most sacred, surely they are the most complete, for in baseball, statistics are kept for almost everything imaginable.

The obvious statistics are all there, of course: most home runs hit in a season (61, Roger Maris, 1961); longest nine-inning game ever played (4 hours, 18 minutes, Los Angeles versus San Francisco, 1962). There are also the negative or bizarre statistics: most errors in a doubleheader by a catcher (4, held by many catchers); most home runs hit in the month of April (11, held by three players); and even "most often hit by a pitch, switch-hitter, complete season" (11, Pete Rose, 1975).

Every aspect of the game is thus measured: fielding is rated by the number of assists (fielding help in putting a player out), putouts, and fielding average (an expression of the number of assists and putouts per attempts). From the point of view of the average fan, the most important statistics are those for batter and pitcher.

The most significant number for the batter, the one you see next to his name on the TV screen when he is up to bat, is known as his batting average. It is found by dividing the number of base hits (a double counts the same as a single here) by the number of official times he has come to bat. (Official times at bat are only those times a batter hits the ball or strikes out; walks and sacrifices do not count, although getting on base as a result of an error does.) For example, suppose a batter is officially at bat three times per game for three games, and in those three games he gets four base hits. His batting average would be .444 (spoken, as are all the statistics in whole numbers: "four forty-four" rather than "point four four four"). Anything above .300 is extremely good and means that the batter is getting a hit three out of every ten times at bat. A very few superstars have compiled season, and even lifetime, records of .350 or even higher, but this is very rare. If the player is a good fielder in a key position, he can be hitting as low as ".250 on the year," but the closer that average gets to .200, the closer the player is to being benched.

Other important statistics for batters include the number of runs batted in (RBI, often called "ribbie"), and "slugging percentage." The RBI figure is simply a total of the number of runs a batter "drives in," or those that score as a direct result of his actions. For instance, if a batter gets a base hit and the runner at second scores, that's an RBI, as is a run that scores as a result of a sacrifice fly or bunt. A batter even gets an RBI if the bases are loaded and he walks, forcing home the man at third. The player who hits a grand-slam home run is credited with four RBIs, one for each of the runners and one for his own score.

Slugging percentage is a statistic that shows how *effectively* a man is hitting: it is obtained by dividing the total number of bases he hits to (that is, a single counts as one base, a double as two, and so on) by the number of times at bat. The slugging average is generally a good deal higher than the batting average, especially for power hitters.

The most important statistic for a pitcher is his earned run average, or ERA. It is a measure of how many *earned* runs a pitcher gives up; that is, how many runs that score are a direct result of his actions as a pitcher and do not result from errors on the part of his teammates. The ERA is found by dividing the number of earned runs given up by the number of innings pitched. The result is then multiplied by nine to give an average of runs given up per nine innings. For example, a pitcher gives up six runs in three games in which he pitched a total of 23 innings:

$$\frac{6}{23} \times 9 = \frac{54}{23} = 2.34$$

His ERA is 2.34, meaning that he can be expected to give up between two and three runs in nine full innings.

The lower the ERA the better, and anything under 3.00 is considered very good, while lower than 2.00 is exceptional. (The Yankee superstar Ron Guidry finished the 1978 season with a phenomenal 1.74!)

Like all baseball statistics, the ERA is cumulative and changes throughout the season. And like the other meaningful statistics, a separate cumulative record is kept for the pitcher's lifetime as a player.

Next to his ERA, perhaps the most important statistic for a pitcher is the number of wins as opposed to losses. In any baseball game, no matter how well the teams played as a whole, it is the pitchers who get the "win" or the "loss." This statistic is always expressed with the wins number first; thus, a 10 and 3 pitcher has won 10 and lost 3 games so far this year. The magic number of wins for a pitcher is 20—any pitcher who achieves it during a single season is considered very, very good; no more than a handful of pitchers manage it during any given year.

If a pitcher's record for the year is 20-3, that still doesn't tell the whole story. He has undoubtedly started in many more than 23 baseball games, but receives credit only for those in which he was the "pitcher of record."

The pitcher of record is usually the pitcher who starts the game, but not always. To be credited with a win, a starting pitcher must not only pitch at least five *complete* innings, but his team must be in the lead at the time he is replaced, and must remain in the lead throughout the rest of the game. (For example, Hunbacher's team is leading by a score of 5-4 in the sixth inning when Hunbacher is pulled for a pinch hitter. In the next inning, the seventh, the opposition gets three hits off Darby, the relief pitcher, to go ahead 7-5, but in the ninth Hunbacher's team pulls it out and wins 8-7. Hunbacher does not get the win.)

As far as a loss goes, the pitcher who was pitching when his team first fell behind, as long as they never again tie or assume the lead, is charged with the loss, no matter how many innings he had pitched up to that point. On the other hand, any time the score becomes tied, all preceding pitchers *not currently pitching* are out of contention for wins and losses. (In the above example Darby would have been charged with the loss if his team had not managed to win at the end, no matter how many subsequent innings he pitched.) Any runs that are scored by men who were on base at the time a pitcher was removed from the game (assuming he is removed in the middle of an inning), will be charged against him for purposes of his ERA.

A rather bizarre example of how all this works occurred in a game early in the 1979 season between the San Francisco Giants and the San Diego Padres. Both starting pitchers, Mickey Lolich for the Padres and Vida Blue for San Francisco, were apparently having off-days. Blue, who pitched 8 innings, was the winning pitcher (his team won 14-10), even though he gave up 11 hits, 10 runs (9 of them earned), and 4 walks. Lolich, who only pitched 2 2/3 innings, was charged with the loss because his team went behind and stayed behind while he was pitcher of record. Altogether Lolich gave up 3 hits, 4 walks, and 7 runs—only two of them earned, however.

Saves can be earned only by relief pitchers, and by only one per game. A reliever earns a save if he is the last pitcher to pitch in a game that his team wins, provided that his team wasn't ahead by more than three runs when he came into the game; he can also be credited with a save if the potential tying run is already on base or is one of the next two batters up; or if he pitches for at least three full innings.

Other important figures for pitchers include the number of strikeouts pitched, both per game and during the season. When I first started watching baseball, my team, the New York Mets, had three of the best strikeout pitchers in the game at the time. The team itself was terrible most years and won very few games, but the pitchers—Tom Seaver, Jerry Koosman, and Jon Matlack—were terrific. Watching these three great starters not only spoiled me, but gave me a mistaken idea of what baseball was like: I just assumed that 8 to 10 strikeouts per game was normal. I have since learned better.

Ten strikeouts per game works out to slightly more than one per inning, and most pitchers do not even begin to approach that mark, being satisfied with 4 to 6 per game or—usually—even fewer. Anything over ten per game is phenomenal. In face, the record for most strikeouts for a nine-inning game is 19 (shared by Tom Seaver and Steve Carlton—Carlton, incidentally, was the losing pitcher when he set the record in 1969).

The final important records for pitchers have to do with very good games. The most common of these is a shutout. In a shutout, the opposition is able to get at least one or more base hits off the pitcher, but the hits are "scattered," meaning they don't add up to any runs, and so the other team doesn't score at all.

Much rarer and more exciting than a shutout is the fabled no-hit game, in which nobody gets a base hit off the pitcher. (Men may get on base, however, on balls or an error.) There is a lot of excitement and superstition attached to even the possibility of a no-hit game. For example, if a pitcher "has a no-hitter going" no one is supposed to mention that fact, or a curse will descend and the next batter will hit one out of the park.

A "perfect" game is a no-hitter in which the pitcher doesn't even walk anyone, and these are the rarest of all games. In fact, fewer than ten perfect games have been pitched in the major leagues since 1900!

SCORING

Obviously, somebody has to keep track of all these statistics, and so for each game there are official scorers, who are usually local baseball writers who have been following baseball for at least ten years. Not only is it their responsibility to decide and assign such statistics as strikeouts and RBIs per game, but they also make decisions for the record on errors, wild pitches, fielder's choices, and other judgment calls not decided by the umpires.

The official scorer's decision on any questioned play is posted on the scoreboard as soon as it has been made (a hit as opposed to an error, for example). TV and radio announcers will keep you informed if you're following the game at home.

As an example of just how complicated the scorer's job can get, the following play occurred in a game I saw. With no outs, the man on first tried to steal second base, but as he ran there was a pitchout, and the catcher quickly threw to the second baseman. Since the runner was not forced, he had to be tagged out, and in the rundown that followed, the second baseman dropped the ball and the runner ran to second, where he was declared safe by the umpire. Statistically all this had to be accounted for, and after a few minutes, the official scorer's decision came down: the runner took second base on an error after apparently being thrown out.

HOW TO KEEP SCORE   One of the best ways to get to know your team, and to make the game even more exciting, is to keep a score sheet for yourself during the game. This is not as complicated as it sounds and will greatly add to your enjoyment of the game, especially at the park.

The first thing you need to know in order to keep score is the number assigned to each defensive player. These are: pitcher—1;

catcher—2; first base—3; second base—4; third base—5; shortstop—6; left field—7; center field—8; and right field—9. (Until you know these numbers by heart, it helps to write them at the top of your score sheet.)

Many teams provide a blank scorecard in the program for the game, but you can easily make one yourself by copying the following on some lined paper:

INSERT HOME TEAM NAME HERE		1	2	3	4	5	6	7	8	9	AB	R	H	RBI
INSERT PLAYERS' NAMES HERE	INSERT PLAYER POSITION													
↓	↓													

INSERT VISITING TEAM NAME HERE		1	2	3	4	5	6	7	8	9	AB	R	H	RBI
INSERT PLAYERS' NAMES HERE	INSERT PLAYER POSITION													
↓	↓													

As soon as you know the lineups for both teams, put the names of each team's players (and the positions they play) in the announced batting order in the left-hand column. If you are watching a National League game, you will list the pitcher in the batting order; if an American League game, note who pitches at the bottom of the scorecard, and put the designated hitter (DH) in his proper position in the batting order.

In addition to the boxes that record the players' progress through the innings, there are spaces as well for times at bat (AB), runs scored, hits, runs batted in, and errors. At the bottom of the innings column there are spaces to record the total of runs scored by each side during the inning. I usually don't record anything but the players' progress around the base, but if you want to you can reconstruct just about everything that occurs during the game.

Here is how you do it. When each batter comes up, find the square that is opposite his name and underneath the number of the inning he is batting in. In that square, you will keep track of his progress around the bases.

If the batter is out on a fielding play, simply write the number of the fielder or fielders involved. For example, if he hits a high fly to center field, write an *8*. If he hits a ground ball to the shortstop, who throws it to first for the out, write 6-3. (6 caught the ball and threw to *3*). If he strikes out, write a *K*. Yes, a *K*. Strikeouts are always recorded this way, and are sometimes even called "K's"; this is because the man who made up the scoring system, a writer who covered baseball in the nineteenth century, had already assigned the letter *S* to steals. Arbitrarily, he decided to use the last letter of the word "struck."

If the batter reaches base, the scoring gets a little more complicated. There is an official method of scoring baseball, which is used by game scorers, but it is rather confusing and hard for an amateur to reconstruct later. Another method, which my friends and I use, is called the "diamond" method.

The idea is to follow the man around the baseball diamond as far as he gets. If he hits a single, for example, start the diamond at "home plate" (the center of the bottom line of the square) and draw a straight line to "first" (the center of the right-hand side of the square). Mark a little dot at "first" to indicate that he hit a single. If he reaches second on a double, draw half of a diamond and mark the dot at "second base" (center of the top of the square). Now, as the player advances, advance the line, but without marking a dot at the new base. If he advances on a hit by the following player, you will be able to see that by glancing at your scorecard and seeing that the following player got to first base. If he advances by stealing, write an S to the right of second base. If he advances on an error, write an E in the same place. If he is put out on his odyssey around the bases, indicate how. For example, if he is put out on a double play, write 6-4 (shortstop to second) to the right of "second base" in your diagram, and then 6-4-3 in the box of the batter who hit into the double play.

If your man scores, fill in the center of the diamond. If he scores on a home run, mark a dot at the bottom of the diamond for "home."

Other abbreviations commonly used in scoring include FC (fielder's choice); HP (hit by pitch); WP (wild pitch); PB (passed ball); SH (sacrifice hit); BB (base on balls, or walk); and BK (balk).

You needn't include all of these details, of course; the idea is to put down the things you are interested in. I always like to know what a batter has done in previous innings, so I can say to myself, "Well, McGillicuddy already struck out twice—he's due for a hit."

As soon as a side is out, draw a straight line through the box of the next batter so you will remember to start with him in the next inning.

See page 92 for a copy of part of a scorecard kept by my friend Nan during a game between the Yankees and the Dodgers in the World Series, 1978.

Looking at the first inning for the Yankees, we see that Rivers, who led off, hit toward second and was thrown out at first. Next Roy White came up and got a single. White ran to second on the next play, which saw Munson thrown out at first, for the second out; and finally Jackson too hit toward the hole and was put out by a throw from shortstop to the first baseman.

In the Dodgers' first inning, Davey Lopes led off with a home

YANKEES		1	2	3	4	5	6	7	8	9	AB	R	H	RBI
RIVERS	CF	4'3	4'3		7		K			K	IIII, I			
WHITE	LF	>	7		-	K	-	⊗		K	IIII	I	I	
MUNSON	C	6'3	-	K		5'3		K		/	IN		I	
JACKSON	DH	6'3		K		K		◇		K	IN	I	I	II
PINIELLA	RF	-	5'3			-	⊗	8		-	IIII	I	I	
NETTLES	3B	◇	-	8		9	9				IIII	I	I	
SPENCER	1B	⊗		⊁		K	-	5			III	I		
DOYLE	2B	⊗		>		◇		1'3			IIII	II	III	II
DENT	SS	⊁		/		/		6'3			IIII		III	III
		%	½	%	%	½	%	½	%	%				
HUNTER	7	GOSSAGE (DAVALIS)												

DODGERS		1	2	3	4	5	6	7	8	9	AB	R	H	RBI
LOPES	2B	◇	⊁		-	5'3		K			IIII	I	II	II
RUSSELL	SS	⊁	⁴⁺			7		5'4			III		I	
SMITH	RF	K	4'3			5'3		-	7		IIII			
GARVEY	1B	K		-	5'3		-		⊁		IIII			
CEY	3B	-	7		6		/		2		IIII		I	
BAKER	LF	6'3		6'3			7				III			
MONDAY	CF	4'3		-	K		6				III			
FERGUSON	C	-	◇		8		-	>			III	I	II	
DAVALIS	DH		3'1		5'3		5'4				III		I	
		½	%	½	%	%	%	½	%					
SUTTON	5'3	WELCH (DENT)						(SPENCER)						

run, which, as I recall, upset Nan a lot; he was followed by Russell
with a single, who was subsequently thrown out trying to steal
second. (We know this because there is no other way 4, the second
baseman, could put him out on a throw by 2, the catcher.) The
following two players, Smith and Garvey, were both strikeout vic-
tims. (The inverted *K*, by the way, stands for a swinging strike.)

READING ABOUT BASEBALL

Most of the terminology used in newspaper accounts of baseball games is given in these chapters. Generally, stories about a local
team will go into quite a bit of detail about any game just played:
"In the first, Frankfurter and Murphy were retired in order, and then
Martinez walked," but you shouldn't have much trouble figuring
out what happened.

Somewhat more complex is the box score, a tabular presentation of the important statistics of a game. Because baseball keeps so many statistics, a box score can be quite detailed. Following is a major-league box score from the *New York Times.*

Milwaukee	ab	r	h	bi	Toronto	ab	r	h	bi
Molitor 2b	4	1	1	0	Bosetti cf	5	2	3	2
Money 1b	3	2	2	0	Bailor rf	4	0	2	0
Muser 1b	1	0	1	3	Howell 3b	4	0	2	1
Bando 3b	5	1	1	1	Carty dh	4	1	1	0
Hisle lf	4	0	2	1	Maybry 1b	4	1	1	2
Davis dh	4	2	2	2	Ashby c	4	0	0	0
Wohlfrd rf	5	1	4	1	Woods lf	4	1	1	0
Yount ss	5	2	1	0	TiJhnsn 2b	3	0	1	0
GThoms cf	3	0	0	1	Gomez ss	2	0	0	0
BMartnz c	4	1	1	0	Upshw ph	1	0	0	0
Total	**38**	**10**	**15**	**9**	**Total**	**35**	**5**	**11**	**5**

```
Milwaukee          0 0 1  1 2 1  0 4 1—10
Toronto            1 0 0  0 1 2  1 0 0— 5
```

DP—Milwaukee 2, Toronto 1, LOB—Milwaukee 7, Toronto 5. 2B—Molitor, Wohlford, Money, Hisle, Woods. 3B—Wohlford, Bando, Yount, Muser, Davis. HR—Bosetti (4), Mayberry (17), Davis (5). SF—Davis, GThomas.

	IP	H	R	ER	BB	SO
Milwaukee						
ERdriguez	5 1-3	7	4	4	2	2
Replogle	1 1-3	3	1	1	0	0
RStein W,3-2	2 1-3	1	0	0	0	0
Toronto						
Undrwood	4	8	4	3	2	6
TMphy L,4-8	3 2-3	4	5	5	2	1
Willis	1 1-3	3	1	1	0	1

PB—Ashby. T—2:29. A—21,511.

As you can see, there is an amazing amount of information locked up in these numbers and letters. To begin with, we are given the number of times each player was at bat, the number of runs he scored, and his hits and RBIs (here called BIs).

For the pitchers too we have a great deal of information: the number of innings pitched, the number of hits given up, the number of runs given up, the number of earned runs, the number of bases given up on balls, and the number of strikeouts pitched.

Below the statistics for batters we see inning by inning when the runs occurred in this rather high-scoring baseball game; the eighth inning in particular produced a lot of runs for Milwaukee.

Below the individual statistics for batters and pitchers we now come to the really complicated shorthand. Don't expect to see all of these initials in every box score that you read; but following is the kind of statistical information that may be included:

First, the fielding and hitting statistics: E—error; DP—double play(s); LOB—number of men left on base; 2B—double; 3B—triple; HR—home run; SB—stolen base(s); S—sacrifice bunt; SF—sacrifice fly.

For pitching statistics, you are likely to see WP (wild pitch); PB (passed ball); HBP—hit by pitch, expressed this way: Walker (by Flanagan); save, balk (spelled out, because of all the other S's and B's).

In some box scores I have seen, the winning pitcher is designated by WP and the loser by LP. In this case a wild pitch is sometimes designated by EP (error on pitcher).

In addition to all this statistical information, our box score records how long the game lasted and the attendance figure. It gives us more information on the players, too—by looking at the HR statistics we can see that Bosetti hit his fourth of the year while Mayberry has already hit 17.

An interesting reconstruction can be made of the fortunes of the Toronto pitching staff. Underwood, who started the game and pitched four full innings, gave up eight hits and four runs in that time, although only three of those runs were earned, the other apparently occurring on the passed ball by the catcher, since no other errors are listed for the team. He was then replaced in the fifth inning by the reliever T. Murphy. Murphy himself gave up five runs, all of them earned, and was ultimately marked the losing pitcher, but clearly it was Underwood who was pitching at the time his team first fell behind. So why, then, isn't he the losing pitcher? The answer comes in reading the inning-by-inning account of runs underneath the batting statistics: Here we see that while Toronto was trailing after the third inning, in the seventh they got a run to tie it up, so all preceding pitchers were removed from contention for wins or losses. Finally, of course, Milwaukee went on to score five more runs in the last two innings and win it—with their reliever, Stein, getting the win, even though he pitched only two and one-third innings.

TV AND RADIO

Unlike other major team sports, baseball is a game you can fully enjoy on the radio, because most of the action is so clear-cut that announcers are able to describe plays precisely as they happen. It's true that you will miss the thrill of seeing a spectacular catch, but because its location and method will have been described to you exactly, you will be able to imagine it in your mind as it must have been. So adaptable to radio is baseball, in fact, that before the days of widespread live media coverage there were radio announcers who made a specialty of re-creating a game in its entirety from wire service reports, even to taped sound effects of bat striking ball and crowd cheering.

A typical radio announcer of today will keep you posted on what is going on at every moment:

"And now with two men out, bases loaded, Jackson comes up. The pitch . . . and it's low. Ball one. Now Murchison goes into the stretch, fast ball! Strike one. It's one and one . . . " This particular sequence might end, "Now the count is full; the pitch . . . and Jackson fouls it back. With the count holding, the pitch, and Jackson hits it deep into right field. Golom is running, running, it's deep, and it's off the wall! Herkison scores . . . Murphy scores . . .

and the throw to second . . . not in time!" It takes very little imagination to see that entire sequence in your mind.

Television announcers give much the same information as radio announcers, although in less detail. Much of the terminology is traditional, although announcers, in their zeal to be original, coin new expressions constantly. One of the standard expressions you will hear often is "away"—meaning out—as in "one away." You will also hear the announcer say, whenever a batter comes up, that he is "one for three," or "0 [meaning zero] for two," and the like. This means that he has got one hit three times at bat, or no hits two times at bat.

The best TV camera view during the confrontation between pitcher and batter is directly behind the pitcher, which allows you to see him making a move toward first or second if he's trying to pick someone off, as well as to watch his moves as he goes into the windup or stretch before pitching. This position also gives a good view of the hitter, but makes it extremely difficult to tell what sort of pitch is being thrown, or even if it's a strike or a ball. Sometimes the camera will show the pitch from behind the plate. Although you get a good view of the pitch from this vantage point you can see little else.

Once the ball is hit, the camera will usually follow it, so you'll be able to see all the important plays wherever they occur, although you may not be able to follow all the base runners if there are several things happening during a given play. Sometimes when there's a man on first the TV director will use a split-screen technique and have a shot of the runner at first leading off toward second while the pitcher is facing the batter.

Between half innings, the TV screen always shows a table of the runs, hits, and errors that occurred during that half inning.

In general TV has had less of an influence on the structure of baseball than on the other major team sports. This is so largely because there are so many natural breaks for commercials that no new ones have had to be created, as they have been in hockey, football, and basketball (and perhaps someday soccer). The only times commercials are shown other than during half innings are when a pitcher is changed, because the new pitcher needs time to warm up, or if an unusual incident, such as a player injury, causes a delay in the game.

Likewise the rules of baseball have not been seriously affected by the presence of TV, although the DH was created to "add more excitement" to the game, which is a euphemism for attracting a bigger TV audience. The principal influence that TV has had on baseball is that many more games than in the past are played at night, particularly during the postseason play-offs, to attract prime-time viewers. For the same reason, the season itself has been somewhat extended, and the gentle summer game is now played in cold weather, occasionally in conditions that would ordinarily result in the game being called. The most flagrant example of this occurred during the National League play-offs in 1977, when the Dodgers and Philadelphia Phillies played an entire game in a pouring, chill rain. It was so wet and muddy that runners slipped while running the bases and everyone had trouble holding on to the ball. Most observers felt that this game was a disgrace to baseball.

AT THE BALL PARK

A very important reason for going to baseball games in person is that baseball tickets are still the cheapest of all the major sports. Also, as with any sport, there is an atmosphere and excitement in the stadium that you simply can't pick up on the tube or radio. If you want a preview of the action, you can even go early and watch batting practice, an entertaining spectacle in which the teams take turns practicing their skills on the field.

Although there is some argument about this, many fans think the best place to sit at a game is directly behind home plate. Naturally, then, this is where the seats sell out first. Next best is to sit opposite first base or third base. Whether to sit high or low in the stands depends on whether you are most interested in watching the pitching or the fielding. The higher up you are the better overall view you will have; the closer you are, the better you'll be able to watch the pitcher-batter duel. I should add that the higher seats are less expensive, as are those by the outfield.

It is a time-honored tradition in baseball to buy cheap seats and then to sneak around until you are sitting where you want to. My boyfriend and I once managed to get into super seats right behind home plate in the mezzanine, next to a little boy and his grandmother who were enjoying the doubleheader as much as we were. Unfortunately, as the first game drew to a close the seats near us began to fill up with legitimate ticketholders, and we knew it was only a matter of time until we would be sent back upstairs with the proletariat. Finally, at a most exciting point of the ball game, the sneering usher walked up: "All right, let me see your tickets." Sheepishly, I reached into my pocket, but Gene grabbed my arm to stop me and gestured at the old woman and boy next to us who were rising to make way for the legitimate holders of their seats!

Although I think it's a good idea to keep score for yourself, the scoreboards in most parks are extremely informative. They are divided into sections for each inning, and spaces for cumulative totals for errors and hits as well as the starting lineups for each team. In addition, there may be a sophisticated computerized light display, and the scores of other major-league games already played or in progress.

ALL-STARS, PLAY-OFFS, AND THE WORLD SERIES

All pro sports in this country have divisions within which teams play and compete against each other for standings, but only baseball has two clearly separated leagues, with slightly different rules, each containing teams that play only other teams in their own league during the regular season.

Thus the play-offs in other sports usually occur between teams who have faced each other before in the course of the season. In baseball, when the championship teams meet in the World Series, it is for the first time that year.

As a result of the lack of interleague play, baseball spawns rivalries that are somewhat different from those in other sports. While you might be a fan, say, of the Montreal Canadiens hockey team, you would not then automatically dislike a team in another hockey division, since the divisions are arranged only for convenience of scheduling and ranking. But in baseball, many fans are die-hard followers not only of their team, but of one league as opposed to the other, sometimes even more than of one team over others. Age-old baseball arguments rage about whether the National League is superior overall to the American.

Apart from the World Series, the only way this question is ever tested during the season is at the All-Star game, which occurs precisely in the middle of the season, in early July, and which pits the National League All-Stars, as chosen by fan votes, against the American League stars, similarly chosen. The manager for each league is the man who coached the winning team in his league the previous year, and he picks the pitchers he will use.

The All-Star game is supposed to be a very big deal, and it certainly attracts a lot of media hype. I wouldn't miss if for anything, but I must point out that most All-Star games are not very good exhibitions of baseball. This is so for a variety of reasons. One obvious reason is that the game simply doesn't mean anything. Although it's true that the National League usually creams the American, nobody really cares very much. The players usually aren't playing at their best; they are tired after half a season, reluctant to take a chance on injuring themselves for the rest of the season, and they haven't played together as members of the same team before.

The time between the last game of the first half of the season and the first game of the second half is known as the All-Star Break, and it is followed by the annual pennant race, which actually begins with the first game of the year, but which "takes shape" following the All-Star Break.

Here is how it works. Each league is divided into an eastern and western division of an equal number of teams (in the AL this is seven each, in the NL six). The teams within each league are competing the entire year for the best won-lost record in their division of their league. Thus four winners—one each for the eastern and western divisions of the two leagues, emerge. (Very infrequently two teams will tie for division winner, as happened when New York and Boston, both of the American League East, finished the 1978 season with identical records of 99 wins and 63 losses. To determine the division winner, one very exciting game was played the day after the season ended.) The East and West division winners within each league now play each other in a best three out of five series, and the winners of those contests become the league champions, or pennant winners.

Because the standings are determined solely by number of games won and lost, and because there are so many games within a year, the pennant race can be very exciting, particularly toward the end of the season, if there are close races in any division. The closeness of the race is judged by the "games behind" statistic, which is the number of games any team would have to win against the division leader in order to tie with it. In other words, if Boston is first in its division and New York is three games behind, New York would have to win three games against Boston itself; or New York would have to win three games against other teams while Boston lost three to any other team. (Expressed another way, any victory or defeat by one team counts as a half game in the statistics.)

As the pennant race draws to a close, you will hear about the "magic number." This is the combination of wins by the division leader combined with losses by the closest runner-up in that division, which guarantees a win by the leader. For example, if team X has a magic number of three, it means that if X wins three of the remaining games; or Y loses three; or X wins two and Y loses one; or any other combination adding up to three, there is no way mathematically for team Y to catch up, and so team X is the division champion and will go into the league play-offs. (The remaining games of the year are still played, however.)

Once the pennant races have been decided, then comes that most exciting of American sporting events, the World Series.

This contest is a best four out of seven play-off between what should be the top team of each league. And unlike the All-Star game, the Series often results in some really spectacular play, unless, as sometimes happens, one team is hopelessly outclassed by the other. The players generally perform their heroic best during the Series, making more dramatic catches, hitting more home runs, and so on, for the glory and prestige, and, of course, the extra money that is a feature of postseason play in all sports.

The use of the designated hitter alternates in the World Series from year to year, so that every other year American League pitchers have to take a turn at bat like everyone else.

AWARDS

Baseball, like all sports, has awards and rankings at the end of the year. For batters within each league there are the individual honors (or at least recognition), for highest batting average, most runs, most RBIs, most hits, most home runs, and most steals; for pitchers there are awards for best record, lowest ERA, number of shutouts, strikeouts, and saves. Fielding excellence is recognized by a number of awards, including the Golden Glove, which is not mathematically determined, but rather is voted on by baseball writers for the player in each league considered to be the best at his particular position. (Thus there is a separate Golden Glove in each league for third base, center field, and so on.)

The most important awards in baseball, however, are the Cy Young and MVP. They are awarded after the World Series and are, again, voted on by a majority of sportswriters.

The Cy Young award is given to the pitcher in each league who is judged to be the most outstanding pitcher of the year, in terms both of overall performance and of value to his team. Winning twenty games or more will put a pitcher in the running but is no guarantee of a Cy Young, and the vote is often close and controversial. For the first time ever in 1977, a relief pitcher, Sparky Lyle of New York, won the Cy Young, reflecting the growing importance of specialty relief pitching.

Shortly after the Cy Young is voted on, the winner of the MVP, or Most Valuable Player, is announced. This award goes to the player who, in the opinion of the baseball writers, was the most valuable to his team. The MVP usually goes to a slugger who is also an outstanding fielder, although it has occasionally been awarded to pitchers, and traditionally (if not always) to a player on the pennant winner.

The announcements of the Cy Young and MVP winners mark the official end of postseason baseball.

PART 3
FOOTBALL

══FOOTBALL FACT SHEET══

Where played: large rectangular field.

Game divisions: four quarters of 15 minutes each, with a 15-minute break between "halves." Sudden-death overtime in case of tie.

Average duration: three hours.

Offense/defense considerations: coin toss determines goals and which team starts on offense.

Governing body: National Football League (NFL).

Number of players on the roster: 45 men may be in uniform for a game.

Equipment: one football, made of inflated rubber covered with leather. Players required to wear hard plastic helmets and heavy padding over much of their body.

Regular season: September through December (play-offs continue into January).

TEAMS

AMERICAN FOOTBALL CONFERENCE

Eastern Division
Buffalo Bills
Baltimore Colts
Miami Dolphins
New York Jets
New England Patriots

Central Division
Cincinnati Bengals
Cleveland Browns
Houston Oilers
Pittsburgh Steelers

Western Division
Denver Broncos
San Diego Chargers
Kansas City Chiefs
Oakland Raiders
Seattle Seahawks

NATIONAL FOOTBALL CONFERENCE

Eastern Division
St. Louis Cardinals
Dallas Cowboys
Philadelphia Eagles
New York Giants
Washington Redskins

Central Division
Chicago Bears
Tampa Bay Buccaneers
Detroit Lions
Minnesota Vikings

Western Division
Atlanta Falcons
San Francisco 49ers
Los Angeles Rams
New Orleans Saints

CHAPTER
10 SUNDAY AFTERNOON MAYHEM

Winning isn't everything—it's the only thing.

—VINCE LOMBARDI

There is no question that football is one of our most popular sports. During its brief four-month season, in fact, it is possible to spend an entire weekend doing virtually nothing else but watch football: high school games are staged on Friday evenings, college games are played Saturday afternoons, and Sunday afternoons are reserved for pro football. As an added attraction, the *Professional Game of the Week* is televised each Monday night.

In spite of its immense popularity, however, football often seems inaccessible to women, and this is so for two reasons. One of these is that very few women have ever had experience playing football; the other is that of all the sports, it relies most heavily on extreme physical aggression and an almost military approach to playing the game.

If you watched the movie *Patton*, you may have noticed that military strategy was often discussed in terms of sports: the generals discussed moving their troops "around end," for example, and spoke of "quarterbacking" (planning and leading) offensive movements. Most of the terms used were borrowed from football, which is itself often described in military terms as a "battle" for "possession of territory," in which the players make use of such "weapons" as the "bomb," the "blitz," and "offensive formations."

There is historical precedent for this warlike terminology, as well as for the undeniable violence that takes place on a football field. Men have been kicking balls around for sport since prehistoric times: modern soccerlike games are thought to have evolved from ancient Celtic rituals in which warriors kicked and ran with the skulls of defeated enemies. Ultimately this sort of "sport" led to soccer, rugby, and then to American football. While rugby and soccer players still kick the ball and run on the field, in American football kicking and running are now the specialized talents of a very few players, and the nature of the contest has become more purely physical, relying heavily on raw power and courage.

It is important to point out that the violent hitting and tackling that take place on the football field are not faked; they are real and result in hundreds of incapacitating injuries every year at all levels of the sport. It is a rare pro—or college—game, in fact, in which one or more players are not injured severely enough to be taken off the field. (The announcers' usual observation about a player who lies motionless or writhing in pain is that he was "shaken up on the play.")

All this is not to say that the point of football is for men to injure each other—although there are undoubtedly some sadists in the pros for whom that *is* the point—but rather for them to overpower each other, in accordance with strict rules that nevertheless allow for a great deal of physical contact.

Although violence will probably always remain an important part of football, each year the NFL institutes new rules and requires better equipment to protect players from serious injury. It is also true that in spite of (and to a certain extent because of) the brutality of the game, football is one of the most exciting of all spectator sports.

Furthermore, once you get past the military approach to the game, football is one of the easiest of all sports to follow. Although the strategy and tactics employed are often quite complex, that complexity matters usually only to the players and coaches. The basic play of the game is always easy to see, and there are few occasions in which even a novice viewer is left wondering what just happened.

For most new-time viewers, women and men, the only real difficulty presented by football is its terminology. Once you know the words, you should have no trouble enjoying and following the game in person, on TV, or in print.

CHAPTER 11

THE BASICS

Two things about football make it markedly different from the other team sports in this book and affect the way it is played. The first is that the football (also called pigskin) is not round but an elongated oval, pointed at both ends. This is because it is designed primarily to be carried and passed (thrown from one player to another); thus it does not bounce as truly and predictably on the ground, nor does it sail through the air in the same way as a round ball.

The second difference is that football is played by "squads" of 11 men each. In the other major team sports, the same men almost always play both offense and defense, alternating as possession of the ball changes. In football each side has completely separate teams for offense and defense. When one side loses possession of the ball, its members go off the field and are replaced by 11 different men whose specialty is to play defense (some men on some teams overlap and play more than one position, but this is increasingly rare). Meanwhile, the other side's defensive players leave the field to be replaced by 11 offensive teammates. There are also squads in football that are used only in special situations, such as for kicking.

Football is played on a grassy field 120 yards long and 53 1/3 yards wide, which is marked off in its central 100 yards into five-yard segments. At either end of the field are two large goalposts, ten yards behind the "goal lines." The area between the goal line and the goalposts is known as the "end zone." At each of the four intersections of the goal lines and sidelines there is a small pennant, known as the "corner flag." The only other notable markings on the field are a series of short horizontal white lines painted in two rows down the center of the field; these are known as inbound lines or "hash marks."

Below is a diagram of a pro football field.

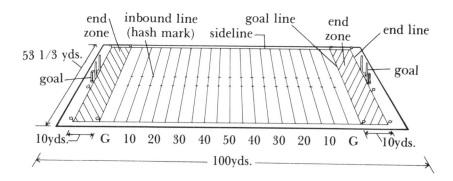

The object of the game is simple: each team tries to move the football across its opponent's "goal line" for a score. This is generally done on a series of plays.

The game begins when the two team captains meet with one of the officials in the center of the field to toss a coin. The visiting captain calls the toss and the winner is given the choice of either starting on offense ("receiving") or of picking which goal to defend. Although wind and other weather conditions can make one goalpost easier to defend than the other, the winner of the toss almost always chooses to receive the ball. At the start of the second half of the game the other team gets to make the choice.

Once the toss has been made, play begins with the kickoff, which is one of the most dramatic ways in sport to initiate a game. Special squads for both teams come onto the field; the men on the team that will be defending begin to run toward the opposition's goal line. One of these men kicks the ball from his own team's 35-yard line as deep as possible into the other team's half of the field. Usually the ball is caught by one of the men on the receiving team, and he and his teammates now begin running down the field toward the kicking team's goal until the man who is carrying the ball is stopped, usually by being thrown to the ground ("tackled"). The players then leave the field while the regular offensive and defensive players take their places; now the next phase of the game begins at the spot where the man with the ball was stopped.

A normal play in football begins when members of both teams line up in a regular pattern, facing one another across an imaginary line on the field. This is known as the "line of scrimmage." In the center of that line is the football; several players from each team will be crouched almost head to head across it, while other members of the team stand farther back. All men remain motionless for a moment, then play begins when one of the offensive players "snaps"—hands—the ball to the player standing directly behind him. At this moment, several things will begin to happen at once. The players who were crouching opposite each other will begin to grapple with one another. The remaining players of both teams will run or attempt to run toward each other across the line of scrimmage, and the man who received the ball, the quarterback, will usually either throw the ball to one of his men who has run past the scrimmage line, or will hand it to a man who will attempt to run with it toward the opposition goal. Whenever an offensive player in possession of the ball is forced to the ground or "out of bounds" (beyond the sidelines), or when the ball has been thrown but is not caught (an "incomplete pass"), an official blows his whistle and play ends momentarily. The members of the offensive team now gather shoulder to shoulder in a circle, known as a "huddle," where the quarterback gives them instructions. Then the two teams line up as before to begin another play. After several such plays, two things become clear: that the offensive team is trying to move the football ever closer to the goal that the other team is defending, and that they do not have unlimited chances to do so.

DOWNS

A "down" is a play in football that includes all actions taking place from the time the ball is snapped until an official has blown his whistle to signal a pause in the action. In order to retain possession of the ball, the offensive team must advance it toward the opponents' goal a minimum of ten yards by the end of four downs. There are two ways to advance the ball: passing—throwing it to another player—or running with it. If they fail to gain ten yards in four downs, they lose possession of the ball to the other team. As the field is clearly marked off into five-yard segments, it is easy to gauge a team's progress. TV announcers or the stadium scoreboard will keep you advised of the downs-and-yardage situation. On the first play, they will refer to "first and ten," meaning that ten yards must be made and this is the first attempt to do so. If on that first play the offense manages to advance the ball four yards from, say, the 20-yard line in their own territory ("their own twenty") to their 24-yard line, at the beginning of the next down the situation will be "second and six"—or second down with six yards yet to be gained in the four-down series. The spot to which the ball has been advanced is now the new line of scrimmage, in this case the 24-yard line. If the offense now advances the ball two more yards, the next play will be "third and four" from their own 26. Once the team has gained a total of ten or more yards from the original line of scrimmage on any of the four downs, it has gained a "first down." It then begins a new series of four downs, with ten yards to go.

Sometimes, because of a penalty or because of aggressive defensive actions—which may include forcing the man with the ball to the ground before he has reached the scrimmage line—the offensive team will be unable to advance the ball beyond the line of scrimmage, or will even be forced to move back toward their own goal line (when the man with the ball is himself forced back). In the latter case the team is said to have lost yardage, but it must still gain ten yards from the *original* line of scrimmage. In the above example, if on the third down the offensive team is forced back to their own 19-yard line, the situation at the beginning of the next down will be "fourth and eleven," because they have to make up the lost yard as well as gain ten yards from the original line of scrimmage.

If a pass is not completed, the yardage situation remains the same but the down is lost. For example, it's second and ten on the Hornet 20-yard line. If a pass is thrown but not caught by the Hornets, the next down will be *third* and ten on the Hornet 20.

Although the offensive team is given four downs in which to progress ten yards toward the opposition goal, in practice they must attain that yardage by the end of three downs. This is because they cannot be certain the final yardage will be made on the fourth down, and if it isn't, they may have to give up the ball nearer their own goal line where it may be easy for the opposition to score.

Thus, except in certain critical strategic situations or if it is deep in its opponent's territory, the offensive team does not advance the ball on the fourth down in the way we've just described: that is, by running with or passing the ball forward. Instead, a special man is brought in for "punting." A punt is a special kick: the punter receives the ball about 15 yards behind the line of scrimmage, then drops it and kicks it (before it touches the ground) as far as possible away from his own goal. The receiving team now "returns" the punt, running forward until the man in possession of the ball is brought down. Once again, new squads of men are brought onto the field, and the receiving team begins its own series of downs at the spot where the man who returned the punt was stopped.

Normally, and especially if the teams are well matched, the ball will move very slowly from one end of the field to the other, changing hands after several series of downs. Gradually, however, the balance of the game will begin to shift, and play will begin to edge closer and closer to one team's goal line until a score is made.

SCORING

There are four ways to make a score in football, each of which is awarded a different number of points.

TOUCHDOWN This is by far the most dramatic method of scoring. A touchdown is made when a player carries the ball across the goal line or receives a pass across the goal line. Because a touchdown (often called simply "TD") is the most difficult regular score to make, it is worth the most points of any score, six. According to Jimmy Cefalo, a young football player whose college career was followed by the *New York Times,* "Scoring a touchdown is the best sensation I've ever experienced. It's total satisfaction . . . like finding the perfect girl or winning the lottery." The sheer exhilaration of making a touchdown is displayed by many players who jubilantly throw the ball to the ground ("spike it") as soon as they cross into the end zone.

After a touchdown, the scoring team is entitled to a:

TRY FOR POINT A try, also called "conversion," or "point after touchdown" (PAT), is an opportunity to score an extra point. On a try attempt, the teams line up at the goal line, as though for a regular play from scrimmage. The ball is snapped to a "holder" behind the line of scrimmage, who places the ball on the ground where it is kicked by a kicking specialist, also behind the line. If the ball passes across the horizontal bar above the goalpost, the try is good, making the total score seven points. If it goes wide of the goalpost, or if it is "blocked" (knocked down) by the defensemen, no point is awarded. Whatever the outcome of the try, possession of the ball now passes to the other team. They receive the ball with a kickoff, as at the beginning of the game.

FIELD GOAL If a team on offense gets very near (usually within 30 yards of) the opposition goal at the end of three downs, the normal play is to try for a field goal on the fourth down. A field goal attempt is made with a kick, similar to a try for point, and can be blocked; if it successfully passes over the crossbar it is worth three points and the other team is awarded the ball, which it receives on a kickoff.

SAFETY   A safety, worth two points, is a kind of penalty score. It is awarded to the defensive team if a member of the team on offense who is in possession of the ball is either forced to the ground or pushed out of bounds in his own end zone, or if he catches the ball and runs into the end zone. This situation is most likely to occur when the offense, deep in their own territory, are forced behind their own goal line by aggressive defensive play. Not only is the offensive team penalized by the two-point score to the defense, it also loses possession of the ball, and must kick off to the opposing team from its own 20-yard line.

TIES   If two teams are tied at the end of regulation play, the game is continued in "sudden-death overtime." After a three-minute intermission, the teams assemble on the field for the toss of a coin, after which the winner of the toss receives the ball on a kickoff. Whichever team scores first by whatever means is immediately declared the winner; usually this is the team that won the toss of the coin.

THE KICKING GAME

As we have seen, the ball is not kicked often during a football game, but each kick is extremely important. Each type of kick is executed according to strict rules, and each has a specific purpose. Below is a summary of the kicks you will see in a football game.

The *kickoff,* which starts each half and puts the ball in play after a field goal or try, is delivered from a stationary "kicking tee," and is supposed to be very high, long, and straight. The idea is to get the ball as deeply into enemy territory as possible so that the team that is receiving will have a long way to return it. If the kickoff is too deep and goes into the end zone, where it is taken by the receiving team, it is called a *touchback,* and the line of scrimmage is automatically moved to the receiving team's 20-yard line. If the ball rolls out of bounds between the goal lines, it must be rekicked.

A team will sometimes employ a risky maneuver on a kickoff known as an "onside" kick. This usually happens late in a game when the kicking team is behind and desperately needs to regain the ball in order to score. In this case, the kickoff is made shallow and along the ground. As soon as it has traveled ten yards, members of the kicking team are eligible to take possession of it—the idea is for them to reach the ball before the receivers do, or try to take it away from the receiver.

A *punt,* as we have seen, is used to send the ball into enemy territory when a team has not advanced ten yards in three downs. A punt resembles a kickoff in two ways: it is kicked as deeply as possible, and a punt kicked into the end zone is a touchback. However, a punt that is kicked out of bounds is *not* rekicked; rather a new line of scrimmage forms where the ball went out of bounds. A truly great punt is one that is kicked deep to a far corner of the field but rolls out of bounds just before getting to the goal line. Sometimes you will see a group of receiving players watching closely as a bouncing, rolling ball heads toward the corner of the field. They are hoping for a touchback, of course, but sometimes the ball rolls out of bounds at, say, the three-yard line, and they then have a long, long way to go.

Sometimes the receiver of a punt will raise his hand, catch the ball, and then just stand there. In this case he has made what is known as a "fair catch," and the line of scrimmage will be at the spot where the catch was made. Once a player has signaled for a fair catch he may not be molested by opposing players, nor may he advance the ball. A fair catch is usually made when the receiver sees that he will have difficulty advancing the ball.

With both a punt and a kickoff (unless a fair catch is made on a punt), the man who catches the ball is allowed to return it down-field—toward the enemy goal line—as far as he can run before being tackled or forced out of bounds. If he can evade all defenders, he can even score. This sort of touchdown is rare and very exciting. Because the men on the kicking team cannot advance beyond the kick until after it has been made, the higher the ball goes and the longer the time it spends in the air before being caught the better, as it allows them to run toward the receiver. Ball time in the air, called "hang time," is often measured by a stopwatch superimposed on the television screen. Any hang time longer than four seconds is considered outstanding.

WHO'S WHO ON THE FIELD

One of the most confusing things about football is the seemingly infinite number of names and positions assumed by offensive and defensive players. This confusion is most obvious when you are watching a game on TV or listening on radio: you will sometimes hear the same player referred to as a back, a running back, a flanker-back, a setback, a halfback, or other names. This seeming schizophrenia has to do with the player's responsibilities on a given play and with where he is standing in relation to other players.

There are rules about where players may stand and how many may be on the line or in the backfield at a given moment. (The "backfield" for each team is the part of the field between the line of scrimmage and the team's own goal.) Within these restrictions, however, there is quite a bit of freedom about how the players may line up (particularly for the defense), and for years coaches have been outdoing one another thinking up fancy "formations" out of which they can run new plays or simply as a means of confusing their opponents. It is this variety of formations that leads to all the names for player positions. We will examine basic formations in detail in Chapter Thirteen. For now let's take a look at the men on the field and their general functions.

OFFENSE

The offense is divided into two categories: seven linemen and four backs, who stand behind the line of scrimmage. The linemen are the members of the team who engage in a physical struggle with the defensemen at the beginning of a down, and they can go through an entire game without so much as touching the football.

The offensive linemen consist of the center, who is responsible for snapping the ball to the quarterback or the kicker; two guards on either side of him; and two tackles who stand outside the guards. These five players are responsible primarily for protecting their teammates, especially the quarterback, from the defensive players on the other team. They also attempt to create "holes" in the defensive line by "blocking," or overpowering the defensive linemen. (A hole is opened so that a man carrying the ball may run through it or, as the late coach Vince Lombardi said, "run to daylight.")

Beyond the linemen, at either end of the line, are two players called ends, whose primary responsibility is to receive passes thrown by the quarterback. One of the ends usually stands several feet to one side of the other linemen, and is known as the "split end," because he is detached, or split, from the line. The other end, who stands beside one of the tackles, is known as the "tight end" ("tight" in football refers to a close formation). In addition to receiving passes, the tight end is also responsible for helping the other linemen block the defensive men. The side of the formation with the tight end is usually called the "strong" side, because of his blocking potential and because there is usually an extra man on that side.

The backs are the players you will probably watch most, because they are the ones who most often handle the ball.

The most important member of any football team is the quarterback. It is he who decides and calls the strategy for each play (sometimes with the advice of his coach), and it is he who is given the football to begin any nonkicking play.

The quarterback is also responsible for making most or all of the passes in a game; he sometimes runs with the ball; and he is responsible for giving the ball ("handing it off") to another back who usually will run with it.

In addition to the quarterback, there are two halfbacks and one fullback. The fullback is often somewhat larger than the halfbacks, and is more likely to be stationed behind the quarterback, while the halfbacks usually stand to his side. All three backs are primarily responsible for running with the ball (also known as "rushing"), and for receiving passes. They may also help in blocking the opposing defensemen. Depending upon where they stand in relation to the other players, they may be called by the variety of names mentioned earlier. There is a third, overlapping category of offensive players, to which the ends technically belong, and that is the receivers. Legally, only an *eligible* receiver is allowed to catch a "forward pass," a pass thrown toward the opposition goal line from behind the line of scrimmage. On the offense, there are five such receivers: the two ends, the two halfbacks, and the fullback. A receiver who stands away from the line of scrimmage, such as the split end or a detached back (standing wide to one side of the other backs), is known as a "wide receiver."

DEFENSE

The defensive men are divided into three categories: the linemen, the linebackers, and the secondary.

In a typical formation, the "line" will consist of one or more tackles, flanked by two defensive ends. The primary function of these defensive linemen is to prevent the offensive team from advancing the ball. To do this, they first have to overpower the blocks of the offensive linemen.

Behind the linemen are the linebackers, usually known as middle, right, and left linebacker (although there may be fewer or more than three men in this position; if there are four, they are usually referred to as inside and outside linebackers). Their duties are generally the same as those of the linemen. In addition, they are also responsible for stopping any member of the opposition who manages to break through the line of scrimmage toward the goal.

The remaining defensemen are known collectively as the "secondary," and they are responsible for covering all action in their own backfield, especially that of the wide receivers. The secondary men are really the last line of defense for a team: they are the final hope for stopping an offensive man with the ball from crossing the goal line, or preventing a receiver from catching the ball near or behind the goal line.

The secondary usually consists of four men: two safeties and two cornerbacks. The cornerbacks generally line up to the outside and behind the linebackers, while the safeties are even deeper in the backfield. One safety usually lines up on the same side of the field as the tight end and is called the "strong safety," while the other is free to go where he is most needed, and is thus called a "free safety."

All members of the defensive team are considered eligible receivers, which means any defender may legally "intercept" the ball; that is, catch a pass intended for someone else.

In addition to the defensive and offensive players named, there are men who participate in the game only in special situations. These include kickers and the players who specialize in "returning"—catching and running with—the ball on punts and kickoffs. These players are said to play on "special teams." Regular starters may overlap and play on special teams, although these positions are more dangerous, primarily because kick returns involve high-speed running and thus the threat of high-speed collisions. Valuable players are therefore usually restricted to their ordinary starting roles.

Until you have been watching football for a while, it can be difficult to determine just what position a man is playing: The players are all dressed alike, so heavily armored that they display as little individuality as Darth Vader's storm troopers in *Star Wars*. Therefore, to make for easier identification by fans, other players, and officials, football jerseys are numbered according to a strict formula. This is most important in determining who is eligible to receive a forward pass; however, a player who is being moved from guard, say, to end on a given play may inform the officials before the play begins and thus be eligible to catch even though his number is not that of an eligible receiver.

The numbers players can wear according to their positions are as follows:

quarterbacks and kickers: 1 to 19
offensive halfbacks and fullbacks, and defensive safeties and
  cornerbacks: 20 to 49

offensive centers and defensive linebackers: 50 to 59
offensive guards and tackles and defensive linemen: 60 to 79
wide receivers and tight ends: 80 to 89.

Numbers above 90 are used rarely during the regular season, and only with the permission of the commissioner of football (in the 1978-79 season, a star wide receiver sported the number 00).

The players are not alone on the field, of course; to regulate their complex and often violent maneuvers, football has no fewer than seven officials.

OFFICIALS

The officials in football, often referred to as "zebras" because of the black-and-white-striped shirts they wear, are both more numerous and more subject to criticism than officials in any other team sport. Because the number of games in the football season is sixteen, and because these games are played once a week, football officials are hired on a part-time basis and paid by the game, unlike officials in other sports who are hired on a full-time basis. The seven field officials must work together as a unit and are formed into "teams" early in the exhibition season. They spend the rest of the season traveling to games together, studying films of games together, and learning to work together each weekend.

Although it is against NFL rules for coaches publicly to criticize officials, they are often attacked in the press for mistakes—especially mistakes that result in a team winning a game because of a bad call. There were several such bad calls in the 1978 season, each one of which caused a furor. This is because officiating mistakes are very costly in football, where each game is extremely important. In the other sports, the seasons are longer and many more games are played. Bad calls in basketball, for example, where over 100 points may be scored in a game and there are 82 games in a season, generally even out. In football, there simply aren't enough games and there isn't as much scoring per game to allow mistakes to balance.

To further complicate the lives of the NFL officials, most of their contested decisions are judgment calls, and in the heat of battle on a football field, with 22 rampaging players flailing away, it is easy for officials to have their view of a play blocked or partially blocked, or to be looking at one part of the action when something critical may be taking place elsewhere. The magnitude of the officials' job and perhaps the impossibility of it was put in perspective by NFL commissioner Pete Rozelle, quoted in *Sports Illustrated.* According to Rozelle, the number of judgments a single official may have to make in a given game can be found by multiplying the average number of plays per game—about 160—by the number of players, 22; this gives 3,520 different possibilities for contested plays!

Possible solutions to this difficult problem include hiring an eighth official who would watch instant videotaped replays of contested action and overrule the field officials' decisions in mistaken calls. Another proposal would allow the coaches of each team the opportunity, two or more times a game, to challenge a decision and have the challenge settled by referring to an instant replay. Some combination of these solutions may be instituted on a trial basis in the next few years.

In the meantime, the game will continue to be controlled by these seven beleaguered men:

The most important official is the referee, who stands behind the offensive team during scrimmages. He is in ultimate charge of the game, settling all disputes and making all decisions at the end of a down as to the placement of the football and awarding of penalties.

Because the football field is so big and so much goes on during a down, the rest of the officials specialize: some are responsible for watching the linemen during a scrimmage; others cover the area around the goal, looking for pass violations; others cover the sidelines. The various aspects of keeping track of time and time-outs are also delegated. These six officials are known as the umpires and field judge, who stand in the defensive backfield; and the head linesman, side judge, back judge, and line judge. These men stand on the side of the line of scrimmage, two to each side of the field.

In addition to the field officials, who are on the field at all times, there is a further group of four men called the chain crew (or "chain gang"). These men stand on the sidelines during most of the game, where they are responsible for the yardage chain, a ten-yard length of chain fastened between two poles. This chain is moved up and down the sidelines as play progresses. One end of the chain is always planted on the sideline opposite the spot of a first down. If there is doubt about whether a new first down was made, the referee signals the chain crew to come out on the field and measure, with the chain, from the previous first down to the place where the ball has come to rest, to determine whether the offense has indeed advanced ten yards.

This measurement is one of the most suspenseful events in football, with fans and teams eagerly awaiting the outcome. When the chain has determined the true yardage situation, often by inches, loud cheers will go up from fans of the winner—for the defense having "held the line" or for the offense having made the first down.

All the field officials blow whistles when the ball is dead in their area, and if they observe a violation during a down they throw a bright yellow flag onto the field. Sometimes only one official spots a violation; sometimes more than one will spot it or sometimes multiple violations are called, and the announcers report, "There are flags all over the field!"

The basics of football as outlined in this chapter are all you really need to know to follow a game. However, there are a great many complexities in the rules that are important in determining the tactics and strategy used by both teams. To give you a better idea of these finer points, we'll take a closer look at some of the key football rules in the next chapter.

CHAPTER 12

HOW THE GAME IS PLAYED

WHO CAN DO WHAT AND HOW

Because each play in football involves so many men, and because the potential for injury is so great, there are many rules about which players are allowed to perform what actions, and under what circumstances. Following are some of the more important of these rules that are likely to affect games you will see.

BLOCKING AND TACKLING   As we saw in the last chapter, offensive linemen try to open up holes in the defensive line and to protect the backs, while the defensive linemen try to hold the line and nullify offensive protection. The physical methods these men use are called the "block" (offensive) and the "tackle" (defensive). The main difference between blocking and tackling is in the use of the hands. Until recently, blockers were not allowed to use their hands at all; now they can push their hands straight out in front of them, palms open, to run into or ward off an opponent. A tackler may use his hands and arms to grab or encircle an opponent, or even to throw him to the ground.

There are other maneuvers, such as striking an opponent on the head, which used to be legal by the defense but are now outlawed because they are too dangerous. There is still plenty of opportunity for violent physical contact, however, and this is why the scrimmage area is sometimes referred to as the "pit."

PASSING AND CATCHING   In order for a forward pass to be considered complete, the receiver must be in complete control of the ball and must catch it inbounds (in the area between the sidelines). If he catches it just as he is being shoved out of bounds but does not gain control before actually going out of bounds, the pass is considered incomplete. Likewise, if the receiver is knocked down and the ball is immediately jarred loose, he is not considered to have caught the pass.

To be legally caught, a ball must also be caught and held firmly in the hands. If the receiver grasps the ball between an arm and the ground, he has "trapped" rather than caught the ball, and the pass is ruled incomplete.

Once a player has possession of the ball he must be very careful to hold on to it. If he drops it (or has it taken away from him), he has committed a "fumble." A fumbled ball can be recovered by either team and can be advanced. (In contrast to a fumble is a "muff." A ball is muffed when a player fails to catch and control it on any pass other than a forward pass or on a kick. A muffed ball may also be recovered by either team but is immediately dead and may not be advanced.)

Not only is the offensive team limited to five eligible receivers who must catch the ball in the prescribed manner, but it is limited to one forward pass per play, thrown from behind the line of scrimmage. Any number of lateral or backward passes may be made, but again, only behind the line of scrimmage. A fumble that rolls forward and then is recovered by the offensive team is considered to be a forward pass; if intentional, it is illegal (although, since this is a judgment call, a team may get away with the occasional forward fumble to gain some yardage).

A final restriction on the offensive team is the 30-second rule, which states that a team has 30 seconds to put the ball in play (with a kick or a snap) after the referee blows his whistle to start play.

Sometimes when a team is planning a particularly thorny play, or when the play is switched at the last minute, this time limit is not observed, and the team is penalized.

SPOTTING THE BALL   The most significant overall factor at any point in a football game is the position of the football on the field. An obvious example of this importance occurs when a team receives a kickoff or punt and tries to return the ball as far as possible toward the opposing goal. Any time ir manages to bring the ball as far as its own 40-yard line or farther, it is said to have achieved "good field position" for beginning a series of four downs.

The exact point at which any down ends is also crucial, because it is normally the place where the next line of scrimmage forms. However, this is not necessarily the point at which the ball comes to rest on the field.

There are a number of rules governing the placement, or "spotting," of the ball for a new line of scrimmage.

For instance, at the end of an ordinary running play, or a passing play that is completed inbounds, the ball is considered positioned at the point where its tip comes to rest on the field, nearest the opposition goal. In this case the actual spot will be at the nearest inbound marker ("hash mark"—see illustration, page 109).

A ballcarrier or receiver is considered "downed" as soon as any part of his body other than his hands or feet touches the ground. However, he is also considered downed if he is so surrounded by opposing players that his forward progress is stopped, even though he may still be on his feet. When this happens, the ball is spotted at the nearest inbound marker opposite the place where his progress was stopped.

If the runner or receiver was forced out of bounds on the play, the ball is spotted at the inbound marker directly across from the spot at which the ball went out of bounds. On an incomplete passing play, the ball is ordinarily spotted at the original line of scrimmage. There are in addition certain designated spots used in the kicking game (see pages 114-115, Chapter Eleven).

VIOLATIONS AND PENALTIES

"There's a flag on the play."

Those words by a TV or radio announcer signal that a foul (any violation of the rules) has occurred during the play in progress, and usually indicate that the down you just saw will be replayed, or that its outcome will be different from what would be expected. Although fouling does not occur as often as in some other sports, fouls in football come up an average of 13 times during each game, and their enforcement can be perplexing to fans. Even football professionals are sometimes bewildered by the application of the many seemingly conflicting rules of penalties and enforcement, as anyone knows who has watched officials confer on the field. This situation is perhaps best summed up in *Illustrated Football Rules*, in which Red Saunders is quoted as saying, "If you are not confused, you haven't been listening."

It would be impossible to list all the different fouls and their penalties here, but the following discussion should give you some idea of what is going on when there is a flag on the play.

Because the number of the down and the yardage to be gained on any given play are so crucial, a team that fouls is penalized by loss of yardage and sometimes loss of down (or both). That is, if the defense fouls, the offensive team will be given additional yardage, often enough for a first down; while an offensive team that fouls will usually lose field position. As a rule, most penalties are enforced ("counted off") either from the original line of scrimmage on the play where the foul occurred or from the spot where the play ended. (In some cases, the penalty is enforced from the spot where the foul was *committed*.)

Ordinarily, a play during which a foul occurs is considered to have been nullified and is replayed in its entirety. In other words, a new line of scrimmage is formed at a point closer either to the defenders' goal or to the offensive team's goal, depending on who committed the foul, but the number of the down is the same as it was on the play during which the foul was committed.

There are two types of fouls in football, contact and non-contact. Contact fouls are for the most part illegal actions involving physical contact with another player; noncontact fouls are usually procedural violations. The following are mostly procedural fouls. Since they are not likely to result in great imbalance or injury, the penalty is only five yards.

DELAY OF GAME by either offense or defense. This rather large category includes such actions as taking longer than 30 seconds to put the ball in play; undue delay in assembling for the scrimmage after a time-out; making an invalid "fair catch" signal; or having more or fewer than 11 players on the field during a down. In a game during the 1978 season between Louisiana State University and Alabama, LSU kicked a field goal that would have been good. However, after the goal it was discovered that there were only ten LSU men on the field, and the team not only had its score disallowed, but it was penalized for delay of game.

ILLEGAL MOTION by the offense is often called because of a rule that states that only one offensive back may be moving backward or laterally at the snap. No other player may be moving in any direction one second before the snap. Two or more backs are also allowed to "shift," or exchange positions *just prior* to the snap, but they must come to a complete stop for one second, or a foul will be called. This rule is not always easy to enforce, as Tony Dorsett, a brilliant Dallas Cowboy rookie, learned during a game in 1977. He moved forward before the snap of the ball (in what should have been an illegal motion), but promptly pivoted on his left foot and ran parallel to the line of scrimmage, acting as if he were the man in motion. Since there was already another Cowboy in motion, both the defense and officials were confused by this tricky "play." Not only were the Cowboys not penalized, but they gained several yards on the down.

OFFSIDES usually refers to illegal moves made at the line of scrimmage. According to this rule players of either team are not allowed to have part of their body over the line, with the exception of the offensive center, who has his hand on the ball prior to the snap. Offsides is also sometimes called when players on one or both sides make a false start and cross the line before the snap. If this false start results in contact with an opposing player, the foul may be called "encroachment," and the down is replayed with a five-yard penalty.

ILLEGAL PROCEDURE   by the offense includes such technical violations as a false start, having fewer than seven men on the line prior to the snap, or an illegal formation.

There are a very few fouls calling for a ten-yard penalty, and these are all enforced against the offense. The most common such penalty is offensive holding, which is illegal use of hands, that is, using the hands to grasp or encircle an opponent. This foul usually occurs on the line of scrimmage just after the snap, particularly on a passing play where the quarterback needs several seconds to set up his pass; if his linemen find that their blocks are not restraining the defenders, they may resort to more drastic measures.

The following fouls are considered serious, and all call for a 15-yard penalty.

UNSPORTSMANLIKE CONDUCT   This is a catchall category and refers to such violations as abusive or obscene language, arguing with officials, and interference with the game on the part of nonplayers (those on the bench, or coaches, for example). If considered "flagrant" or repeated, unsportsmanlike conduct may also result in expulsion from the game. It is an interesting comment on the development of football that the actions included as illegal under this category are such violations as concealing the football under one's jersey, painting a football on one's jersey, or wearing a radio receiver in one's helmet.

ILLEGAL BAT   This refers to "batting" the ball with the hands while it is in the air. While the defense can bat a pass at any time in any direction, the offense is allowed to bat it toward the goal only once; more than that calls for a 15-yard penalty.

ILLEGAL KICK This is any kick by any player that is not a legal kickoff, try for point, or punt from scrimmage. The rule came into effect after Larry Kelley, a Yale end in 1936, kicked a loose ball down the field soccer-style in a crucial game against Princeton. He recovered the ball for a touchdown and was given the award for outstanding college player of the year. However, the officials realized that such enterprise could change the game of football forever, so the illegal kick rule was introduced.

The remaining violations have to do with violent contact. They include such obviously gross violations as striking an opponent in the face, clubbing him, kicking him, and fighting. Others are:

CLIPPING, which is throwing one's body across the backs of the legs of an opposing player. (It is, however, legal for the defense to tackle the ballcarrier from behind.)

ILLEGAL CRACKBACK This is an illegal block made by a wide receiver who has started to run downfield but then returns to the line and blocks an opponent, often from his blind side (the side he isn't looking from).

PILING ON It is impossible not to notice that the end result of many a play in football is a writhing mass of intertwined bodies, with the passer, receiver, or ballcarrier somewhere on the bottom. The pileup generally results from several men being involved in a play at once, particularly when more than one defensive player is trying to tackle an offensive player. It is illegal for the defense to wantonly pile onto an already existing pile once the target has been downed, because this increases the chance of injury to one or more of the players involved. An extreme example of piling on occurred in a college game several years ago. On one play all 22 players fell on the ball after a fumble. When the players were finally separated, they found the ball at the bottom of the pile, flattened.

Like many violations, piling on is a judgment call on the part of the officials.

FACE MASK VIOLATION In their desperate struggle to gain some advantage over the other men, or to ward them off, players will sometimes grab anything handy, such as an opponent's face mask. If this grabbing is merely incidental, the penalty is five yards. But if a player gets a good hold on another's face mask, and particularly if he twists it or pulls it, it calls for a penalty of 15 yards.

TRIPPING You will often see runners tackled around the legs or even ankles, and this will certainly look like tripping to you. However, under football rules, tripping is an illegal act only if it is done to someone who is not a ballcarrier; or if the act of tripping itself is done by using the feet or legs.

ROUGHING THE KICKER, ROUGHING THE PASSER The kicker, whether he is kicking a field goal, a try for a point, or a punt, is protected by the rules, and may not be touched unless such contact is incidental to actually blocking the kick. The passer's situation is a little different. He may be tackled at any time *until* the pass has been thrown, at which point his person is considered sacrosanct. Furthermore, under a new rule instituted during the 1979 season, the officials are supposed to blow their whistles as soon as the quarterback is "in the grip of" any tackler. However, if a defenseman is already committed to the tackle before the passer throws and his own momentum cannot be stopped, the resulting contact is not illegal. A tackler who simply jumps on the quarterback for the fun of it is charged with roughing the passer and gives his side 15 yards.

There are a variety of other fouls that are obviously not only unfair but dangerous, such as tackling someone who is out of bounds. Most of these are lumped under the general term *unnecessary violence.*

PASS VIOLATIONS Although an incomplete pass is not a foul, it is treated as though it were and, as we have seen, is penalized by the loss of the down but no loss of yardage.

An *intentional* incomplete pass is considered a foul, called "intentional grounding." This foul is most often committed when the quarterback is unable to find a man to receive a pass, or when the offensive line has failed to hold off the defense long enough for him to throw. Under these circumstances the quarterback will often "throw the ball away"—that is, throw it into an area of the field where no defenders can intercept it, or throw it out of bounds. As long as the quarterback throws in the general direction of one of his eligible receivers, intentional grounding will probably not be called on him. The penalty for intentional grounding is ten yards *plus* loss of down.

Because of the penalty against intentional grounding, some quarterbacks will allow themselves to be tackled rather than receive a ten-yard penalty, particularly if they are close to the line of scrimmage. Going down before the ball has been thrown is known as "eating" the ball.

PASS INTERFERENCE   is any act on the part of the defense that would prevent the offense from legally receiving a pass. Because there is a rule that a pass receiver cannot be molested once he gets five yards beyond the line of scrimmage, the defensive players who are covering him are restricted to deflecting the ball or catching it first, or to tackle him as soon as he catches it and hope it will jar loose from his hands. Any other contact with him is considered pass interference.

However, since all defenders are eligible receivers, they are considered to have equal rights to the ball, and the offensive receiver is prohibited from interfering with *them*. What this usually means in practice is that if two men seem to have an equal chance at the ball, they will crash into each other, which is considered incidental and therefore legal contact.

Pass interference by the offense calls for a ten-yard penalty from the line of scrimmage. By the defense it is one of the most serious of all fouls, and results in the offense being awarded a first down at the spot of the interference as if the pass had been completed. Furthermore, if the interference was caused by a foul that draws a yardage penalty, such as unnecessary roughness, that penalty is enforced from the spot of the interference as well. If the interference occurs in the defenders' end zone, the offense is given a first down on the one-yard line.

DELIBERATE FOUL TO PREVENT A SCORE   If a foul during a scoring situation appears to the officials to have been deliberately initiated solely in order to prevent a score, the offensive team may be awarded the score (touchdown or field goal or conversion).

Most fouls take place during a normal series of downs, where the offensive team retains possession of the ball. What about those situations in which there is an interception, or a recovered fumble and possession of the ball changes during the play? Although there are exceptions here as throughout the foul system, in general, if the foul occurs prior to the change of possession, the change of possession is wiped out and the ball returns to the offensive team *regardless of which side committed the foul.* The penalty is then enforced in the usual manner.

If the foul occurs after the change of possession, the team that has captured the ball keeps it, and enforcement of the penalty generally takes place from the spot at which the change of possession took place.

In addition to how and where penalties are enforced, sometimes the question arises as to when to enforce them. For instance, suppose a foul occurs between downs, or at the end of a half. As might be expected, a foul that occurs between downs is enforced on the next down; a foul occurring at the end of the half is enforced at the beginning of the next half, on the kickoff. A kicking team thus penalized is said to be "in the hole," having to kick from a spot nearer its own goal.

MULTIPLE FOULS   So far we have looked at situations in which only one foul occurs during a play. Occasionally more than one foul occurs on the same play, and the officials must decide how to administer them.

If each team commits a foul, and the penalty for the fouls is the same (say, 15 yards each), then the penalties are called "offsetting," and the down is replayed in its entirety as if it had never taken place. If one foul draws a more serious penalty than the other, the more serious foul is enforced from the previous scrimmage line.

If the same team commits more than one foul on a play, the team that did not foul generally has the choice of which penalty to impose. (There are some exceptions to this, depending on the nature of the foul or fouls; for example, a foul that calls for the expulsion of a player is always awarded, regardless of the choice of the team that was fouled against.)

DECLINING PENALTIES A team that is fouled against, once or more than once, also has the option of accepting or declining the penalty (again with certain exceptions). If the penalty is declined, the game goes on as if no foul had occurred on that play. The decision of whether or not to accept a penalty is sometimes very important strategically. For example, suppose the Gorillas are first and ten on their own 40-yard line. The quarterback throws a completed pass to a receiver who is downed on the Walrus 40-yard line, for a gain of 20 yards. However, during the pass a foul was committed by a member of the Walrus team that calls for a 15-yard penalty.

If the foul is enforced, the ball will return to the scrimmage line and the Gorillas will be given 15 yards, putting them at the first and ten on the Walrus 45-yard line. Clearly, it is to the advantage of the Gorillas to decline the penalty and continue to play the game from the Walrus 40-yard line.

After any foul is called, the violation, the penalty, and the outcome—that is, whether the penalty was accepted or declined—will be announced. Most referees these days wear microphones on the field, so you will be able to hear their decisions both at the stadium and on television. The statements will be accompanied by body language explaining the foul. On the next page is a chart of the most common referee's signals used in football.

**TOUCHDOWN, FIELD GOAL,
OR SUCCESSFUL TRY**
Both arms extended above head.

SAFETY
Palms together above head.

FIRST DOWN
Arm pointed toward defensive
team's goal.

**DEAD BALL OR NEUTRAL
ZONE ESTABLISHED**
One arm above head with an open hand.

With fist closed: **Fourth Down.**

LOSS OF DOWN
Fingertips tap both shoulders
(following signal for foul).

TIME-OUT
Hands crisscrossed above head.

Same signal followed by placing one
hand on top of cap: **Referee's Time Out.**
Same signal followed by arm swung at side: **Touchback**

NO TIME-OUT OR
TIME IN WITH WHISTLE
Full arm circled to simulate winding clock.

DELAY OF GAME OR
EXCESS TIME-OUT
Folded arms.

Same signal followed by forearms
rotated over and over in front
of body: **Illegal Formation
or Illegal Procedure.**

PERSONAL FOUL
One wrist striking the other above head.

Same signal followed by swinging leg:
Running into or Roughing Kicker.

Same signal followed by raised arm
swinging forward: **Running Into Passer.**

Same signal followed by hand striking
back of thigh: **Clipping.**

HOLDING
Grasping one wrist, the fist clenched,
in front of chest.

ILLEGAL USE OF HANDS
Grasping one wrist, the hand open and
facing forward, in front of chest.

Same signal followed by hooking one
foot behind the opposite ankle: **Tripping**

PENALTY REFUSED,
INCOMPLETE
PASS, PLAY OVER, OR
MISSED GOAL
Hands shifted in horizontal plane

PASS JUGGLED INBOUNDS AND CAUGHT OUT OF BOUNDS

Hands up and down in front of chest (following incomplete pass signal).

ILLEGAL FORWARD PASS

One hand waved behind back.

Same signal followed by raised hand flung downward:

Intentional Grounding of Pass.

INTERFERENCE WITH FORWARD PASS OR FAIR CATCH

Hands open and extended forward from shoulders with hands vertical.

INVALID FAIR CATCH SIGNAL

One hand waved above head (following Interference With Fair Catch signal).

**INELIGIBLE RECEIVER OR
INELIGIBLE MEMBER OF KICKING
TEAM DOWNFIELD**
Both hands placed on cap.

**OFFSIDE, ENCROACHING, OR
FREE KICK VIOLATION**
Hands on hips.

ILLEGAL MOTION AT SNAP
Horizontal arc with one hand.

**CRAWLING, PUSHING, OR
HELPING RUNNER**
Pushing movement of hands to
front with arms downward.

**UNSPORTSMANLIKE
CONDUCT**
Arms outstretched, palms down.
(Same signal means continuous
action fouls are disregarded.)

ILLEGAL CRACKBACK
Personal foul signal followed by
the strike of an open hand
against mid-thigh.

ILLEGAL CUT
Bent at waist with both hands at knees.

THE BALL AND THE CLOCK

As in all the team sports except baseball, football must take place within a certain period of time, and the actions of both teams will be influenced to some extent by how much time remains. Furthermore, the clock is often stopped during the game; this stoppage is sometimes deliberate for strategic reasons.

Time remaining and whether or not the clock is running can be crucial in the closing moments of a quarter. Whenever the clock is stopped or the ball is considered "dead," no further play is allowed. However, while the ball is always dead when the clock stops, sometimes the clock continues to run though the ball is dead (that is, no further action may take place). Thus, if a team is behind toward the end of the game, it wants to avoid all situations in which play stops but the clock continues to run, "eating" up the time it has remaining to score.

The clock continues to run but the ball is dead whenever a player in possession of the ball is downed *inbounds*. In almost all other "dead ball" situations, the clock is stopped automatically. This occurs whenever the ball goes out of bounds; when a fair catch is made; when a score, safety, or touchback is made; when a pass is incomplete; at the end of a down in which a foul has occurred; when the kick is allowed to roll dead or is intentionally downed by the kicking team; and in a variety of less frequent situations, such as when the ball accidentally touches the goalposts, or any time an official blows his whistle.

After the clock has stopped the ball is put back into play either by a snap or a kick.

As with all rules in sports, there are exceptions. The most important of these are: after a touchdown the clock does not start again until the kickoff following the try for point; and during the last two minutes of a half the clock does not start after a kick until the kicked ball has been touched by a player.

The clock is also stopped for a variety of time-outs (and the ball is always dead in these situations). Among these time-outs are the "two-minute warning." This is an automatic time-out that is called two minutes before the end of each half; at the end of this time-out the clock starts at the snap and there are two minutes left to play. There are also several automatic "referee's time-outs." These include time-out after a passer is brought down ("sacked") behind the line of scrimmage before he has thrown; and any time there is an event that uses up clock time, such as when the officials must confer. There are also team time-outs. Each team is allowed three time-outs of one and one-half minutes during each half. In addition, the referee allows two-minute time-outs for injuries, and three-minute time-outs for repair of equipment. Either team may take more than three time-outs but is penalized five yards each time it does. This is known as "buying" a time-out.

Finally, there are rare circumstances in which the ball is alive, though the clock has stopped. For example, at the end of a half, if a play is already in progress when time runs out, the play is allowed to continue. Also, if the defensive team commits a foul on the final play of a half during which the clock runs out, the offensive team is allowed one more play.

In the next chapter we'll take a look at the plays that make football such an exciting game.

CHAPTER 13 BEHIND THE ACTION

TUESDAY NIGHT AT THE MOVIES

Second-guessing is one of the most satisfying parts of sports, both for fans and for professionals. In the case of football, it is raised to the level of obsession. Because there are so many players involved in each game, and because there are so many potential plays on both sides, detailed analysis of a game can take the greater part of a week.

Thus the widespread use of film. Every pro football game that is played each week is filmed; the films are then distributed to the teams, who analyze them in depth. Teams review their own mistakes and triumphs as well as those of future opponents, and prepare detailed charts and diagrams that dissect each play and the actions of both teams.

Is football strategy then so complicated that it can only be understood by a computer? The answer to this is yes and no. On a superficial level football can be enjoyed by almost anyone watching for the first time. The basics, after all, aren't that difficult: the offense tries to get the football over the goal line while the defense tries to stop this from happening. The strategy and tactics employed in achieving these ends, however, are quite intricate, with multiple themes and variations. In some cases even the coaches and players aren't certain of exactly what happened until they review the films of a game. So, don't feel bad if you find yourself somewhat puzzled by the specifics of play when you watch a football game. Chances are that even the sportscasters who are speaking blithely of "weak side rotation" and "dogging off the nickel" aren't all that sure what is really going on.

THE PLAYBOOK

In all pro sports, the success of a particular strategy often depends on the successful completion of set plays that have been rehearsed over and over in practice sessions. Although there are certain set plays all teams use at one time or another, it is a point of pride for coaches to be able to develop new, secret plays. The secrecy is important: a coach trying out a new defensive weapon does not want anyone but his own team to see it until it is sprung upon the opposition the following Sunday afternoon.

To help ensure secrecy, as well as to make certain that team members know and understand all the basic plays that are supposed to be in their repertoire, during training camp each player is issued a top-secret playbook, which he is supposed to memorize. These playbooks are considered so important that their loss is usually punishable by a hefty fine. Some coaches claim to have hundreds of plays covering all kinds of situations; others maintain that there are very few basic plays and all else is variation.

When you see the offensive team going into a huddle, the quarterback is delivering the play that will be used on that particular down. The plays are either decided on by the quarterback himself, or "sent in" by the coach. Since unlimited substitutions are allowed in football, the coach can give the information to a substitute player and then send him into the game in place of another player. A player used to deliver the coach's decisions is usually a member of the line, sometimes called a "messenger guard." (The information delivered in a huddle is of course extremely important and is usually given very quickly; however, Don Meredith, former Dallas quarterback and now an announcer for ABC, was remembered by his teammates for going into a huddle—even on crucial plays—and singing a few bars of "God Didn't Make Honky-tonk Angels," before giving his signals.)

Once the play has been given, the team lines up on the field and the quarterback begins the "count," a prearranged series of words or numbers, one of which signals the center to snap the ball. Important team plays have code names, allowing for last-minute changes at the line.

The defense tries to anticipate the offensive play and respond with a counterstrategy of its own. Usually the defensive middle linebacker calls the formations, which will be used to counter the expected offensive play. When either side decides to change strategy at the last minute, the quarterback or middle linebacker calls the new play in code. These changes at the line are known as "automatics" or "audibles."

Although the coach develops an overall game plan for each game based on film and scouting reports of the team to be played, the plan usually must be modified during the course of the game. To assist in determining what patterns are developing and what changes may be needed, each team has one or more "spotters" seated high up in the stands where they can get an overall view of the action. Their reports are relayed by telephone to the sidelines, where the coach evaluates them and decides on any changes necessary.

For the specifics of how this drama unfolds on the field, let's take a look at the elements of strategy for offense and defense.

OFFENSIVE STRATEGY

It is generally believed that fans prefer to see a lot of passing, but statistics show that the teams that win most consistently are those that have a good, consistent "running game."

Running the ball is a reliable way to pick up short yardage. Since ten yards have to be gained before the fourth down, all an offensive team needs to retain possession is an average of three and one-third yards per play; "rushing," or running, is the safest way to do this. When the team needs longer yardage, a long pass, called a "bomb," is generally used.

Of course each team's strategy will be built around the capabilities of its particular personnel, as well as those of the opponents they are likely to face throughout the season. Also, since an essential part of the game is deceiving the opposition for the few seconds necessary to complete a play successfully, a team that is known always to pass in a certain situation might decide instead to rush, and vice versa.

Over many years, strategists have developed a number of offensive formations from which the various plays emerge. Formations are designed to solve certain problems: for example, to open a hole in the defensive line for a back to run through; or to occupy the defense in such a way that a receiver can run deep into the backfield while the quarterback is setting up to throw to him. Some formations are designed to keep the opposition guessing as to which sort of play is likely on the down. Each formation not only has subtle positional variations but can be flip-flopped—for example, the wide receiver can be positioned on the left side of the field instead of to the right.

Often you will see the offensive team line up one way, and then seconds before the snap one or more backs will change position: moving, say, from the right side of the field to the left, or from behind the quarterback wide into a flanking position. This motion is used to further confuse the defense who may have made up their mind what the upcoming play is likely to be. The backfield shift may indicate to them either that the nature of the play has changed (that it will be a running, say, instead of a passing play), or that the direction of the play will be going to the right side of the field rather than the left.

Most formations are designed to allow for a variety of passing or running plays, depending on what the defense does. Some formations lend themselves more easily to running plays; others to passing plays. As a rule, the fewer wide receivers there are, the fewer options there will be for passing, while a formation such as the "shotgun" maximizes passing chances by increasing the number of possible receivers.

Below and opposite is a series of diagrams showing some of the formations you are likely to see in pro football games.

right safety   left safety
○   ○

right cornerback   left cornerback
○   ○

middle linebacker
right linebacker ○   ○   ○ left linebacker

right end   right tackle left tackle   left end
○   ○   ○   ○

line of scrimmage
— — — — — — — — — — — — — — — — — —

wide receiver   left guard   right guard   tight end
○   ○   ○   ○   ○   ○   ○

left tackle   center   right tackle

quarterback ○   ○
                                   wide receiver

○   ○
running back   running back

NOTE: Alternatively, the wide receiver on the left could be split from the line as a split end.

PRO T

SE: split end
T: tackle
G: guard
C: center
TE: tight end
QB: quarterback
RB: running back
WR: wide receiver

WISHBONE

FB: fullback

BASIC I

TB: tail back
FLB: flankerback

SHOTGUN

SLB: slot back

PRO T OR PRO SET FORMATION   This is one of many variations on the *T* formation, in which the three backs line up side by side behind the quarterback. In the *Pro T*, two of the backs line up side by side behind the quarterback as running backs, while the other back lines up behind and to the side of the line of scrimmage as a wide receiver. On the other side of the formation one of the ends is split as another receiver. This is a versatile formation, allowing for a variety of running or passing plays to either side. Variations of the Pro T include the *Wing T*, which looks the same except that both ends play in on the line of scrimmage (thus leaving only one wide receiver, who is called in this position a flankerback); and the *Slot T*, in which one of the backs lines up behind the slot between the split end and the tackle as a "slot back."

WISHBONE FORMATION   This formation is actually another variation on the T. In the wishbone formation the three backs are all lined up behind the quarterback, with the fullback directly behind him and the two halfbacks slightly behind the fullback and to either side. (The back formation is thus supposed to resemble a wishbone.) This formation is much more widely used in college ball than in the pros, and like the T is considered a versatile formation, with particular emphasis on the running game.

I FORMATION   Also a popular college formation, the *I* formation has nearly as many variants as does the T. In any I formation, two or more backs line up directly behind the quarterback, as "setbacks" (the one on the end is called a "tailback"). In the basic I formation, one of the backs lines up outside the line of scrimmage as a wide receiver, leaving two setbacks; in the power I, this player moves closer in and lines up as a running back next to one of the setbacks; while in the "stack" I, all three backs line up behind the quarterback. I formations are used primarily for strong running through the line, with passing capabilities provided by the flankerback (as wide receiver) in the Basic I.

SHOTGUN FORMATION   The first time you see the shotgun you may think that something is wrong, because the quarterback is no longer in his accustomed position directly behind the center but is standing several yards behind the line. The other backs line up as flankerbacks or slot backs. The purpose of this formation is to increase the chances of completing a long pass when long yardage is needed. Not only are the halfbacks and fullback near the line of scrimmage, where they can function as receivers rather than runners, the quarterback has extra time to set up for the pass. (Because he is farther in the backfield, it will take the defense longer to break through the offensive barriers and get to him.) This is in some ways a risky offense, because there is always a danger that the long-distance snap won't be delivered and received correctly, and if the defense breaks through and sacks the quarterback, a great deal of yardage will be lost.

There are many variations on these and other formations. Once you have been watching football for a while you will become familiar with those favored by your own team in different situations.

The choice of plays always depends on the overall situation: the score, the time remaining in the half (or game), the yardage to be gained, and the down. For example, on a first down, anything is possible, although a running play is most likely. If the average three and one-third yards is made, then probably another running play will be called. But on a third or even second down when long yardage must be made, the quarterback will usually choose a passing play, although it is more risky than a run.

Field position is also important in determining plays. If a team is near its own goal line, no matter what the down or how many yards it needs, it generally won't pass because if the defense intercepts, they will be that much closer to making a touchdown. Conversely, the farther downfield a team moves, the safer it becomes to try pass plays, even fairly tricky ones.

The time remaining on the clock is also important. If a team is behind and the game is about to end, the quarterback may begin passing on most plays to move the ball quickly downfield. On the other hand, a team that is ahead in the waning minutes of a game will usually run the ball exclusively, with the runner trying to stay inbounds. When he is downed, the clock will continue to run, even during the time it takes to set up a new line of scrimmage. One or two such plays can effectively "eat up" the remaining time in the game.

When a team is ahead by a narrow margin in the closing minutes of a game and has possession of the ball, it is a time-honored tradition for the offense to do nothing at all on the final play or two. That is, when the quarterback receives the ball he simply holds it tightly to him and falls down. It's true that no yardage will be gained this way, but there is also no danger that the ball will be fumbled during a hand-off or intercepted on a pass play. The New York Giants learned how costly it was to ignore this conventional wisdom in the closing moments of a game at the end of the 1978 season. With a narrow lead in this important game, the Giants had the ball deep in their own territory with enough time left for at most two plays. On the first play the quarterback fell on the ball, drawing resounding boos from the opposition fans. With just a few seconds left, most fans now turned off the television or began walking out of the stadium; the announcers were already summing up the game, pointing out how desperately the Giants had needed to win this one and how good they must be feeling. On the final play, however, the quarterback did not fall on the ball but chose to hand it off to one of his running backs. Both men had rehearsed this move countless times in practice sessions and in games, yet somehow something went wrong: The hand-off was missed for a fumble, and as Giants players and fans watched in horror, the ball went skidding behind the quarterback onto the field, where it was recovered by a player for the opposition who ran into the end zone for a touchdown. The Giant coach, John McVay (who was later fired), summed this play up as "the most horrifying end to a football game I've ever seen."

STANDARD OFFENSIVE PLAYS

When the quarterback intends to pass on a play, he drops back after receiving the ball into an area of relative safety known as the "pocket." This area is created and maintained by the offensive line whose sole duty on a passing play is to give the quarterback "pass protection," allowing him time to make his throw.

On any pass play the quarterback will look for his "primary receiver," the man he hopes to throw to. If that man is not where he is supposed to be, or if he is being heavily covered by the defense, the quarterback will then pick out another receiver, and with perhaps a deceptive "pump" of his arm, faking the moment or direction of release, will throw the ball.

Meanwhile, the intended receiver (or receivers) has been "running a pattern" to arrive at the preagreed spot downfield where he is supposed to catch the ball. These patterns usually consist of fast sprints with deceptive feints and cuts, designed to draw the secondary men in the wrong direction or to elude them altogether.

Common patterns include the "fly," in which the receiver runs directly downfield; the "sideline pattern," in which he starts downfield, then breaks to the sideline; the "flag pattern," in which the target is the flag at the corner of the field; and the "post pattern," in which the receiver starts to head for the sidelines but then breaks for the end zone. Both of the latter patterns call for the quarterback to throw a high, lobbing ball *over* the defenders. In the short patterns the idea is for the receiver to maneuver himself between the secondary men and the quarterback, so that a short, straight pass can be caught in front of them

Among shorter pass plays, one of the most common is the "screen pass." The idea is for several linemen to move to one side of the line at the snap, setting up a physical barrier between the defensemen and a receiver. The receiver is then relatively free to receive a pass in the "flat," or area to the side of the line of scrimmage.

On running plays, the runner has three choices of where to go with the ball: to the right, to the left, and through the middle. A run around the end of the formation is known as a "sweep," and is usually accomplished with the help of one or more linemen who have pulled away from the line at the snap to precede the runner, blocking any defenders in his way. A run through the middle is usually accomplished by the creation of holes in the line. In the "inside trap" play, a lineman allows a defensive player to penetrate across the line of scrimmage and then blocks him from the side or the back while the runner heads for the space the defensive lineman has vacated.

PLAY-ACTION PASS   This is a maneuver that looks like an ordinary running play until the last minute, when it usually develops as a long pass. It is initiated when the quarterback fakes a hand-off to one of his runners. He then throws to a receiver at the last minute.

This deception works because when the quarterback hands off to a runner, the runner immediately cradles the ball with his bent arm. Because it is difficult to see the ball in this position, a runner who seems to be holding the ball will often be able to deceive the opposition long enough for the quarterback to pass without serious opposition. To ensure success, the runner must play his part to the hilt, charging into the line of scrimmage toward a hole, or sweeping around the end. Defensive players who realize they have been tricked are likely to hit the runner just as hard as if he were actually carrying the ball, or even harder. One running back who was tired of being tackled on fake plays told *Sport* magazine that as soon as he reaches the line he calls out, "I don't have it! I don't have it!"

DRAW PLAYS   A draw is conceptually the opposite of a play-action pass; that is, it is a running play that is disguised as a pass play. In the typical draw, the quarterback drops back as if to pass, luring the defensemen away from their running coverage assignments, then at the last minute hands off to one of his backs. In the quarterback draw, the quarterback drops as if to pass, then suddenly cuts and runs with the ball himself. This play, while somewhat dangerous to the health of the quarterback, is often quite effective. A quarterback who is willing to run is quite an asset to his team; if something goes wrong on a potential play, he can always drop back and then run the ball as far forward as possible, sometimes for significant yardage. Some quarterbacks make a specialty of running in these circumstances and are known as "scramblers."

OPTION PLAY An option play is any play in which the quarterback can choose at the last minute whether to pass or hand off the ball. Although most forward passes in a game are made by the quarterback, the other backs are also allowed to pass; this rule gives rise to another exciting play known as the halfback option. In this play, a halfback takes a hand-off from the quarterback and begins to run to the outside of the line. Depending on what the defensive men do, he can keep the ball and continue to run or can pass it himself to one of the receivers on his team downfield.

REVERSE PLAY In a reverse, the quarterback hands off to one of the running backs, who begins to run laterally, committing the defense in that direction. This back then hands off to another back who is running laterally in the opposite direction. The "flea-flicker" is a very tricky variation of a reverse play, in which the second back with the ball may return it to the quarterback, who has dropped back for a long forward pass; or the second back may drop back and throw a forward pass himself, or even return it to the first back for a pass. Since any number of lateral passes are allowed behind the line, there is no violation of the one-forward-pass rule. One drawback to these complicated plays is that they take time; if the defense manages to overpower the offensive line while the plays are being set up, the ballcarrier or passer is likely to get tackled for a loss of yardage. Another disadvantage is that because so many people are handling the ball there is a good chance of a fumble.

DEFENSIVE STRATEGY

In a series of *Sports Illustrated* booklets on football strategy, coach Bud Wilkinson points out that normally there are only two ways a team can gain possession of the football: by preventing the offense from making ten yards in the required number of downs; or by receiving the ball after the other team has scored. Obviously, a defense that consistently limits the opposition's drives to a very few yards is going to give its own offense that many more opportunities to try to score on their own.

Defensive formations are generally more flexible than those for the offense. Since there is no rule about how many men must be on the line of scrimmage, the defensive players may line up in a variety of different positions to counter the offensive play they are expecting on a given down.

Most defensive formations are variations on three-deep or four-deep defenses, which means that either three or four men play in the secondary. Commonly, the front line will consist of one or two tackles flanked by ends (making a total of three or four linemen); occasionally another lineman will join them to play as defensive "nose guard" or tackle. (This player lines up directly opposite the offensive center.) Defensive formations are usually referred to as 4-3-4 (four linemen, three linebackers, and four men in the secondary); 3-4-4; 4-4-3; or 3-5-3. In addition, there are various named defenses, the most famous example of which is the "flex" defense used by the Dallas Cowboys. In the flex, the linemen are staggered, with only two men actually on the line. This formation is said to be one of the most effective against running plays because it is difficult to break through.

As a rule, a team that is expecting a running play will position its backfield men closer to the line of scrimmage; on an expected passing play, the secondary will be strengthened and moved back. "Prevent" defenses are used when the defense knows that the offense needs desperately to gain long yardage. The "nickel" defense is a prevent defense in which one or more linebackers play essentially as members of the secondary, with five men assigned to cover the five offensive eligible receivers one-on-one.

Just as the quarterback is expected to read defenses, so the defensemen are expected to look for opposition "keys," or tip-offs as to the nature of the offensive play. If, for example, the offensive linemen start to run downfield, this is a sign that a running play is coming, because they are not allowed to run across the line of scrimmage ahead of a pass. Similarly, if on the line of scrimmage the guards lean one way or the other, this may be a tip-off as to the direction the play will be run.

4-3-4 DEFENSIVE FORMATION

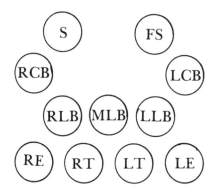

S: safety
FS: free safety
RCB, LCB: right and left cornerback
R,M, and LB: right, middle, left linebacker
R and LE: right and left end
R and LT: right and left tackle

Just as it is a prime tactic of the offense to fake plays and try to conceal their intentions till the last minute, the defense sometimes initiates "stunt" plays, which involve last-minute switches of assignments between players in order to disorganize the offense. For example, an end and tackle might switch assignments to throw the backs off-guard, or a tackle and middle linebacker might switch, with the tackle dropping back while the linebacker moves forward through the "hole" just vacated by the tackle.

One of the most exciting defensive plays, which is loved by crowds everywhere as long as it isn't used against their own team, is the "blitz," in which the idea is to tackle the quarterback on a passing play before he can throw the ball. A blitz is initiated by the linebackers or the secondary (if a safety is involved, it is called a "safety blitz"); it is carried out with the aid of the front linemen, who overpower the offensive line, opening holes for the backfield men to come pouring into. One or more men may participate in a blitz, and when it is successful it results in sacking the quarterback, or forcing him to get off a too-hasty and usually inaccurate pass. This maneuver is also referred to as "red dog" or "dog," and a blitzing team is often said to be "dogging." A quarterback who is good at "reading" the blitz can often counter it by handing off the ball to a runner who may then be able to rush through the holes now created in the defensive line for a long yardage gain.

Because the maneuvers we have been talking about are so complex and varied, it is sometimes difficult, especially in a close game, to see which team is stronger on given plays. The best way to gauge your team's effectiveness is to watch for consistency and continued possession of the ball. On passing plays, does your quarterback usually have plenty of time to throw his passes, or is he constantly being sacked or getting off bad throws? If the quarterback is having trouble, then the front line is not doing its job, and your team will have to rely much more on its defense. On running plays, look for a consistent gain of three to five yards per play. Less than this, or frequent loss of yardage, indicates a breakdown in "rush blocking"—blocking during a running play—or mistaken judgment on the part of the quarterback. When watching your team's defense, of course, just reverse the perspective.

CHAPTER
14 FOLLOWING THE GAME

Football, more than any other sport, is a game governed by numbers. When players are chosen for the draft, not only is a man's talent taken into consideration, but also how fast he can run, how tall he is, and how much he weighs. If a man does not fit physically into the correct mold for, say, a middle linebacker, then unless he can play at another position he is not likely to make the pros.

Just as players are judged on their numbers, so are teams. When you are reading about football games, you will find it almost impossible to follow the gist of a story unless you know what is meant by the various statistics.

Many newspapers provide their readers with statistical comparisons of offense and defense between teams about to compete in an important game. These figures are printed not only to give fans a good idea of what to watch for in a game, but also to help them decide how to bet. An injury update is also printed before big games, to prevent teams from concealing any injured players until the last minute, thus invalidating the betting line.

These team reports are generally very complete. In the semifinals of the 1978–79 season play-offs, the Houston Oilers, a young team who had never got this far in the play-offs before, were matched against the Pittsburgh Steelers in what was supposed to be one of the greatest games of the decade. Below is a table showing some of the statistics the two teams were compared on:

STEELERS-OILERS STATISTICS

STEELERS

	Steelers	Opponents
First downs	316	264
Third-down efficiency	48.1	39.0
Rushing yards per game	143.6	110.9
Passing yards per game	168.1	149.6
Yards penalized	943	954
Fumbles lost	17	21
Touchdowns	46	22
Points	356	195
Conversions	44	21
Field goals	12-26	14-26

OILERS

	Oilers	Opponents
First downs	276	292
Third-down efficiency	45.7	40.7
Rushing yards per game	154.8	129.5
Passing yards per game	146.1	177.6
Yards penalized	833	957
Fumbles lost	21	17
Touchdowns	35	34
Points	283	298
Conversions	31	32
Field goals	14-18	20-31

Note that for each statistic, there is a figure for the team as well as for the team's opponents. These are cumulative totals for the season: total number of first downs; total third-down efficiency, which refers to the percentage of times that the team achieved a first down by gaining the required number of yards at the end of third downs; the average number of yards gained per game by passing and running; the number of yards penalized during the year; the number of fumbles recovered by opposing teams; the total number of touchdowns made; the total number of points made on all scores in the season; the number of conversions, or successful tries for a point; and, finally, the number of field goals made and total field goal attempts. Comparing these numbers, we see that the Oilers made 14 field goals in 18 attempts; the Steelers were far less successful, making only 12 field goals in 26 tries, but they made a significantly greater number of touchdowns. The total points are a sum of the number of touchdowns (times six points); the number of tries for point; and the number of field goals (times three points).

Following the team statistics are ratings for individual players. For quarterbacks, the significant statistic is passing, which most tables will present as follows: att.—the number of pass attempts; comp.—completions; pct.—percentage of attempts completed; yds.—total number of yards gained by passing; TD—number of touchdown passes thrown; int.—number of interceptions thrown; and sacks—number of times the player was sacked. Over 50 percent pass completion is considered good for a quarterback.

For running backs, the important statistics are for rushing; these are broken down into number of runs made (no.); yards gained running (yds.); average yardage gain per rush (avg.); longest gain on a run (long gain); and number of runs for a touchdown (TD).

For defensive players, the number of interceptions made is followed by yards gained on interceptions; longest yardage made on an interception; and number of touchdowns scored as a direct result of interceptions.

The kicking game is also evaluated by statistics for individual kickers. These include number of punts made; total number of yards punted; average yardage per punt; and number of punts blocked by the opposition.

The punt return is considered by many fans to be the most exciting play in football; its popularity is reflected in the fact that it is analyzed statistically. For each punt returner the figures are number of punts returned; number of yards gained on all returns; average yardage per return; longest run on a punt return; number of touchdowns scored on punt returns; and number of fair catches made. Kickoff returns are analyzed in the same manner.

Glancing at these figures will give you a fair idea of the relative strengths of both teams, as well as effectiveness of individual personnel. What is not really reflected here, however, is the performance of linemen and linebackers, except for sacks and interceptions.

Because there are no statistics kept on successful blocks, the performance of offensive linemen must be inferred. For example, a team with a lot of sacks of its quarterback can be assumed to have a weaker offensive line than a team with few sacks, since the linemen's job is to protect the passer until he has thrown. Likewise, a team with a good rushing record by several of its backs must have a good offensive line—one that is able consistently to open holes in the defensive line and to block for runs.

In addition to comparisons of teams before a game, the sports pages also feature a summary of games in the form of a statistical table or box score. Following is the box score of a game between the Dallas Cowboys and the New Orleans Saints played in November 1978.

Points scored in each quarter are followed by game totals for both teams. Thus we see that the New Orleans Saints leaped out to a 7-0 lead over Dallas in the first quarter, but remained scoreless for the rest of the game while Dallas racked up 27 points.

The source of each score is presented next: New Orleans scored its touchdown on a run from the one-yard line by Muncie; the try for point was successfully completed by Mike-Mayer. Dorsett scored the first touchdown for Dallas with a similar run from the Saints' two-yard line; he was followed by Staubach with a one-yard touchdown rush. The third touchdown sounds exciting: It was a 24-yard touchdown pass from Staubach to DuPree. After each touchdown Septien was successful in his try for an extra point. Dallas's remaining six points were made on field goals of 24 and 26 yards respectively by Septien. The well-attended game drew 57,920.

When we next look at individual game statistics, we find that New Orleans passed for almost twice as much yardage as Dallas, throwing 40 passes for 25 completions; in contrast Dallas threw only 15 passes, of which 9 were good.

COWBOYS 27, SAINTS 7

New Orleans Saints .... 7 0 0 0— 7
Dallas Cowboys .... 0 14 7 6— 27
    N.O.—Muncie, 1, run (Mike-Mayer kick).
    Dal.—Dorsett, 2, run (Septien kick).
    Dal.—Staubach, 1, run (Septien kick).
    Dal.—DuPree, 24, pass from Staubach (Septien kick).
    Dal.—FG, Septien, 24.
    Dal.—FG, Septien, 26.
    Attendance—57,920.

	N.O.	Dal.
First downs	15	17
Rushing yardage	62	198
Passing yardage	215	106
Passes	25-40	9-15
Interceptions by	0	3
Punts	6-39	5-46
Fumbles lost	1	0
Penalties	6-50	6-65

INDIVIDUAl LEADERS
    RUSHING — N.O.: Muncie, 7-26; Galbreath, 8-22.
Dal.: Dorsett, 25-152; Laidlaw, 11-33.
    PASSING — N.O.: Manning, 25 of 39, 235 yards;
Harris, 0 of 1, 0. Dal.: Staubach, 9 of 15, 141.
    RECEIVING — N.O.: Galbreath 7-66, Harris, 6-66.
Dal.: DuPree, 3-73; P. Pearson, 2-29.

Dallas intercepted three New Orleans passes, however, and achieved more total yardage on punting, with an average of 46 yards per punt to the Saints' 39-yard average. Furthermore, New Orleans also lost the ball on a fumble and was penalized 6 times for a total of 50 yards.

The box score concludes with figures on individual leaders for each team. The New Orleans running back Muncie, for example, ran 7 times for an average gain of 26 yards, while Dallas's superstar

Dorsett ran 25 times for a total gain of 152 yards. The Saints' quarterback Manning gained 235 yards by completing 25 out of 39 passes, while Staubach completed 9 of 15 for 141 yards. Although the two New Orleans receivers each caught several passes totaling 66 yards, the winning Cowboys' top receiver, DuPree, achieved 73 on just three catches.

It appears then, that Dallas won easily, advancing toward New Orleans's goal with a steady, consistent rushing game, combined with accurate passes when necessary.

FOOTBALL AND THE TUBE

The main reason for football's amazing growth throughout the sixties and seventies is that in many ways the sport is made to order for television viewing. Although there is a great deal of congestion during most plays, the TV viewer actually has a better opportunity to see what is going on than the fan at the stadium. This is because the TV director can choose from among five or six camera shots; any important play will not only be shown from the best angle as it happens, but can be replayed from several perspectives. Furthermore, because all action stops at the end of each play, there is time to set up the cameras to follow the most likely actions on the next play.

On the other hand, TV fans who are interested in watching an isolated part of the action—the struggle between the front linemen, say, or the darting patterns run by wide receivers—will find themselves out of luck most of the time, because sports directors assign the cameras to what *they* feel is the most important part of the action. Almost invariably this means following the ball—as the quarterback drops back and tries to pass, or as a running back takes it and plunges toward a hole in the front line. Again, though, the instant replay can often show you most of what you may have missed during a given play.

For most fans, such minor drawbacks to television football are more than compensated for by the convenience and high technical level of sports broadcasting. TV football draws bigger audiences than any other sport, with the exception of a very few special events, such as the World Series in baseball. In return for delivering a large viewing audience, the NFL is well rewarded by the networks—the contracts signed in 1978 guaranteed payments of over five million dollars per team. To make their money back, the networks charge a fortune for commercials on the football shows, even while they increase the number of commercials shown to what may be a saturation level. In the 1978 season, each game was interruped by 22 minutes of commercial time plus an additional minute of public service announcements by the NFL, which works out to more than ten percent of the three hours allotted to the average game.

While it's true that football does have many natural breaks in which to insert commercials—time-outs by each team, intervals after punts, recovered fumbles, and scores—there are never enough for all those commercials, so extra time-outs must be called for the express purpose of selling products. You know this sort of time-out is coming when the announcer reports "time out on the field" with no explanation. While many fans at home don't object to all this commercialization, it can be quite annoying to fans at the game, who must wait through excessive time-outs and artificially extended periods between plays, without even a Lite-beer mini-drama for distraction.

Still, like it or not, there is no sign that the number of commercials during football games is likely to decline. Because so much money is changing hands on the weekends, the NFL, the networks, and the commercial interests all want to make sure that the fans are getting what is being paid for, which brings us to the real heart of the relationship between TV and football.

That relationship is made possible by the fact that football is infinitely changeable. Unlike baseball, which remains very much as it was in the nineteenth century, organized football has been willing to experiment with all sorts of changes—in equipment, size and markings of the field, and the playing rules. Many recent changes have begun as just such experiments to make football more "exciting." To network executives the word "exciting" for any sport means high scoring—American fans are presumed to be too unsophisticated to be able to appreciate a good defensive game. Because there is so much money invested in football, then, there have been many rules changes designed to increase overall scoring.

Among these were two new rules instituted in 1978: one provided the passer with better protection by allowing the offensive linemen to use their hands in blocking; the other provided an extra field official to make sure receivers are allowed to run their patterns unmolested. Because it was believed that fans find field goals boring, a few years ago the goalposts were moved from the goal line, where they had always been, to ten yards behind the goal line. Many other such changes have been and will continue to be made, although the basic mix of violence combined with action will undoubtedly remain.

There have been signs in recent years that football's popularity is waning somewhat, which may be only natural after the uninterrupted growth it has enjoyed for nearly two decades. A friend of mine who is a longtime fan attributes any possible decline to the superabundance of football on TV. "It really is possible to have too much of a good thing," he says. "I mean, last New Year's weekend I could have watched twenty-one hours of football if I'd wanted to, between the pro and college games. Actually, I did start out to watch them all, but by the fourth game everything started to look the same. I had a splitting headache, and I'd only seen about half of what was available."

Because football is so jargon-heavy, it is harder to follow the announcers in this sport than in any other. Many tend to talk in a kind of shorthand, which can be intimidating to a new viewer. Unless, for example, you know that "dogging" means "blitzing," and that the "nickel" is a type of defensive formation, you may be tempted to give up when you hear the announcers speak of a team's "dogging off the nickel" (running a blitz play from a nickel formation). Likewise, announcers often refer to the passing game as the "aerial" game, and call the offensive backs by as many names as they can think up, without providing any clues for new fans. Other shorthand includes the following: Of a quarterback: "He's eight of eleven for sixty-eight today." Translated, this means the player has thrown 11 passes for 8 completions and a total of 68 yards. "Thread the needle" means throw a pass. (More specifically, this term refers to a pass thrown between two defenders who are closely guarding a receiver.) "The Vikings are oh and two for third-down conversions" means they've tried to achieve first-down yardage from a third down twice, and have so far failed to do this.

Because TV announcers tend to speak so much as insiders or to concentrate on folksy color stories, sometimes to the exclusion of nearly everything else, fans are increasingly turning to radio as a supplement to TV broadcasts. And, because the commercial time on TV is in such demand, with exclusive contracts limited to a few products, advertisers are beginning to support good commentary on nationwide radio networks. Letters to the editors of major sports magazines show that many fans of all levels find the radio commentary informative and interesting.

Whether or not you get your audio from radio, when you watch a football game on TV you'll be able to pick up several things that the fan at the stadium can't. For example, decisions of referees are broadcast, and so sometimes are strategy sessions at the bench during a time-out; occasionally even the quarterback's calls in a huddle are broadcast by a shotgun mike. Instant replays can be extremely helpful as well, giving you a perspective impossible to the live audience. Another sight the TV cameras often pick out is that of players on the bench gulping deeply from oxygen masks after particularly grueling plays.

A final advantage to watching football on TV is that various statistics are flashed on the screen at regular intervals, giving you a good idea of the relative effectiveness of both clubs as well as a clue to what's happening if you tuned into a game late.

After any touchdown, an analysis of the drive (series of downs leading to a score) is presented, including the total number of downs played; the total yards gained; and the amount of time of possession. Whenever a kicker comes up for a punt, field goal, or kickoff, his longest kick and average yards per kick will be mentioned. Periodically a quarterback's stats too will flash on the screen (completions, attempts, percentage yardage). Most useful are the stats that are shown at the end of each period, comparing how the teams have done up till then. These figures compare number of first downs; yards gained rushing; yards gained passing; total yards; number of completed passes; turnovers (loss of the ball through interception, fumble, or other error), and time of possession. The most important figures here are those for first downs and time of possession. If one team is way ahead at the half, almost certainly it has a heavy edge on these two statistics, which indicate that the offense has been able to keep control of the ball while the defense holds the opposite team to few plays and few yards gained (or even negative yardage—in a game I saw between the New York Jets and the New England Patriots, the Jets' total yardage at the end of the first quarter was minus seven!).

GOING TO A GAME IN PERSON

Football in person has an image that is more social than sport-oriented; that is, a football game is thought of as a place to go on a date much more than is, say, a hockey game. In addition, there is the common practice of "tailgate parties" in the parking lot before the game and of course the cheering image of happy fans bundled up in blankets, sipping additional warmth from flasks smuggled in under heavy coats.

For reasons explained earlier, you will probably be able to see more of the action of a game if you watch it on television, but there is something so exhilarating about attending a game in person that most stadiums with good teams sell out even in the dead of winter. Which is, of course, the only real drawback to going to a football game in person. Unless you live in the South or Southwest, any game you attend, particularly late in the season, is likely to be bone-chillingly cold, with the possibility of snow or rain, since football games are almost never canceled or postponed.

Although the scoreboard will keep you informed as to the number of the down and the yardage yet to gain (and on the sophisticated electronic boards, relevant statistics for individual players as well), it can be helpful to take a pocket radio (with earplug) along, to help you understand what has happened on any really congested play.

Most fans agree that the best place to sit at a game is somewhere near the 50-yard line, above field level. While it might seem that you would be able to see more by sitting very near the field, such is not the case; not only do TV crews and other sideline wanderers get in your way, but you are so close to the level of action that it's difficult to watch plays as they develop. The higher up you sit, the closer your perspective will be to that of the TV viewer; but remember that the higher seats are more likely to receive the effects of wintry winds.

PLAY-OFFS AND RANKINGS

Just as the NFL has never been hesitant to tamper with the rules to increase TV audiences, so it has elaborated its postseason schedule to the point where football has the most complex play-off system in all of sports. So bewildering is this system that Tom Landry, coach of the then champion Dallas Cowboys, remarked during the 1978 season that if his team made the play-offs he hoped someone would tell him about it.

To understand the play-offs, it's necessary to start with the standings of the teams at the beginning of the season. Pro football teams are divided into two conferences, the American and National (both of which used to be separate leagues); each conference is further subdivided into three divisions, eastern, central, and western. Each conference is made up of fourteen teams, so the divisions consist of either five or four teams each.

The regular season schedule is set up so that, in theory, at least, the worst teams have the easiest schedules. This scheduling is partly to keep local audiences happy and partly to increase the chances for any team to make the play-offs. Each team must play two games against each other team in its division—one as a home game for either team. Beyond that, the teams play outside their divisions in a way that is designed to provide competitive balance (for example, a fifth-place team plays a total of four games with other fifth-place teams). Thus, the weaker teams do not have to play the stronger teams except those that happen to be in their own division.

At the end of the season, the rankings determine which teams get into the play-offs. Overall, the teams are rated against each other within their own conferences on the basis of won-lost records. However, in a 16-game schedule, there are often ties in the rankings, so an elaborate tie-breaking method has been devised, which consists of nine steps. Tie-breaking moves logically from step one—which of the teams did better in the two games they played between them—through comparison of touchdowns against common opponents, all the way to step nine, which is the toss of a coin.

Once the rankings have been determined for the season, the play-off schedule is arranged. The winners of each division within each conference are automatically in the play-offs (six teams). In addition, each conference has two wild-card teams, which are second-place teams with the best overall records.

In the first round of the play-offs, the four wild-card teams play each other in two intraconference games.

The following week, the second round takes place, pitting the surviving two wild cards, plus the division winners, against each other in four games, again by conference. No two teams in the same division play each other until the third round. Another complex formula determines which teams are opponents and who has home-stadium advantages. The four survivors, two from each conference, then play each other the following weekend in the conference championships. The final winners of the conference championships then go on to play in the Superbowl, which is held at a "neutral site" later in the month of January.

The Superbowl itself is perhaps the biggest sports event in America, both in terms of hype and in size of audience. As a sporting event, however, it has generally left something to be desired. After all, by the time the Superbowl rolls around, the players and fans are tired of football, especially after the holiday-season glut of college and pro games. Furthermore, by this late in the season many of the top players have been sidelined or at least diminished in effectiveness by injuries. As Howard Cosell remarked on the last Monday night football game of the 1978 season: "With sixteen games on the schedule and a limited roster, injuries ultimately determine who wins and who loses."

Because of injuries and the complicated play-off system, then, and perhaps especially because of the grueling 16-game regular season schedule, the Superbowl is usually *not* an exhibition of the best in football. Superbowl XII in 1978, for example, was a boring mismatch between the mighty Dallas Cowboys and the "Cinderella" Denver Broncos, who had come out of nowhere to win their conference title. The most interesting aspect of this game, in fact, was the regularity with which Denver failed to complete its passes; the Denver quarterback completed only 8 of 25 attempts, for 35 yards gained passing. Dallas, in contrast, completed 19 of 28 for 182 yards! On the other hand, Superbowl XIII, in 1979, was a very exciting contest between the Cowboys and the Pittsburgh Steelers; the Steelers' decisive defeat of the Cowboys seemed to signal an end to their longtime leadership of pro football.

Even when a Superbowl isn't a good game, the hype surrounding it can be entertaining—in fact, such is its mystique that television programmers generally schedule a full weekend of pre-Superbowl special shows. (The game itself rotates among the networks.) Furthermore, it is one of the biggest betting events in pro sports, and because the "betting line" (see page 35) makes it potentially profitable to bet on either team, even a terrible mismatch can become an exciting game for those with money on the line. Finally, the Superbowl is a universally American Big Event: even people who don't ordinarily watch or like football somehow find themselves drawn toward the tube on Super Sunday. As the critic John Leonard writes in the *New York Times*, "In a world in which almost everything else is problematical . . . there will be definition, conclusion and certitude, live and in color; and once a year at least I would like to be doing what everybody else is doing, and 95 million people is a lot of everybody elses."

At the end of the season, the great players at each position are nominated to an All-Pro team (there are rival All-Pro teams chosen by the wire services and by professional football writers). The ultimate outcome of this is the Pro Bowl, which takes place two weeks after the Superbowl, and which pits the best players of the AFC against those of the NFC. The most notable thing about the Pro Bowl is that it mercifully draws a curtain on football until the following fall.

CHAPTER 15

THE COLLEGE GAME

College football is one of the three most popular televised sports in this country. (The others are pro football and baseball.) Except for a few small schools, football is played on every college campus, if only on an intramural level.

Not only does a winning football team provide its school with big money in the form of lucrative TV contracts and bowl offers, but it also attracts alumni donations in a way that few other appeals can. Unfortunately, all this money and media attention have an inevitable dark influence on the college sport. No one who reads the sports pages even occasionally can miss widespread charges of recruiting violations, including a variety of bribes paid to young players as inducements to attend a particular school. Furthermore, the large amount of money and attention given to athletic departments for football help keep women's collegiate athletics in the dark ages, though this is beginning to change thanks to HEW Title IX, which mandates that schools must spend the same amount of money on women and men athletes. Still, certain big money-making sports such as football are exempt from some of the Title IX requirements, an acknowledgment that for many colleges the most important thing about football is to have a winning team.

This is not to say that a college football team should not try to do its best. But while winning truly *is* everything to a pro team—the pros are being paid to win, after all, just as a lawyer is paid to win cases or a salesman to make sales—the wholehearted acceptance of the pro winning ethic has led to some abuses in college football. In pro football, the players are knowingly risking their health in exchange for a lot of money and glamour. In college football, the chance of bodily injury is less, but it still exists, and many young players simply don't understand the risks. Furthermore, since many men on football scholarships are only nominally scholars, those who don't make it to the pros are sometimes left at the end of their four years without an education (and sometimes with a crippled body). I don't mean to imply that college football is evil or that all coaches are sadists who teach morons to play a dehumanizing game. However, in the major football schools football is such a big business that common sense and fair play are sometimes forgotten in the pursuit of success on the field. The ultimate result of this ethic is perhaps epitomized in the sad story of Woody Hayes, longtime coach of Ohio State University. During the Gator Bowl, one of the postseason games, Hayes became enraged at a rival player who intercepted a pass late in the game when OSU was losing. While his horrified players tried to restrain him, Hayes began to hit the player in the throat, oblivious to the TV cameras, which recorded the entire incident. This behavior was considered excessive even for Hayes, who had previously been in trouble for assaulting a TV cameraman and whose players reportedly wore their helmets in the locker room when they had lost. The result was that the Ohio State administration fired him the next day.

The attitudes on the part of some administrations and coaches that culminated in the Hayes incident are not, happily, the dominant ones in a sport that has millions of devoted fans. For the majority of these fans college football is good plain fun, played in a festive atmosphere where the joy of rooting for one's alma mater surpasses emotionally the kind of thrills provided by pro sports. Also, because of that same loyalty (as well as the desire to win pro contracts), college players display an enthusiasm usually lacking in the pros. Dale Fuller, an avid football fan for years, puts it this way: "The players really give one hundred and ten percent in college ball. You know that even if a team's really far behind they could still come back. The thing about college ball is that they care."

Even those who don't particularly enjoy the sport often attend college games, if simply for the excitement and pageantry of elaborate half-time shows with marching bands. And, at least at the top-ranked schools, there's the opportunity to watch first-rate football.

MAJOR DIFFERENCES BETWEEN COLLEGE AND PRO BALL

The regulating body for college ball is the NCAA (National Collegiate Athletic Association); however, there are few *major* rules differences between the pro and the college game. Among those that are most noteworthy are the following:

THE FIELD   The playing field is the same size for both college and pro ball, but the inbounds lines for spotting the ball in the NCAA are much farther toward each side of the field (nearly 20 feet) than in the NFL.

TIMING   The NCAA, like the NFL, has 15-minute periods. However, a game can last longer than a pro game because the clock is always stopped when a team has achieved a first down (which results in more playing time). Games can end in ties in the NCAA and so do not go into overtime.

PROCEDURAL DIFFERENCES   In college football, only four officials are needed to regulate the game, while the NFL has seven. In the NFL, the defense may run with a recovered fumble; in college, a ball fumbled on the ground is dead as soon as it is recovered. The ball is also dead if it goes into the end zone on a punt (in the NFL such a ball can be run).

SCORING   One of the most striking differences between college and pro ball is that in addition to touchdown, try for point, safety, and field goal, college players have yet another way to make a score. Instead of kicking on a try for one point, the team has the option of running the ball or passing it across the line for a two-point touchdown.

Most other rules differences have to do with variations in definitions of fouls, or in yardage or spot of enforcement for penalties. For example, grasping the face mask is always penalized by 15 yards in college ball, while the same violation in the NFL may result in only a five-yard penalty. Intentional grounding in college on the other hand, is penalized by only five yards, while it costs an NFL quarterback 15 and loss of down. Play is similar in both college and pro football, though the college game employs somewhat smaller men, resulting in less bone-jarring violence. Most college teams rely on variants of two offensive formations: the Wishbone and the I (see page 148).

When reading about college football, you will often see the term "redshirt." This refers to an injured player who sits out a year of college play. The rule is that a player may play for a total of four years, even though he may attend school for five years. Thus, even if a player has to miss, say, his sophomore year, he may still be eligible to play the following three years. Redshirted players are allowed to practice with their team, if they are able.

RANKING THE TEAMS

Since there are thousands of colleges in the United States and a good number of them have football teams, ranking and scheduling of college teams could present a real problem. This is circumvented by putting teams of potentially equal strength together into different divisions. The top division, consisting of 139 teams, is IA, followed by IAA, then II, III, and so on down the line. Each division is further subdivided into conferences, mostly along geographical lines, and includes independent schools, or those with no conference affiliation.

At the beginning of the season the top 20 teams in Division IA are ranked by polls (based on their records of the previous year); the rankings change then throughout the year, with some unranked teams moving up, others falling out of the top rating.

Because there are so many teams involved, and because the football schedule is limited to few games, the rankings are always inexact, comparing teams that played quite different schedules. Thus, the rankings are always based to some extent on the opinions of those polled, and as a result no team can be said at the end of the season to be a true national champion: any postseason play-off between the two *best* teams is a matter of chance.

To further confuse things there are two polls: the UPI poll, which is a polling of top coaches, and the AP poll, in which football writers rank the schools. This system led to a conflict of the polls at the end of the 1978 season: AP gave top rank to the University of Alabama, while UPI ranked USC as the number-one team. This was after several weeks in which the number-one team in the nation was unanimously considered to be Penn State, the only undefeated team in the nation until it met Alabama in a postseason showdown at the Sugar Bowl. In that contest Alabama beat Penn State; and since USC had beaten Alabama earlier for its only defeat, the UPI decided USC was better, even though it had won its own postseason bowl game on a controversial fumble-touchdown.

All this confusion is obviously a result of the fact that college football does not have a regular play-off series. Conference championships are determined by overall team records, and while the postseason "bowl" games almost always feature conference champs and other top teams, none of them is truly a championship contest. There is a good chance that within the next few years a true play-off system will be initiated, the various rounds to be rotated among the bowl games.

The major Division IA conferences include most of the traditional name football schools. Among them are the Big Ten; Atlantic Coast; Southwest; Pacific Ten; Western Athletic; Big Eight; Southeastern; Ivy League; Southland; Missouri Valley; Midamerican; Pacific Coast; and Southern conferences. Most of the teams you hear about (apart from local teams, of course), come from these conferences. These include such independents (teams unaffiliated with a conference) as Penn State, Pittsburgh, Notre Dame, and Army and Navy.

Just as big-time college football attracts a lot of money to a school, so it costs a lot of money to maintain, and more and more colleges have been getting out of major competition for this reason. In coming years there will be far fewer colleges actively in contention for national football exposure.

Which brings us to the postseason games, all of which are known as bowl games. In recent years these have begun to proliferate in response to the money provided by nationwide TV exposure. The bowl contests are scheduled at the end of the football season, with the various bowls "bidding" for participants from among the top-ranked teams. Some bowls have a contract with one or more conferences, while others may invite any teams that they wish. The idea is to match up teams that are nearly equal in skill and record, although it doesn't always work out that way.

The four most important, so-called major bowls are the Rose, Orange, Sugar, and Cotton Bowl. Of these the best known is the Rose Bowl, which is played in Pasadena, California, on New Year's Day, preceded by the famous "Tournament of Roses Parade." The participants in the Rose Bowl are always the champions of the Pacific Ten and Big Ten conferences. The Orange Bowl, which is played in Miami, has a contract with the Big Eight, pitting its champ against another top-ranked team. The Sugar Bowl features the winner of the Southeastern Conference as host to a top team from another Division IA Conference. Finally, the Cotton Bowl pits the Southwest Conference champ against a visiting team, and is played in Dallas.

Other bowls include the Fiesta, Holiday, Liberty, Sun, Tangerine, Peach, Gator, and Bluebonnet bowls. One of the most interesting bowl games is the Hula Bowl, which is played in Hawaii. This contest is a sort of a college all-star game, with teams competing on a geographical basis (Eastern versus Western All-Stars). The Hula Bowl is worth watching not only for the chance to see some of the top young players in action (the stands are reputed to be loaded with pro scouts), but also because of the rather strange rules, reflecting play of teams who have not played together for more than a very few practice sessions. The most interesting of these rules is the one that allows a team trailing by more than a touchdown to receive the kickoff after a score, even if it was the trailing team itself that scored. The other major rule change is that blitzing is not allowed, a blessing to all the fourth-year quarterbacks who, having survived college football, don't want to be wiped out before their pro careers even start.

There are individual postseason awards for players and teams within each division and conference, but the most important award by far in college ball is the Heisman Trophy. This may be given to any player in any position who is voted by sports reporters and broadcasters as being "the outstanding college football player of the United States" for that year. Heisman winners are almost guaranteed a lucrative pro contract, while their schools receive reflected glory and prestige, making it easier to bring promising young high school players into their recruiting programs.

PART 4
BASKETBALL

═BASKETBALL FACT SHEET═

Where played: indoor wooden court.

Game divisions: four quarters of 12 minutes each. As many five-minute overtimes as necessary to break a tie.

Average duration: two hours, ten minutes.

Offense/defense considerations: visiting team chooses its own basket for first half; the teams change baskets for the second half.

Governing body: National Basketball Association (NBA).

Number of men on the roster: 11.

Equipment: one basketball, two baskets.

Regular season: 82 games. The season extends from October through April (followed by the play-offs).

TEAMS

EASTERN CONFERENCE

Atlantic Division
Boston Celtics
New Jersey Nets
New York Knicks
Philadelphia 76ers
Washington Bullets

Central Division
Atlanta Hawks
Cleveland Cavaliers
Detroit Pistons
Houston Rockets
Indiana Pacers
San Antonio Spurs

WESTERN CONFERENCE

Midwest Division
Chicago Bulls
Denver Nuggets
Utah Jazz
Kansas City Kings
Milwaukee Bucks

Pacific Division
Golden State Warriors
Los Angeles Lakers
Phoenix Suns
Portland Trail Blazers
San Diego Clippers
Seattle SuperSonics

CHAPTER 16

BASKETBALL: THE MAN-MADE SPORT

Of all team sports, basketball is by far the most schizophrenic, always struggling to decide whether it is ruled by a collection of individuals or a team of them.

—FRANK DEFORD

Basketball shares a great deal in common with the other sports mentioned in this book: like them, it requires individual skill and team cooperation, it relies on strategic and tactical planning, and its rules have continually evolved as it has become more popular. But basketball is completely different from the other sports in one important respect: of all the major team sports, it is the only that was actually invented from scratch.

In 1891, a young Canadian named James Naismith was working at the YMCA training school in Springfield, Massachusetts. The head of the physical education department had noticed that calisthenics bored the boys who attended the school, yet because of the harsh winter they could not go outside to play strenuous sports for physical exercise. He asked Naismith to try to come up with a system of exercise or game that would not only allow the young men to get plenty of exercise indoors, but would keep their interest through the winter. Naismith took a look around the gym and realized that any such activity should involve a lot of running but must minimize physical contact, because the space was small and the players might be injured on the hard wooden floor. He also decided to make use of a ball and some sort of goal, as in soccer. Since this was to be an indoor game, perhaps the ball could be tossed into a container of some sort by one team, while the other tried to prevent a successful toss. The janitor of the YMCA school made a major contribution to the history of sports by supplying Naismith with his containers: two empty peach baskets that he had found in a storage room. The peach baskets were nailed to the wall at either end of the gym, Naismith explained his original 12 rules, and basketball was born.

Of course the game has changed a great deal since then. The peach basket, which had to be emptied with the help of a ladder each time a goal was scored, has been replaced by a round metal hoop hung with a bottomless cord net. Although most of Naismith's basic rules still remain in spirit, there have been many additions and elaborations of them (although the basic number of rules is still only 12). Even more important, the game of basketball has developed into a full-fledged sport, one of the most popular in the world. Basketball is played in over 142 nations, including China, which proudly displays its 7'6" center, Mr. Chu.

Among the many changes in the sport that could not have been foreseen by Naismith, who devised his game as a healthy recreation for everyone regardless of size or skill, is the growing reliance on very tall players. While Mr. Chu is still unusual, it is becoming increasingly common to see one or more players on a team nearly seven feet tall. Kareem Abdul-Jabbar of the Los Angeles Lakers, for example, is 7'3", while the two shortest men in the pros in 1979, Calvin Murphy of Houston and Mack Calvin of Denver, are 5'10"— a size that would be considered short only in the king-sized world of basketball.

The game of basketball is still as strenuous as Naismith intended it to be—a starting player may run as much as seven or eight miles a game. However, for several reasons, including the height and finely honed skills of today's pro players, basketball has evolved a kind of "star system," which can result in mediocre teams having winning seasons because of one or two very good players. More common and detrimental to the sport is the deterioration of the concept of team play, as some stars, concerned only with their own playing statistics, prefer to shoot or hold on to the ball as much as possible, ignoring their teammates. While this style of play may be de rigueur in street-style basketball, it does nothing to improve the quality of the game in the pros, and is in direct contradiction to Naismith's original intentions when he created the game.

Because of this recent undue emphasis on star players, as well as growing competition from other sports, men's pro basketball is facing something of a crisis and will probably have to change during the eighties in order to keep its audience. (Ironically, women's pro basketball, with its greater emphasis on team play, is continuing to grow in popularity even while the men's league is in trouble.) Whatever the ultimate future of pro ball in the NBA, however, there is no question that basketball itself will remain popular with people of all ages all over the world—as a sport, an exercise, and an exciting entertainment.

CHAPTER 17 THE BASICS

In city ghettos and suburban backyards, basketball is played by varying numbers of players on surfaces of concrete, grass, and asphalt. On an organized level, basketball is played by two teams of five men each on a rectangular wooden court in a gymnasium.

The short sides of the rectangle are known as the "base lines," while the long sides are called the "sidelines." Everything between these lines is considered in bounds; the lines themselves and everything beyond them are out of bounds. The court is marked with a line dividing it into two halves; in the center of this line is a circle known as the "center circle." At each end of the court the baskets, made of netting, hang from metal hoops mounted on rectangles of glass or wood, known as "backboards" or, simply, "the boards." Underneath each basket, extending 18 feet, 10 inches into the court from the base line, is painted a 16-foot-wide "free throw lane." At the end of this lane nearest center court is a circle, called the "free throw circle." A line parallel to the base lines, the free throw line (or foul line), bisects the circle. The whole thing—lane and circle—is known colloquially as the "key."

The object of basketball is the same as it was when James Naismith invented it: to score more points than the other team by

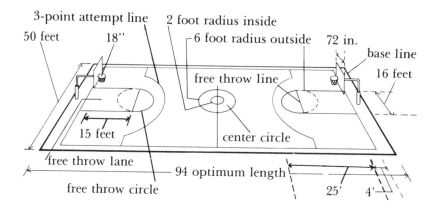

throwing the ball into the basket more often. (Players, by the way, shoot at their own, not their opponents', basket.) Because there is no one player charged with stopping goals, as in hockey and soccer, and because basketball is a very fast-moving game, it is the highest scoring of all the team sports, with total scores of over 100 points by each team common in the pros.

The game begins with a "jump ball." This is a maneuver that takes place in the center circle. The players from both teams stand around the circle while two players, usually the tallest men on each team, face each other. The referee, one of three officials in gray shirts, tosses the ball high into the air between the players. The two men jump, arms up, and vie to tap the ball in the direction of a teammate. Once someone has possession of the ball, the game proper begins.

The first time you watch a basketball game, it may appear to be a wild melee, as players run from one end of the court to the other. The action during a game is most furious whenever a shot is attempted—you will see players waving their hands and arms in the shooter's face, and moving quickly from one part of the court to another. If the ball does not go into the basket, several players will scramble for it. If the shot is made ("sunk") there is only a momentary pause while one member of the nonscoring team tosses the ball to a teammate from out of bounds to start play again. And so the game continues, from one basket to the other, in a regular progession, whether or not the ball actually passes through the basket on any given shot. From time to time the action is interrupted by the sound of an official's whistle.

Whenever the whistle blows, all play comes to a stop and one of three things happens (unless this is a regular time-out). A player may walk to the free throw line while other players (but not all nine of them) line up outside the free throw lane. The player at the line now receives the ball from an official and attempts one or more unimpeded shots at the basket.

Or there may be a "throw in," where one member of a team receives the ball out of bounds along the sidelines or base lines and tosses it in to one of his teammates, whereupon play resumes.

Finally, and very rarely, there may be another jump ball, similar to that which started the game. This happens most often if two players attempt possession of the ball at the same time and it is not clear who has control.

In any case, once the ball is put back into play the movement from end to end of the court resumes. After you have watched the game a while, you will notice that all this running is being done by every player on the court except one: the man with the ball. This is because there are strict rules about the way the ball may be moved.

When James Naismith invented basketball, he realized that if players were allowed to run freely with the ball it would be very difficult to stop them. So, while encouraging vigorous running in all other aspects of the game, he decided to restrict the way the ball could be moved on the court, to make it easier for the defense to get possession of the ball. Therefore the ball may be moved in only three ways: it may be passed to another player, shot at the basket, or "dribbled." A dribble is a bounce, and a man may run while dribbling the ball, but the ball must be kept moving, bounced between the palm of the hand and the floor. A player who is dribbling well looks as if he were working a yo-yo up and down: the ball seems to be connected to his hand by an invisible string.

Except for some key rules regarding physical contact, this is all there is to basketball: to move the ball from one end of the court to the other and to try to throw it into the basket.

Because that structure is so essentially simple, there is a great deal of room in basketball for individual elaboration, and this may be why basketball, more than any other team sport except baseball, produces individual stars of strikingly different styles. In order to better appreciate what these men do, let's take a look at the rest of the skeletal structure of the game.

SCORING AND REBOUNDING

There are two ways to score in basketball: by making a field goal, which is worth either two or three points, and by making a free throw, which is worth one point. By far the most exciting is a field goal, which is a shot taken "from the floor" in the middle of the action. The majority of field goals are made in the area of the basket and are worth two points. Shots taken beyond the three-point line, a semi-circle approximately 22 feet from the basket, score three points, if they are successful.

It is not surprising that only a certain percentage of field goal attempts go through the net during any given game: not only are the shooters harassed and crowded by their opponents on most shots, but they are usually forced to shoot from less than ideal position. Furthermore, a shot may be "blocked," or knocked away by a defender. When the ball does not go into the "hoop," it generally bounces off the rim of the basket or off the backboard. At this point it is in neither team's possession (a "loose ball"), and both teams have an equal right to it. The fight for possession of that ball is an important part of the game of basketball, and whichever team gets to it is said to have made a "rebound." A rebound made by the team that took the shot is an *offensive* rebound, and the player who made it generally tries to take another shot at his basket. If a rebound is captured by the opposite team, it is a *defensive* rebound, and the normal procedure is for the rebounding team to move the ball as quickly as possible to their own end of the court, often with an "outlet pass" thrown quickly by the rebounder to a teammate at midcourt.

Each rebound is extremely important because it gives the rebounding team possession, or the opportunity to shoot at its own basket.

FREE THROWS

The other way for a team to make a score in basketball is by shooting a free throw, also called a "foul shot." This is an unimpeded shot taken by a player standing in the free throw circle. It is awarded under certain circumstances after a foul or violation, and while each free throw counts only one point, a player may be given one or two opportunities to make that point, or in some cases two or three opportunities to make two points. A *successful* free throw is called a "conversion."

Most fouls are called for violations of basketball's rules restricting physical contact. Whenever a foul has been committed, the guilty party is supposed to raise his hand, and the official scorer, one of several men sitting at a long table on the side of the court, records his name and the foul. A player is allowed to commit only five fouls in the entire game—on his sixth foul he is automatically out of the game.

We will go into the specifics of the foul and penalty system in the next chapter.

THE PLAYERS

A basketball team consists of five men: two guards, two forwards, and a center. All team members shoot baskets and get rebounds. Each man is also responsible for "guarding," or trying to limit the effectiveness of his opposite member on the other team: the center guards the opposing center (and vice versa); forwards guard the opposing forwards, and so on. These individual contests are called "matchups." In addition to their general functions, each player position has special duties and requires special skills.

The two guards, sometimes called "backcourt men," are the smallest men on a team, although "small" is a relative term in the world of basketball. They are also usually the quickest. As the name implies, a guard tends to be more of a defensive player than the others. The guards generally spend the most time in actual possession of ("handling") the ball, although they may not shoot and score as often as their larger teammates.

A guard's most important function is to act as a catalyst for the team, to make things happen. The guards are responsible for moving the ball from their *backcourt* (where the opponents' basket is located) to their *forecourt* (where their own basket is). The guard who does this most often is usually called the "ball-handling" or "play-making" guard. He is also the player you will most often see giving hand signals to his teammates or calling out to them. Mack Calvin, a play-making "small" guard, described his job in *Sport* magazine as that of a "field general . . . I have to react on the run. The most important job for every ball-handling guard is to make sure that the big men get involved early in the game."

By this he means that one of the primary functions of the guards, who generally remain in the back part (near the center line) of their own forecourt, is to try to pass the ball to an "open"— temporarily unguarded—forward or the center. If an opportunity comes up for a guard to move ("drive") unimpeded to the basket for a shot, or if he is able to take accurate shots from "outside"—the area away from the key—so much the better.

The forwards are sometimes called "corner men" because they usually position themselves near the corners of their forecourt—that is, near the basket—where they are in position to shoot and to rebound. A good forward should be strong enough to prevent his opposite number on the other team from shooting effectively and rebounding. A forward is usually either a "small forward," who moves quickly and scores a lot, or a "power forward," who excels at getting rebounds.

The "big man," the center, is indeed very big. Very tall centers, those men seven feet and taller, are usually not the clumsy giants you might expect but skilled and talented athletes who move with speed and grace. A center who can also shoot well is nearly impossible for another team to stop.

In spite of their dominating size, centers generally are *not* responsible primarily for scoring, but rather for defensive moves and for helping their teammates on offense. In fact a center's main duties follow naturally from his size: obviously a man that tall is going to have an advantage in grabbing any rebounds, and his sheer physical presence can intimidate the other team. If he is taller than everyone else on the court he can serve as a relay for passes and take shots almost at will. Furthermore, all a very big man has to do to block a shot is to raise his arms and there is nowhere for the ball to go.

Because basketball is such a fluid and fast-moving game, the functions of all men on the team overlap. And whatever a player's position, whether his team is on offense or defense, one of the most important realities is that he is never alone. That is, there is always (almost always) a man from the other team with him—either guarding him or trying to break free from him.

It is obvious that basketball players, more than most athletes except soccer players, must possess, in addition to the fine skills specific to basketball, all-around athletic ability. No matter what his position, a player must be able to run quickly and for long periods of time; to shoot at the basket with either hand; to jump and even turn in the air while jumping; and to perform all these actions without any protective equipment and with very little rest.

SUBSTITUTIONS

Because of the strenuous nature of basketball, substitutions are made often throughout the game. Most commonly, a substitute is sent in to allow a starting player to rest, but men are often substituted as well for strategic reasons, or because an important player is in foul trouble or temporarily injured.

Unlimited substitutions are allowed, meaning that a player may leave and reenter the game any number of times, but there are strict rules about when a substitute may enter and how. A substitute is allowed to enter only when the ball is dead and the clock is stopped. Furthermore, he must report to the official scorer before entering and wait until he is beckoned onto the court by an official before he comes in to replace his man.

POSSESSION

A team can get possession of the basketball in a variety of ways. The most obvious is to receive it out of bounds after the other team has made a field goal or free throw, but this is clearly not the way to win basketball games. Good teams work on getting possession through defensive rebounds and by forcing the other team to commit "turnovers." A turnover occurs whenever the offensive team loses possession of the ball. Often a turnover occurs because an offensive player passes badly, thereby allowing an interception, or because he is dribbling when he should perhaps pass to a man who is in a safer position. The most exciting turnover is a steal: a defensive man comes out of nowhere and simply knocks the ball away from the man who has possession. Other common reasons for turnovers include a number of rules violations.

Another way to lose possession of the ball is to have it knocked out of bounds. The last man to touch the ball before it went out of bounds is considered to have been responsible, even if the ball only grazed him before it left the court. The team that was not responsible for the out of bounds gains possession of the ball with a throw-in at the spot where the ball went out of bounds.

Sometimes you will see a player leap headlong at a ball that is about to go out of bounds and save it by batting it in the air to a teammate. This is a somewhat risky move, however, not only because the player who saves the ball may end up crashing into the nearest seats, but also because there is always a danger that the opposition will benefit from his desperate move. I've seen this happen several times when a rookie player misjudged the situation and "saved" a ball about to go out of bounds near his opponents' basket—the ball was immediately grabbed by an opponent and thrown into the basket.

BASKETBALL AND THE CLOCK

A basketball game is divided into four quarters of 12 minutes each; the first two quarters are separated from the last two by a 15-minute period "between the halves." Although 48 minutes is not a very long period of time, especially when you consider that as much as 100 points may be scored by each team in that time span, the actual time of a game is considerably longer than 48 minutes, because the game clock is stopped often.

Whenever an official blows his whistle, usually because a foul or violation has been committed, the clock automatically stops. If a free throw or throws are awarded, the clock does not start again until they have been completed. The clock also is whistled to a stop when the ball becomes "tied up," that is, when neither of two or more opposing players seem to have clear possession of it. In this case, the play resumes with a jump ball like the one that began the game. The clock also stops when the ball goes out of bounds and is started again as soon as the tossed-in ball has been touched by an inbounds player.

It is important to note, by the way, that the clock does *not* stop after a goal has been scored.

Time is also called for injuries or any other sort of emergency, including damage to the basket or backboard. Finally, there are time-outs allotted to each team, as well as certain automatic time-outs.

Each team is allowed seven time-outs of 90 seconds each during a game. However, those time-outs must be taken according to a formula: there must be at least two time-outs per period (that is, a total of two, regardless of which team they are taken by); and no team can call more than four time-outs in the fourth quarter. If neither team has called a time-out in the first six minutes of the first quarter, then the referee will call an automatic time-out, which will be "charged" to the home team. This rule was introduced to make certain that the required number of commercials will be inserted on TV during each quarter.

Because the number of time-outs is limited, they are used judiciously and tend to be "saved" for critical situations insofar as possible. Time-out is frequently called when a team is in trouble, unable to sustain an attack, for example, or committing a number of turnovers. Likewise, if a team is doing exceptionally well, sinking several baskets in a row, the coach of the opposing team will usually call a time-out to interrupt and perhaps destroy that momentum, as well as to allow his own players a chance to regroup. Very rarely, a team will exceed the number of time-outs allowed, either deliberately or inadvertently. For each such excessive time-out a penalty is assessed (see pages 206–207, technical fouls).

Each team is also allowed one 20-second injury time-out per half. If a team takes more than that, it is charged with a regular 90-second time-out. Loss of a contact lens and ensuing search, by the way, counts as an injury time-out, unless the small piece of plastic takes longer than 20 seconds to locate, in which case it becomes a regular charged time-out. (I always cheer on the players who are searching on hands and knees for a lost lens, because as a contact wearer myself I know how it feels to suddenly lose that vital piece of plastic.) If the lens has not been found by the end of a called injury time-out, play resumes with no further delay.

Even including all the time-outs, there isn't really much time during a game, and over the years a number of other timing regulations have been introduced to pro basketball (not all of which are used on the high school and college level) in order to prevent any delay or stalling by a team that is ahead.

The most important of these restrictions is the 24-second rule. In addition to the game clock, which is displayed on the scoreboard at pro games, there are also digital timers at either end of the court that mark off seconds. Whenever a team gains possession of the ball, this "24-second" clock starts running. The team then has to take a shot at its basket within 24 seconds. If the team does not do so because of exceptionally good defense or for any other reason, the defending team is given possession by a throw-in.

After any missed shot, the 24-second clock is started again as soon as either team takes possession of the rebound.

Other timing restrictions include the five-second rule, which states that a player who is throwing a ball inbounds has only five seconds to do so; and the ten-second rule, which gives a team that gains possession of the ball in its backcourt (usually after a basket, but also for any other reason) only ten seconds to move the ball from the backcourt to its forecourt.

The final timing restriction is known as the three-second rule, and it states that *no* offensive player, either with or without the ball, is allowed to stand in the free throw lane under his own basket for longer than three seconds. This rule was initiated to prevent very tall men from standing by the basket and dropping balls into it.

Violation of any of these rules results in loss of the ball to the opposition, with a throw-in.

OVERTIME   Basketball games do not end in ties; any game that is tied at the end goes into one or a series of overtime periods during which each team tries to outscore the other. If the score is still tied at the end of the first overtime, there are as many more overtimes as necessary until one team is ahead when the buzzer sounds. Each overtime period lasts five minutes, and each team is allowed two extra time-outs per overtime.

In the next chapter we will take a look at some of the reasons why basketball, with its simple rules, is in many ways a difficult game to play, and why it takes years of practice for a talented athlete to become a great player.

CHAPTER
18

HOW THE GAME IS PLAYED

To the average fan watching a basketball game, the action seems fast, flowing, and spontaneous. Behind that seeming spontaneity, however, are thousands of hours of practice by the players to develop their three basic offensive skills: dribbling, passing, and shooting. The use of each of these skills is limited by the very strict rules in basketball regarding movement of men on the court. These rules are most stringent for the player in possession of the ball.

MOVING WITH AND WITHOUT THE BALL

As we saw in the last chapter, a man may move with the ball only if he is dribbling it. Because the ball is not in continuous possession during a dribble (since it is being bounced), dribbling is considered a somewhat riskier means of advancing the ball than passing. Very good dribblers can bounce the ball equally well with either hand and are able to move quickly on a dribble without looking at the ball. A player who takes too many steps between bounces of the ball is charged with a violation called "traveling" (also known as "walking" and "steps").

When a player stops dribbling, he must remain for all intents and purposes rooted to the spot; that is, while he is allowed to move one foot in any direction, the other foot, or "pivot" foot, must remain planted on the floor (though he may turn on the foot to change direction). He may move from this position only if he received the ball on a pass; once a player has dribbled and stopped he may not dribble again. When shooting or passing from the stationary position he is allowed to jump into the air, but the ball must leave his hands before his pivot foot touches the floor, or he will be charged with traveling.

The other main restriction on movement is that players are not allowed to run directly into each other (although this violation is not always easy for the officials to see). This rule causes the most problems for the defense, since they must try to stay between the man they are guarding and the basket; and this restriction is at the heart of many basic offensive and defensive set plays. In fact, on any play part of the contest between two players who are guarding each other is a race to reach a given position first. A defensive man is entitled to block the path of the man he is guarding (with or without the ball) provided that he reaches the spot clearly *before* the man. Also, the defensive man is supposed to be facing his man in most situations. He is allowed to move parallel to a man whose path he is blocking (thus preventing him from running around the block) as long as he doesn't move directly toward his opponent. In playing defense, a player is allowed to raise his hands and arms and wave them in front of the opponent, but he isn't allowed to throw an arm, elbow, or hip into his path.

Once a player on defense has established his position on the floor, his counterpart is not allowed to run into him but must maneuver *around* him to continue on his path to the basket or near it. If a man is dribbling and he finds his path blocked, he must stop and either pass or shoot, unless he is certain that he can get past the defender without contact.

PASSING

The very good teams generally make use of a great deal of passing: the idea is to get the ball to the open man, one who has got free of his man and can take an unimpeded shot. Sometimes a great deal of passing will go on within the 24-second period, because no one is ever truly open.

There are three basic types of passes in basketball. The one most often seen is a short, direct pass between two players who do not have a defender between them. A high, lobbing pass is used to move the ball over a cluster of defenders, or to get it to the tall center. The bounce pass is a low pass made by bouncing the ball in such a way that it will be deflected toward the intended receiver, and is usually used to get the ball to a man who is in motion toward the basket. This pass is also a good way to move the ball a short distance through "heavy traffic," or a number of defenders.

These three basic passes all have variants, which the announcers may refer to by several names: *a cross-court pass*, usually considered risky, is a lobbing pass from one side of the court to the other; *a baseball pass* is thrown high with an overhand motion like that used to throw a baseball; *a drop pass* is a variant of the bounce pass, but instead of the player bouncing the ball directly to a teammate, he starts a dribble, bouncing the ball once, then leaves it for a rapidly moving teammate to pick up. A *hook pass* is an arcing toss with a sweep of the arm, and is generally used to move the ball quickly from one end of the court to the other over the heads of the defensemen. A *jump pass* is released at the top of a jump, again aimed over the heads of the defenders. It is sometimes used by a player who jumps to take a shot, then sees an open player with a better chance at sinking a basket. The most spectacular passes are *behind the back passes*—a successful one can seem as if it has been made using extrasensory perception. One of the most commonly used passes is a very short underhanded pass, which is known as a "hand-off."

Any pass that leads directly to a basket earns the player an "assist" in the official scoring.

SHOOTING

Shooting at the basket is ultimately what the game of basketball is all about. In my neighborhood playground, I have seen boys (and occasionally girls) practice shooting baskets for hours on end, moving methodically from one spot on the court to another. They practice shots standing still, and they practice shots moving. Many other skills are essential in making a good basketball player, but a man who cannot consistently sink baskets will never make it in the pros.

Just as shots are classified as one-handed or two-handed, they are also classified as "inside" or "outside." An inside shot is one taken close to the basket, usually with a great many defenders around. An outside shot is farther from the basket, and is usually taken by a man who is on the periphery of the action, over the heads of the defenders.

A variety of colorful names are used to describe the different shots you will see in a game.

LAY-UP This is perhaps the most basic shot in basketball, and the one that is most difficult for the defense to stop. A lay-up is usually made by a player who has beaten the defense to the basket. He runs toward the basket, then tosses the ball up over the rim, where it gently bounces off the backboard into the basket. Or, as the great player Julius ("Dr. J.") Erving explains in his booklet "Basketball Fundamentals," "You lay the ball on a spot of the backboard . . . so the ball will fall into the basket."

JUMP SHOT OR JUMPER This and its variants is the shot most often used, and refers to any shot in which the ball is released at the top of a jump. Among its virtues are that it is hard to block and can be made at some distance from the basket, even if the court is clogged with defenders. In order to stop a jump shot, the defender must usually jump at the same time as the shooting player. A common practice is for the shooter to pretend to start to jump, drawing the defender into a jump; as the defender comes down, the shooter jumps and releases his shot unimpeded.

HOOK SHOT   This one-handed shot, often used by tall centers, arches high toward the basket. It is one of the most difficult shots to block.

TIP-IN, OR TAP-IN   This is a shot that is made after the ball has rebounded from the backboard or rim. The offensive player jumps and, instead of grabbing the ball for another shot, taps it into the basket. The tip-in is made at the height of a jump.

DUNK, SLAM DUNK, STUFF   This is the tall man's version of a lay-up and is virtually impossible to stop. It is also a spectacular shot. It is made, like the lay-up, by a player who has outraced all defenders to the basket. Instead of bouncing the ball into the basket off the backboard, the man leaps into the air and literally stuffs the ball down and through the basket.

Other more exotic shots you may hear announcers refer to include:

SCOOP SHOT   This is a variant on the lay-up, in which the ball is thrown underhand, rather than overhand against the rim. Also known as a reverse lay-up.

FLOATER   This is a long, lobbing shot that seems to hang in the air before it enters the basket.

RAINBOW SHOT   Similar to the floater, this is a shot taken from far outside the basket area that arcs very high before going in.

SKY HOOK   A high hook shot made close to the basket by an extremely tall player.

FADEAWAY   A jump shot taken while backing or jumping away from a defender, thus giving the shooter more room. It is often a hasty, off-balance shot.

TWISTING SHOT   There are two types of twisting shot, the twisting lay-up and the twisting (or "turnaround") jump shot. In both shots, the player starts with his back to the basket, then twists in the air while in the process of shooting. A twist shot is extremely difficult for the defense to block, since the shooter starts with his back to the basket (and therefore to the defender who is between him and the basket). Some players, such as Bob McAdoo of the Detroit Pistons, specialize in this very difficult shot.

Finally, the most important if usually least exciting shot is the *free throw*. Since a free throw shooter is not harassed in any way by the defense, it should theoretically be possible for a player who practices enough to make virtually all his free throw shots. Yet even the greatest players seldom sink more than 80 percent of their shots, perhaps because of the pressure involved in such a situation, particularly if the score is close throughout—and especially toward the end of—a game. (And also because no human player, no matter how skilled and no matter how much he has practiced, can perform perfectly.) You can learn a great deal about players by watching the way they make their free throws. Almost all of them have a very definite routine they go through before shooting, which seldom varies. For instance, some players bounce the ball a specific number of times, some go through little touching routines on their uniform, others breathe deeply a certain number of times. If more than one shot has been awarded, notice that on the second shot the player will go through exactly the same routine, and that is the point of practicing free throws: to be able to do the same thing time after time.

Theoretically, of course, if players followed all the rules of basketball to the letter there would never be a need for any player to shoot a free throw. This is not a theoretical world, however, and not breaking the rules of basketball is somewhat more difficult for players than it would seem.

CONTACT OR NONCONTACT

When James Naismith invented basketball, he devised safeguards limiting contact in order to avoid injuries. Most of the rules that have been added since then have been designed to strengthen that intent. And yet basketball is very much a contact sport, especially under the basket ("under the boards"), where a great deal of shoving, pushing, and elbowing goes on.

Because of the proximity of players to each other, a certain amount of contact is virtually unavoidable. No matter how scrupulous a player may be, when two men are moving in the same direction at the same time, one trying to shoot the ball while the other tries to prevent the shot or to get the ball, inadvertent contact is bound to occur.

The rules recognize this reality, of course, and are designed to prevent *avoidable* contact. Because intent is difficult for the referee to judge, however, and because so much of the action under the basket is difficult to see, many if not most players don't always observe the letter of the law. Thus as the heat of competition builds, so does the likelihood of deliberate as well as unintentional contact, which may in turn lead to retaliatory pushing, shoving, and even fighting.

Until the 1978–79 season, "handchecking," or continuously touching the player one is guarding, was overlooked by the officials. Although handchecking had always been illegal under NBA rules, the rule against it is now vigorously enforced, and almost any handchecking that is observed by the officials will result in a whistle for a foul.

It was the provocative nature of handchecking that led to its ban: offensive players would become angered by this patently illegal maneuver that was nevertheless used against them often and to telling effect. A Phoenix player discussing the use of this tactic told *Sport* magazine about his arch rival: "He'd look like he was just resting his hand on you, but he was so strong and sneaky that he'd actually be grabbing a whole handful of your gut. By the end of the game you'd be all black-and-blue."

During the 1977–78 season the potential for violence in the game finally exploded in several incidents that both sharply exposed the contact nature of basketball and pointed out the need for better officiating.

The two most widely publicized incidents resulted in injuries and the intervention of Larry O'Brien, commissioner of basketball.

In the first case, superstar Kareem Abdul-Jabbar of the Los Angeles Lakers decked Kent Benson of the Milwaukee Bucks. Commissioner O'Brien fined Jabber five thousand dollars but did not suspend him because Jabbar had broken his hand and would therefore be unable to play for a number of weeks anyway. In a more shocking episode, Kermit Washington, also of the Lakers, was involved in a fight with another player during a game when Rudy Tomjanovich, of the Houston Rockets, intervened. Claiming that he thought Tomjanovich was joining the fight rather than trying to break it up, Washington punched Tomjanovich in the face, injuring him so severely that he had to undergo extensive plastic surgery and was unable to play for the rest of the season. Washington was assessed both a fine and a suspension, and Tomjanovich later filed a 2.6-million-dollar law suit against the Lakers.

Because of these and other outbreaks, Commissioner O'Brien issued a statement promising that "conduct of this nature will not be tolerated." In the future, brawling players were to be fined and suspended.

Each NBA game is controlled by a referee and an umpire. They are assisted in their duties by three other officials: a scorer, who is responsible for keeping all statistics in the game, and two official timers, one to run the game clock and the other in charge of the 24-second clock. These men all sit at the scorer's table, which is located along one of the sidelines.

It is generally conceded that basketball is one of the hardest games to officiate, because congestion on the floor can be so great, and because so many of the calls are judgment decisions in which the referee is supposed somehow to divine the "intent" of the alleged perpetrator. On the next few pages is a summary of hand signals used by the referees to signal offenses.

VIOLATIONS, FOULS, AND PENALTIES

There are three types of illegal actions in basketball: violations, interference, and fouls.

**OFFENSIVE FOUL
CHARGE**

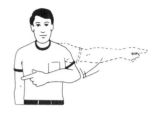

OUT-OF-BOUNDS

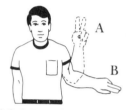

**A) SCORE COUNTS
B) NO. OF FREE THROWS**

PERSONAL FOUL

3-SECOND VIOLATION

TIME-OUT

**PLAYER NUMBER
COMMITTING FOUL**

ILLEGAL DRIBBLE

TRAVELING

TIME IN

BLOCKING

NO BASKET

HACKING FOUL

PUSHING

JUMP BALL

HOLDING

DIRECTION OF PLAY

TECHNICAL FOUL

LOOSE BALL FOUL

BASKET INTERFERENCE

GOAL TENDING

24-SECOND VIOLATION

Violations are breaches of technical rules by the offense and are penalized by awarding of the ball to the other team, with a throw-in from out of bounds.

The most common violations include knocking the ball out of bounds; violating any of the various timing restrictions (3-second, 5-second, 10-second, and 24-second rules); traveling; "palming" (also called "carrying")—allowing the ball to rest on the upturned palm, even momentarily, while dribbling; and "double dribble," which is called for starting a dribble, stopping it, and then starting again.

"Interference," also called "goaltending," is a special category of violation that was made necessary by the increasing number of very tall players in the game; it has to do with interfering with the ball when it is *above* the basket. Defensive goaltending is called when a player deflects a ball that is on its downward path to the basket, preventing an otherwise almost certain goal from scoring. The offensive team is then awarded two points as if the basket had scored. Offensive goaltending is called when an offensive player pushes the ball toward the basket while it is on its downward path above the rim. If made, the basket is disallowed, and the ball is awarded to the other team.

All remaining infractions in basketball are classified either as personal fouls or technical fouls. They are penalized for the most part by awarding one or two free throws to the other team.

Personal fouls are simply contact fouls and, when deliberate, are more tactical than "personal."

The most commonly called foul against the offense is charging:—running into the defending player who has legally stationed himself in the offensive player's path. In practical terms, charging is very difficult to call, and as sportscasters often point out, such a call "could go either way"—against the offense for charging, or the defense for holding or pushing.

The most commonly called foul against the defense is holding, which means touching or grabbing an opponent, especially when he is trying to shoot or get into position to shoot.

Other contact fouls specifically prohibited include pushing or shoving; any contact with the ball holder from the rear; elbowing; hacking or chopping (striking an opponent with the arm); slapping; kicking; and, of course, punching or fighting.

Technical fouls, often simply called "T's," are for the most part concerned with *conduct* (as opposed to contact fouls), and may be imposed on any member of the team, including the coach. The reasons for awarding a technical foul include: illegal defenses (see Chapter Nineteen); extra time-outs (a team that has used up its time-outs may "buy" an extra time-out at the cost of one technical foul); delay of game, which includes such actions as failing to immediately give the ball to an official when the whistle has blown, or batting the ball away from a player about to make a throw-in; illegal substitution; hanging on the basket rim (this violation also carries a hundred-dollar fine); and the most common reason, unsportsmanlike conduct, which covers a multitude of behaviors such as use of profanity or arguing with the officials. The officials have quite a bit of freedom in awarding technical fouls, sometimes penalizing such actions as "excessive griping" or "sarcasm" in carrying out officials' orders.

Technical fouls are called against coaches surprisingly often. One of the rules of basketball states that the coach may not come onto the basketball court at any time without the express permission of an official. For some hotheaded coaches this restriction is too much, and when outraged by an official's decision, such a coach may come off the bench and approach the officials in anger. The referees' response to this is usually to assess a technical foul.

Usually the other players on the bench will try to calm a coach who is known to be particularly excitable. A high school coach in Oregon has perhaps come up with the ideal solution to the "T" problem. According to *Sports Illustrated,* this enterprising if touchy man had a seat belt installed on the bench so he wouldn't jump up and earn technical fouls every time he disagreed with the referees!

A technical foul results in one free throw to the nonoffending team, and two T's on the same player—or coach—results in automatic ejection from the game.

A free throw awarded because of a technical foul may be taken by any member of the team. After the free throw attempt, the ball is returned to the team that had possession when the technical foul was called.

The only really confusing aspect of basketball has to do with the allotment of penalties. We have already seen that a player taking a free throw may have more than one opportunity to make it, or may sometimes have three opportunities to make two shots. Here is how the penalty system works.

Each player is allowed to commit five personal fouls. More than this, and he is ejected from the game (he "fouls out"). A player who quickly accumulates two or three fouls at the beginning of a game, or commits four or five fouls in the last half, is said to be in "foul trouble," and unless his presence is urgently needed on the court, he usually does not play a great deal until the closing minutes. Not only does a player jeopardize his own playing time by getting into foul trouble, he puts his team at a disadvantage, because every personal foul committed by any member of a team also counts as a "team foul" for that team. (Technical fouls are not included in this system.) Each team is allowed a total of four team fouls per quarter. Any more than four puts the team "in the penalty" and gives any opposing player who attempts a free throw (except for a technical foul) an extra attempt to sink any shot that is missed. Thus, if the player is awarded one free throw for a foul, he now gets two opportunities to make that one point. If the foul is worth two free throws, he is given three opportunities if one of his first two shots misses.

Furthermore, until a team is in the penalty, its offensive fouls do not result in a free throw but instead in a loss of the ball to the other team (with the exception of "flagrant" fouls such as fighting).

All defensive fouls are penalized by the award of one or two free throws. One free throw is awarded for any contact with a player who is shooting if the shot is successful. If the shot does not go into the basket, the player is given two free throws. Illegal contact with an offensive man who is not in possession of the ball generally results in the award of one free throw.

Two free throws are always awarded for any "flagrant" foul, such as fighting, and any backcourt foul, which is a foul committed against a member of the offense when he is still in his own backcourt. Backcourt fouls are penalized so severely in order to discourage them, as it is felt they slow the game. If an offensive player trying for a rebound makes contact with a defensive player who gets the rebound, this is considered a backcourt foul "off the boards."

In all of the above cases an extra opportunity to make the one or two shots is given if the offending team has committed more than four team fouls and is thus in the penalty. The most points that can be scored on one play are four: this happens when a player who is fouled while shooting a successful three-point basket also makes a successful free throw attempt.

There are two final categories of fouls, "loose ball" and "double," which are enforced separately.

A double foul occurs when both teams commit fouls on the same play. Each player is charged with a personal foul, but the fouls do not count toward team foul totals, and no free throws are awarded.

If the double fouls occur while two players are vying for possession of the ball, play is resumed with a jump ball; if the fouls occur between two players who are away from the ball, the team that had possession before the fouls retains possession.

A loose ball foul is any foul that takes place while the ball is in the air for a shot, or during a rebound if neither team gets possession. Whichever team commits the foul is charged with a team foul and the guilty player with a personal foul, but no free throw is awarded unless the team is in the penalty.

PUTTING THE BALL INTO PLAY AFTER A FREE THROW

When a free throw is to be followed by another free throw, the referee controls the ball between the two shots. On the last free throw of a series, if the ball goes into the basket, it is put into play out of bounds as if a field goal had been made. If the ball does not go into the basket, the ball is in play: the free thrower's teammates may attempt to tip it in, while the defensive team attempts to get the rebound.

CHAPTER 19
BEHIND THE ACTION

A good basketball player is always in motion, on offense and on defense, with the ball or without it. In fact, movement even without the ball is considered one of the cornerstones of sound basketball. On the offensive side, constant movement not only tends to confuse the defense, but the more a man moves around the better chance he has to become momentarily free of the man guarding him so he can receive a pass or take a shot.

On the defensive side, motion is also important: a good defensive player must not only move with the man he is guarding, but ideally stay between him and the ball or, if the man has the ball, between him and the basket. Because of the restrictions on movement by a player in possession of the ball, many defensive actions are designed to make him violate those restrictions, or to make him lose possession of the ball.

In a close, well-played game, all of this movement and cutting in and out may appear random and unplanned. The fact is that while there is a lot of room in basketball for spontaneity, most teams rely on a number of set plays within their overall strategy. Furthermore, the strategic planning of a game begins before the opening jump (although it may be changed—and changed again—in the course of a game, sometimes in vain).

One of the most important aspects of the game plan is the matchups—the assignment of players to guard each other. Not only are speed and shooting ability considered in determining matchups, but also player height and strength. A very tall center, seven feet or more, particularly if he also is quick and can shoot, is very difficult to stop no matter who is matched against him. In forward match-ups, a difference of two or three inches between players can often determine who "wins" their confrontation.

Because the basketball roster is limited to 11 men, with only five on the court at any one time, the individual capabilities and skills and the "chemistry" between the players, as well as their size, must be taken into consideration by the coach.

OFFENSIVE PLAY

There are two general styles of play in professional basketball. The more elegant is a "pattern" or "control" game, in which the players employ a great deal of passing and run many set plays and variations. A well-disciplined team can achieve championship results with this type of play, even if they lack a superstar.

In contrast to the tight control of a pattern game is the free-wheeling excitement of a "running" game. This style of play is a good deal less disciplined than the pattern game and relies to a greater extent on the talents of a few very good players, who are always on the lookout for opportunities to put their special talents to use.

One type of running game is often referred to as a "fast-breaking" game. The fast break itself is actually a practiced play that begins with a defensive rebound. The man who takes the rebound is supposed to pass immediately to a teammate who has dropped back to center court. Meanwhile, another teammate is streaking down the sidelines toward his own basket. The man at the center line now dribbles toward the basket and/or passes off to the running teammate, who ideally arrives at the basket unchallenged by any defensive player. A team that is good at the fast break and uses it a lot is said to be a fast-breaking team. The fast break is not only a good way to pile up a lot of points in a hurry, but it can also confuse and wear out the opposing team.

Even a well-disciplined pattern-playing team will of course employ the fast break when the opportunity presents itself, depending on the capabilities of team members and the opposition. Teams that employ the fast break often are fun to watch and hard to stop. You will sometimes hear announcers speak of a "three-on-two" breakaway, which means a fast break in which three offensive players are running to their basket with only two defenders in the way. Two-on-one and three-on-one breakaways are also common.

Team cooperation is most important—indeed essential—to a pattern game; close cooperation is also important to the success of a fast-breaking game. There is yet a third style of play, which has become increasingly popular and which is referred to as "one-on-one" play. "One-on-one" is a type of basketball commonly played in streets, gyms, and playgrounds, in which one person plays directly against another, each trying to sink baskets and to stop the other player from doing so. Teams that have one or two shooting superstars sometimes depend on this style of play; while there will of course be some passing, the best shooters on the team will tend to hold on to the ball and shoot whenever they can, rather than trying to find a teammate who is perhaps in a better position to get a clear shot. As a result, the players who are not directly involved in the one-on-one confrontation tend to play less aggressively than they otherwise might.

Sometimes one-on-one is employed as a deliberate tactic when a team is in trouble: one or two very good shooters may simply go for the ball and shoot at every possible opportunity. When this happens, announcers will sometimes refer to the team's "reverting" to one-on-one play. Or a team may resort to one-on-one to exploit the other team's weakness at a given moment: an obvious mismatch, for instance, between two players.

Although one-on-one play is sometimes deplored, occasionally a team can gain a winning record by relying on the talents of one or two exceptional players. The New York Nets (now the New Jersey Nets) were the top team in the old American Basketball Association partly because of their great forward Julius Erving. A former Net was quoted as saying that their offensive strategy was to "get the ball to Dr. J. and let him do whatever he wanted to with it."

POSITION

Establishing floor position is an important part of any game, whatever the style of the team. The center, who is also called the "pivot man" or "pivot," usually stands in what is known as a "high post" or "low post." In a high post he stations himself near the "top of the key," by the free throw line, and moves back and forth through the free throw lane.

A high post is usually taken by centers who are quick and can shoot accurately from the free throw line. When stationed at the high post, the center usually stands with his back to the basket, and is available to relay passes from teammates, shoot, dominate the "middle," and also to draw his opposing center away from the area under the basket. A center in this position is also valuable in grabbing offensive rebounds.

The low post is near the base line just outside the free throw lane. A very tall center stationed here ("posted down low") can take shots and grab offensive rebounds almost at will.

Variations on these two themes include high-low post with the center and a forward positioning themselves at either end of the key; and double low post, in which two men, usually the center and a tall forward, are stationed just outside the free throw lane near the basket. As with all positional offenses the stations used by the team will depend on their own personnel and the opposing matchups.

The "weak side" of the court can also be important in positional play. This is the side opposite the side where the ball is at any given time and where, therefore, there are fewer players. An alert player can make use of the relatively open area on the weak side by cutting toward it to take a relatively unobstructed shot at the basket.

Establishing position is just as important for the defense as for the offense, of course, and a great deal of the movement in a basketball game consists of this sort of jockeying for floor position. Many offensive players are known to have certain spots that they prefer to shoot from, and an alert defensive player who manages to station himself in that spot before his opponent can reach it will have a definite psychological advantage.

SET PLAYS

There are many set plays in basketball, each with innumerable variations and options. Because the game moves so quickly things seldom work out exactly as planned, and opportunity often dictates how and when such plays are executed. Below is a brief discussion of the plays you are most likely to see and hear discussed by announcers.

SCREENS   There are three common ways that an offensive player can get off a successful shot at the basket. He can beat the defender into the basket area and shoot a lay-up; he can shoot *over* the defender (usually with a jump or hook shot—and in this case he must surprise or "fake out" the defender to avoid having his shot blocked); or he can momentarily free himself from the defender and take an unimpeded shot. The most common way for an offensive man to get loose from his defender is by the use of a "screen."

Almost all offensive set plays in basketball make use of screens, or the threat of them. In basketball, screens are usually referred to as "picks," and here is how they work.

We have seen that it is illegal for one player to deliberately run into another; further, that a player who has established himself in a position has prior right to that position, and that if a stationary player is in an opponent's path, the opponent must stop or change direction or move around him.

A player who wants to free himself from the man guarding him can use a teammate as a screen to do so. He does this by maneuvering toward a teammate who is more or less stationary, then moves quickly past him very close to him. The defender, who is moving with the offensive man, must stop when he comes to the stationary man and loses a second or two while shifting direction to get back to the man he was guarding. In the meantime, the player who used his teammate as a screen may have got off a shot at the basket or managed to cut toward it for a lay-up. A player who deliberately stations himself in his teammate's path is "setting a pick." Centers positioned in the high post often do this, although any player may set a pick for any other if he anticipates the play and the direction it will go.

Most of the set plays you hear about in basketball make some use of screens, either those deliberately set or those occurring naturally in the flow of the game. Among them are the following:

PICK AND ROLL This is a tricky maneuver requiring close cooperation between two players. Let's say that Carpenter sets a screen for Breem, who has the ball. As soon as Breem has moved past Carpenter, shaking his defender, Carpenter himself suddenly cuts toward the basket where Breem throws him a clean pass for a shot. This is called pick and roll because the screen, instead of remaining stationary, "rolls" toward the basket himself. It generally works if it catches the defense by surprise.

GIVE AND GO The give and go is similar to a screen play, with one player running toward a stationary teammate. But instead of this being an actual screen, the run toward the teammate is only a fake; the man with the ball passes to the screen, then, changing directions, runs for the basket in time to receive a return pass. Ideally, his defensive man, expecting a normal screen play, will be thrown off-balance long enough for the play to work.

SCISSORS PLAY (also called "slice" or "double cut"). In this case two players, usually guards, cut past and in front of a stationary man at the same time, moving fast, and going in opposite directions toward the basket. The screen, who has received the ball on a short pass from one of the cutters, is then free to pass to either of them or to take advantage of defensive confusion and get off a shot himself.

BACKDOOR PLAY   In most of the above plays, the offensive man is trying to get away from the man guarding by cutting *in front* of him. In a backdoor play, the offensive man suddenly runs behind his defender and around the periphery of the action (rather than directly toward the basket), then cuts toward the basket from the edge of the court, where he is now free to receive a pass.

FAKES AND DECEPTIONS

A basketball player has to be more than a great athlete to make the pros. He also has to be a good actor. This is because in basketball more than in any other sport, deceptive "moves" are important not only in outplaying the opposition, but also, sometimes, in fooling the officials.

The team on offense always has one primary goal—to move the ball to the basket and shoot. Because each offensive man is covered by a defensive man, however, any movement of the ball—by passing or dribbling—is risky. If a defender can guess which way his man is planning to run or to pass the ball, he can block either the player or the ball and sometimes steal the ball as well. For this reason a great deal of all players' effort goes into developing "fakes." For example, before shooting, a player may bend his arms or body ("pump") once without releasing the ball and only then shoot; or he might pretend to start a jump, hoping to draw the defender off-balance. When passing, a player may look directly at one of his teammates and then pass to another. When getting ready to move (or "drive") toward the basket, he may dribble a step to the left, drawing his defender with him, then suddenly cut to the right and continue unimpeded.

When playing defense, players learn to look for and smoke out deceptive maneuvers: looking at an opponent's lower body is supposed to help, because a man can't fake with his pelvic region. Even more important, very good defensive players learn to anticipate what is most likely to happen in a given situation, then to react a split second before the offensive player expects them to.

Not all deceptive moves are designed to fool the opposition: very often players will feign having been fouled—by falling down in a congested area, for example. Since so many actual fouls are not called in the turmoil of a typical game, the few fakes that succeed probably help to even things up.

Sometimes an offensive player deliberately tries to get the man guarding him to commit a foul.

In his book *"Defense! Defense!"* Red Holzman, coach of the New York Knicks, states that 40 percent of all basketball games are decided by one point. Each extra point thus counts for a lot, and "drawing" fouls is a good way for a team to get those extra points. (Committing excessive fouls, personal or technical, also obviously puts a team at a real disadvantage.)

Theoretically, any contact in basketball is illegal, and especially any contact with a man attempting to shoot. Yet the defender must try to stop the shooter somehow—by jumping to block the shot, by waving his arms to distract his opponent, by anticipating the next move. Because the defender can only guess what the offensive man is going to do, while the offensive man *knows* what he will do, the danger of accidental contact is great. An offensive player about to shoot is delighted with some contact that will not spoil his aim but that will be called a foul and give him a free throw after he's made the basket. Thus, the attempt to "draw a foul," which usually consists of faking the direction or timing of the shot to cause the defender to make an accidental contact. Some players are extremely good at drawing fouls, especially good jumpers who can shift their position in midair.

When a team is in foul trouble—either "in the penalty" toward the end of a close game, or when one or more of its most important players are in immediate danger of fouling out—the opposing team on offense has a real advantage and can afford to station its men close to the basket, knowing that the defenders won't dare guard too closely for fear of being called on fouls.

DEFENSIVE PLAY

There are two basic types of defense in the game of basketball, zone and man-to-man. A zone defense is one in which each defending player covers a certain area on the court and guards any man who may come into that area. In a man-to-man defense, each man is primarily responsible for another man, although there is some leeway. Zone and man-to-man defenses overlap considerably, and most teams make some use of both.

A "pure" zone defense is considered the most difficult type of defense to break through, and is the type used almost exclusively in high school and college basketball. However, pure zone defense is illegal in the NBA.

Apart from the growing violence in the game, there is probably no other issue in basketball that arouses as much controversy and makes as many headlines as that of zone defense. Zone defenses were originally outlawed when the league started, in 1946, because they can tend to slow the game and to keep scoring low. However, the introduction of the 24-second clock neutralized the possibility of stalling by forcing teams to shoot quickly, so the original reason for outlawing the zone no longer remained. The rule is still on the books, however, and a pro team that is caught using a zone is warned once and given a technical foul; for a second such warning there is another T and the coach is ejected from the game.

It is very difficult to prove that a team is using a zone, and it is conceded that all the teams in the NBA use a "modified" zone defense at least some of the time, and some of them use it much of the time. This strange controversy led to a game in the 1977–78 season in which one of the league's oldest and most respected umpires was fined twenty-five hundred dollars and suspended three games for announcing that he would not call penalties against zone defense during the game.

During the same season, *Sport* magazine took a poll of the players on the Kansas City Kings, facetiously asking them which team had the best zone in the league. One player filled out his ballot: "They all do."

It is possible that zone defenses will eventually be legalized, although many owners still are afraid that they will slow the game and make it boring. In the meantime, teams will continue to rely on some form of man-to-man defenses, with some admixture of zone coverage.

In a normal man-to-man defense, a defending player must be no more than six to eight feet away from his opponent, although players are allowed to—and continually are forced to—switch assignments of the men they are guarding, and also to "sag" off their man and assist a teammate who needs help guarding a dangerous offensive player. It is known as "double-teaming" when more than one player guards a man; a team will even, on occasion, "triple-team" an especially formidable opponent, although the danger of fouling him is thus increased.

The most exciting type of man-to-man defense to watch is any of the "pressure" or "pressing" defenses. The fastest moving of these is the full court press, which is usually used in desperation, as in a tied game, or when a team is down. The aim is not only to prevent the other team from further scoring but to force them to commit turnovers.

A full court press begins as soon as the offensive team has received the ball through a rebound in its backcourt, and the idea is for each man not only to guard his man much more intensively than usual, but for any defensive player near the man with the ball to help out in guarding that player, double-teaming to prevent effective passing and moving of the ball downcourt. A half-court press uses the same philosophy, but the intense pressuring of the offensive team does not begin until the ball has been brought across the center line of the court.

When you are watching any sort of pressing defense, the defensive men will appear to swarm all over the court. A press not only makes it difficult for the other team to pass and dribble, but also speeds up the game and can disrupt the rhythm of the attack. Some teams use a pressure-type defense consistently, but an all-out press is exhausting and somewhat risky because it makes extensive use of double-teaming, with two defensive men pressuring the man with the ball. If that player manages to pass to his teammate who is temporarily unguarded, a clear shot at the basket is assured.

Whatever the overall defensive strategy, certain tactics are essential to a good defense. Among the most important of these is "switching" defensive assignments to counter an offensive play. When you are at a game you will sometimes hear a defensive man call "switch!" Chances are some sort of screen play is developing, and the defense hopes to neutralize it.

For example, suppose Addams has the ball and is about to run the man defending him into the center, Bryce, who has set a pick. If the man guarding Addams sees this move coming, he may yell "switch!" as a signal to Bryce's defender to switch assignments with him. Thus, as Addams moves past Bryce to drive to the basket, he is immediately picked up by the man who was formerly guarding Bryce, while Addams's original guard is left to guard Bryce. The main disadvantage of switching is that it can create mismatches, leaving a short man guarding a very tall one. But the primary aim is, after all, to prevent the cutting player from gaining a clear path to the basket.

Offensive teams often set picks in order to create such mismatches, and any given play may become a guessing game with each team trying to anticipate what the other is going to do.

Another important defensive tactic, used close to the basket, is known as "boxing out." The idea of boxing out is an extension of the basic defensive principle of always staying between your man and the basket. In this case, the defensive man tries actively to maneuver so that he is between his man and the basket when they are both very near it. Not only does this position make it hard for the offensive man to shoot, but it puts the defender in a better position to grab a rebound. A player who is boxing out is usually very close to the man he is guarding, and since there is a lot of congestion under the basket, it often results in contact. This contact usually takes the form of surreptitious pushing or leaning against the offensive man, and it is seldom observed or called by the officials. As the great center Kareem Abdul-Jabbar complains, "If you elbow a little guy, it's a foul; if you elbow a big guy they call it boxing out."

DOWN TO THE WIRE

Most sports-watchers would probably agree that there is nothing more exciting than a very close basketball game in its final moments. The possibility of a turnaround in one team's fortunes or of a tie (and overtime) is always there; this possibility is usually reflected by the changing strategy of both teams as the final seconds tick away.

For one thing, at the end of a game it's not unusual for one or more star players on each team to be in danger of fouling out. If one of these players is your top scorer and there is a real chance that the game might tie and go into overtime, this can be serious indeed. Any player in that position must be very careful how he plays, and not allow the man he is covering to maneuver him into fouling.

Besides the foul situation, two other things are important toward the end of a game: the time remaining on the clock and the number of time-outs left for each team.

For example, if a team in possession of the ball is ahead by three or more points with a minute or less to go, they will probably "slow down play"—take their time moving the ball down the court, trying to use up as much of the 24-second clock as possible before shooting.

Conversely, when a team with the ball is behind, it may be more rash, moving and shooting as quickly as possible, trying to force a steal or a turnover whenever the other team gets possession. To conserve time, the losing team almost always calls a time-out (if it has any left) as soon as the winning team has made a basket. This is because the nonscoring team is then awarded the ball at midcourt rather than the base line in the final two minutes of play, and thus can more quickly move the ball to its own basket.

The use of fouls in the closing minutes of a game is also important. As a general rule if you are ahead you do not foul; if you are behind, sometimes you must foul deliberately. For example, suppose the opposing team is ahead by two points in the final seven seconds of the game and they have the ball. The practice is for a defender to deliberately foul the worst free throw shooter on the team. The hope is that he will miss the free throw, and on the rebound the defense will be able to get possession and score, at least forcing a tie. To counter this tactic, the team that is ahead might put in all its best free throw shooters.

A losing team may try other desperation moves as well, which sometimes work. It is a common tactic for the team that is down to knock the ball out of bounds deliberately when the other team has possession. Then, when the offensive player out of bounds tries to throw the ball in, one or more defenders will put a great deal of pressure on him, waving their arms through all of the nearby air space, in the hope of causing him to pass badly or to violate the five-second clock.

I once saw the New York Knicks do this. They were behind one point with six seconds to play; their opponents had the ball out of bounds at the midcourt line. Two Knicks put a lot of pressure on the man who was throwing in, who nearly took the full five seconds. At last he tossed in and at that split second one of the Knick guards came running through, stole the ball, and dribbled toward the Knick basket for a last-second lay-up to win the game!

While such dramatic last-minute turnarounds are rare, they happen often enough to make it a mistake to turn off the tube or leave your seat until a basketball game is definitely over.

CHAPTER 20 FOLLOWING THE GAME

WATCHING BASKETBALL

It has already been noted that pro basketball's TV ratings have been declining in recent years. Observers attribute this decline to several factors: there are no exciting teams in the major cities, or "media markets"; the nature of the game has changed to a point where it is not as enjoyable to watch; the season is too long and too many games are telecast. There is probably some truth in all of these suggestions, but a further reason that is seldom mentioned is that basketball is not easy to watch on television. While any sport is much more exciting in person, this is especially true of basketball.

Unlike the field sports, which take place on the vastness of a grassy field, and unlike hockey, where the players are hidden by protective equipment and skate on an ice rink walled off from the audience, basketball is played on a relatively small wooden court, closely surrounded by spectators. The front seats, in fact, are very near to the edge of the court. There is thus a sense of audience participation at a basketball game that simply isn't there for any other team sport. In basketball you can usually see the players' expressions and hear their voices. At the same time, no matter where you are sitting, you can watch the whole court and follow the plays as they develop.

In a televised game the camera tends to follow the man with the ball, which prevents you from seeing most of what is going on away from him. Furthermore, because the action moves so quickly in the congested area around the basket, the director must often switch camera angles in the middle of a developing play, and by the time your mind and eyes have refocused to the new viewpoint, the play may be over and you will be left wondering what just happened. (Fortunately, however, you can often see it in instant replay.)

Of course it's true that basketball is not seriously affected by the need to insert commercials, because of its frequent time-outs. Still, you will almost certainly enjoy the sport more if you attend a few games in person.

The question of where to sit in basketball is not as easily answered as with the other sports. I prefer to sit near midcourt, as low as possible, because I personally like to watch the players and their expressions. Many fans prefer to sit halfway up in the stands behind the baskets, where they can have a nearly unobstructed view of the sometimes frenetic and always congested action under the boards. On the other hand, it's easiest to follow the development of plays and patterns very high up and near midcourt.

Most basketball arenas have scoreboards that will not only keep you informed about the time left in each quarter, but also give the fouls on each team and time-outs remaining. Whenever a basket or foul is made the player's name and number are announced on a loudspeaker.

If you miss the game either live or on TV, you can read about it in the papers the next morning, but even that is not as easy with basketball as with some other sports.

READING ABOUT BASKETBALL

For a fan interested in following the specifics of a game she didn't see, basketball reporting can be particularly frustrating. Because so many points are scored in each basketball game, the papers do not give as much of a play-by-play account as they do for other sports. Rather, they give cumulative totals per quarter and discuss the trends within each quarter or half. Thus, you may learn that the Golden State Warriors dominated the first half of a game they played against the Boston Celtics, only to commit seven turnovers in the last quarter and lose the game in the final moments. You will also learn who the high scorers were, but it may be more difficult to get an idea of how any given player performed in the game.

In a humorous column in the *New York Times* that dealt with just this problem, columnist Roy Blount, Jr., speculated that basketball is perhaps a game with "too few quantifiable phrases." Whereas the other sports seem to keep statistics on every phase of a game, for basketball the emphasis is almost entirely on points scored. Blount suggests that the game would be more fairly reported if it started keeping track of " 'dunks slammed,' 'picks executed,' 'fast-break baskets,' " and even " 'bad shots taken.' "

Until the unlikely day when Mr. Blount's suggestions are adopted by the NBA, reading a box score will only give you the bare skeleton of a particular game.

Following is the box score from a game between the Seattle SuperSonics and the Washington Bullets. For each player three numbers are given: the first refers to the number of field goals he scored; the second, a hyphenated figure, tells how many free throws he made in how many attempts; and the final figure is his point total. Thus in the example we can see that Dandridge, playing for Washington, shot ten field goals for a total of 20 points, sank six out of seven free throws attempted, and had a total for the night of 26 points.

After the player statistics are the point totals for each team for each quarter, followed by the game totals. Scanning these figures we can see that Washington dominated Seattle in all but the last quarter, when Seattle managed to make as many points, though the team still lost the game by a large margin. Below the team point totals is a listing of players who fouled out; the total number of personal fouls; the total number of technical fouls; and attendance at the game.

Some box scores, especially those for local teams, will give you a bit more information about the performance of your favorite

SEATTLE (110)
J. Johnson 4 7-9 15, Shelton 6 0-0 12, Sikma 5 3-5 13, D. Johnson 2 4-4 8, Williams 5 4-5 14, Silas 6 4-5 16, Snyder 2 0-0 4, Brown 5 3-3 13, Hassett 4 0-0 8, Awtrey 3 1-1 7. . Totals 42 26-32 110.
WASHINGTON (132)
Dandridge 10 6-7 26, Hayes 11 10-13 32, Unseld 6 5-6 17, Henderson 6 4-4 16, C. Johnson 4 2-2 10, Chenier 1 1-3 3, Wright 2 6-11 10, Corzine 4 0-0 8, Ballard 4 2-2 10. Totals 48 36-48 132.

Seattle .... 29 26 22 33— 110
Washington .... 37 27 35 33— 132
Fouled out—Silas. Total fouls—Seattle 36, Washington 21. Technical fouls—Shelton, Washington coach Motta, Seattle trainer Furtado. A—19,135.

players. This information may include the following: minutes played (min.); field goals made (fgm.); field goals attempted (fga.); free throws made (ftm.); free throws attempted (fta.); rebounds (reb.); assists (a.); personal fouls (pf.); and total points (pts.).

Although detailed reports on games do not appear in the paper, a significant body of statistics is kept by the NBA. For example, rebounds, blocked shots, and steals are all recorded, as are such team statistics as number of turnovers committed and "points against," which is the average number of points scored against the team per game.

Likewise, cumulative totals are kept for player scoring and rebounding throughout the season, and awards are given to the top men in each category. The two categories that get the most publicity are the points per game average (above 30 is superstar performance) and rebound average (15 rebounds or better per game is the mark of a star). Also important is the field goal percentage, which is the percentage of field goals attempted that are actually made. Anything above .500, which means that the player makes half of all his attempts, is considered excellent.

THE PLAY-OFFS

The NBA is divided into two conferences, the Eastern and the Western; each conference is further subdivided into two divisions, one containing five teams and the other six.

The teams are ranked in order within each division according to the number of games won and lost. These numbers are then converted to a won-lost percentage, expressed as a three-figure decimal. Thus, a percentage of .500 means that the team has won and lost the same number of games. A team that doesn't achieve at least .500 usually has little chance to make the play-offs. Very good teams have percentages in the high six hundreds or even seven hundreds, meaning they win up to 70 percent or more of their games.

The NBA has a very lengthy postseason play-off system, which is sometimes referred to by exhausted players as the "second season." This system is designed not only to include as many teams as possible in the play-offs, but also to give those teams that do make it a fair chance to compete against one another. A total of 12 (out of the 22 teams in the league) make the play-offs. These are the number-one teams in each of the four divisions, as well as the four teams in each conference (regardless of division) that have the best won-lost records. The play-offs are then conducted in four rounds.

The four division-winning teams sit out the first round, which is a best two-out-of-three series pitting the eight other teams against each other, by conference. In this contest, the top-ranked runner-up team in each conference plays the fourth-ranked team, while the second- and third-ranked teams play against each other.

In the semifinal round, each of the four division winners (which did not play in the first round) plays against one of the victors of the first round in a best four-out-of-seven series.

The four winners of the semifinals then go on to the conference finals, another four-out-of-seven matchup. In this series the two remaining teams from each conference play against each other for the Eastern or Western Conference championship.

The two conference champions then go on to play each other in a final four-out-of-seven play-off, for the World Championship of Basketball.

THE FUTURE OF THE NBA

Because of declining television revenues and gate attendance, as well as what some observers feel may be a deterioration of the game, the NBA instituted several changes beginning with the 1979-80 season, and may well make further changes in the coming years.

The most important change, from the point of view of players as well as fans, is a revision of the playing schedule. Up until the 1979-80 season, each team played the same number of games against each other team in the league. Since 1979, however, the schedule has been weighted so that teams play more games against their own divisional rivals. Not only is this expected to heighten the excitement of local rivalries, in the minds of many observers it will also produce better basketball. The large amount of travel required by the past schedule required players to spend an inordinate amount of time on the road, where they had to cope with fatigue, time zone changes, and travel delays caused by bad weather. This was reflected in the fact that for almost every team in the NBA, the road record was sharply worse than that at home, and many teams about to go on a road trip virtually conceded that they would lose most, if not all of their games.

A second change, instituted as an experiment in the 1979-80 season, is the three-point field goal, which was used in the old American Basketball Association. Most fans who followed the ABA teams liked this rule because it not only encouraged spectacular and exciting shots from far beyond the normal area of shooting, but also gave the trailing team a chance to come back rapidly at the end of a game. Although the three-point shot was attempted fewer than five times in an average game during the 1979-80 season, such observers as Red Holzman feel it "adds a dimension to the game" and will probably remain a permanent fixture in the NBA.

The NBA may be in the doldrums at the present time, but there is no question that basketball remains one of the most popular spectator sports. In fact, on the college level, attendance is up.

THE COLLEGE GAME

There are a number of differences between the NBA rules and those of the NCAA (National Collegiate Athletic Association, which governs all college sports); most of these are minor. Some of the rules have a significant effect on the nature of the game, however, resulting in a sport that is markedly different from the pro game. The most important are these four: first, the game is divided into two 20-minute halves, rather than four 12-minute quarters; second, there is no rule requiring a team to take a shot at the basket within 24 seconds of taking possession; third, the zone defense is legal in college; and finally, a player is ejected on committing his fifth foul.

What these rules add up to is a somewhat shorter and slower-moving game with less scoring and less fouling, but with much more opportunity for elegant team work. Because the offense does not have to shoot in a hurry, and because the zone defense (which is used almost universally in college) is extremely difficult to penetrate, an offensive team takes its time setting up shots, using intricate and exciting passing patterns until a player is in good position to shoot. Because there is so much passing, there are often spectacular steals as well.

Although this is one of those unresolvable sports debates, many fans prefer the college game to the NBA game. To purists, in fact, the college game approaches "true" basketball much more closely than its professional counterpart. While there may be a lower score, there are also fewer interruptions for free throws, because there are fewer fouls when the offense is not pressured to score. On the other hand, the fact that the offensive team can take as long as it needs to shoot can also lead to stalling tactics, particularly toward the end of the game. Thus, a team that is ahead by a small margin late in the game may move the ball upcourt slowly, then simply pass from player to player till the clock runs out, never letting the defense get near and never taking a shot. This tactic is known as "freezing" and can be maddening to watch, particularly when it is your team that is behind. Freezing is also sometimes used as an overall game plan by inferior teams who hope to keep the scoring low so they will have a chance for an upset. This tactic can lead to a very boring game, and it was to eliminate its use that the NBA instituted the 24-second clock.

COLLEGE BASKETBALL CHAMPIONSHIPS

As with college football, college basketball's system of determining the best teams is extremely complicated. This is so not only because there are hundreds of teams to choose among, but also because opportunities for the top teams to compete against one another are limited. Therefore, a weekly polling system is used to rate the best teams. Since polls rely in part on opinion, this system often leads to controversy, and to further confuse things there are two polls: the AP poll, conducted among sportswriters, and UPI poll of basketball coaches.

Most of the best teams in the country belong to one of several NCAA-sanctioned conferences, such as the Big Eight and Ivy League, which are divided more or less along geographical lines. Each team plays a majority of games against conference rivals, though there are many intraconference matchups as well.

In the postseason, there are interconference play-offs for the conference championships. To determine the overall top team, the NCAA holds a play-off tournament, to which it "invites" the eight top-ranked teams in the country. (A college is not allowed to turn down such an invitation.) These teams play in four regional preliminary games, then the remaining four teams go into a semifinal series and finally the top two teams play against each other for the NCAA championships.

Unlike the NBA season, which with the play-offs goes practically into the summer, the college basketball season is over by the end of March.

The reason an invitation to the NCAA play-offs cannot be refused is that there exists a rival championship play-off series, known as the National Invitational Tournament, which is held in

Madison Square Garden. Originally, a team that received bids to both tournaments was permitted to make a choice, but because the NIT was more attractive to many teams, the NCAA passed a rule stating that teams could not play in any other postseason tournament if they declined an NCAA bid. In effect, the NIT now invites the second level of the top collegiate teams to compete. These teams are only marginally less great than the top teams, and both tournaments, which are televised nationally, showcase the best of the college sport.

PART 5
HOCKEY

HOCKEY FACT SHEET

Where played: indoor ice rink.

Game divisions: three periods of 20 minutes each. No overtime except in play-offs.

Average duration: two and one-half to three hours.

Offense/defense consideration: home team defends goal of its choice first and third periods.

Governing body: National Hockey League (NHL).

Number of men on the roster: Unlimited. Each team can dress (have in uniform) 17 skaters and 2 goaltenders for each game. Teams usually carry 2 or 3 extra players.

Equipment: one puck, a small, round rubber disk. Each player wields a long, L-shaped wooden stick, and wears extensive protective equipment, which may include a helmet, face mask, and heavy padding.

Regular season: October to early April (followed by the play-offs).

TEAMS

CAMPBELL CONFERENCE

Patrick Division	Smythe Division
Atlanta Flames	Chicago Black Hawks
Philadelphia Flyers	St. Louis Blues
New York Islanders	Vancouver Canucks
New York Rangers	Winnipeg Jets
Washington Capitols	Edmonton Oilers
	Colorado Rockies

WALES CONFERENCE

Adams Division	Norris Division
Boston Bruins	Montreal Canadiens
Toronto Maple Leafs	Los Angeles Kings
Quebec Nordiques	Pittsburgh Penguins
Minnesota North Stars	Detroit Red Wings
Buffalo Sabres	Hartford Whalers

CHAPTER 21 THE VIOLENT SPORT

I went to a fight the other night and a hockey game broke out.

—RODNEY DANGERFIELD

Unless you have lived in Canada, chances are that your first introduction to hockey of any sort was in high school or college, when you played field hockey, long a popular sport for women. If you're anything like me, this was a new and exciting experience. I still remember the exhilaration of running up and down the field, trying to control the ball with my stick (and failing miserably, since I was the world's worst athlete at that time). Despite my clumsiness, though, I loved the movement and order of the game, the sense that if only I stayed in my position and ran with the other women (and handled the ball as little as possible), all would be well.

Ice hockey is similar in many ways to field hockey, which is not surprising since it is a descendant of the earlier game, having first been played on ice with rules very similar to those of field hockey. The similarities are striking in the positioning of players, in some basic strategies, and in the idea of getting the ball (puck) into the goal.

The dissimilarities, however, are even more striking, at least as ice hockey is played in the National Hockey League. For one thing, ice hockey is probably the fastest game there is in sports (you can move much faster on skates than by running, obviously); for an-

235

other, professional hockey in the United States and Canada is conspicuously violent. This is so not only because the rules of the sport emphasize heavy body contact, but also because of frequent individual attacks by players upon one another. While fighting is officially discouraged and deplored, it is, in fact, recognized as a part of the game in the rules, and players and fans alike seem to relish the mayhem as much as the finer points of skill and strategy. When I first started watching hockey it took me a long time to get past this aspect of it. If I want to watch men beat each other up, I reasoned, why not watch boxing, where that is the whole point? Gradually, though, I became seduced by the beauty and excitement of the game and learned to accept the fights as a sort of "boys will be boys" price one must pay for watching.

Also, as I learned fairly quickly, those ferocious-looking fights are often more show than real: even the occasional blood-spatters one sees look worse than they are, because red shows up so well on the gleaming white ice. An occasional bench-emptying brawl can even be amusing because it's all so silly.

All that said, I must issue a warning to anyone with a weak stomach: violence and fighting *are* a basic part of the game, and despite mutterings in the press about reform, it is unlikely that this aspect of hockey will change, at least not given the gladiatorial mood of current American male sports.

The frequency of fighting is without a doubt one of the reasons for hockey's popularity, but I believe this aspect of hockey is most enthralling only to those who know little about the sport itself—which can be fast, exciting, and breathtakingly beautiful.

CHAPTER 22

THE BASICS

Even if you know nothing about hockey, you can enjoy your first game on an aesthetic level. For the fact is that hockey, especially when played between two good teams, combines the thrill and daring of Olympic speed skating with the grace and intricacy of ice dancing. And, once a few basic points are understood, hockey becomes an easy game to follow and get caught up in.

Before we go into the rules of hockey, it's necessary to take a close look at the playing field, or rink, because its many markings have a direct bearing on some of the most important rules regarding player movement.

An official ice hockey rink is a long rectangle (200 feet by 85 feet in most arenas), surrounded by a low wooden wall ("the boards") that is topped by Plexiglas panels for most of its length. The brilliant white ice is clearly marked with lines and circles in vivid red and blue.

A red center line divides the rink into two equal halves. Toward the end of each of these halves is another, narrower, red line, ten feet from the end of the rink. This is the goal line, and situated in its center is the goal (also called "net" or "cage"). The two goals are each composed of two four-foot-high goalposts six feet apart. These are set directly on the goal line and are connected by a crossbar. Behind the goalposts a large net extends to catch the puck if it is directed into the goal. Directly in front of the goal a red rectangle is marked off, four feet deep by eight feet wide. This is called the "crease."

The two remaining lines on the ice are situated 30 feet to either side of the red center line. These "blue lines" divide the rink into three playing areas. The area between the blue lines (which includes the red line) is known as the "neutral zone." (This area is often referred to by announcers as "center ice.")

Everything between the blue lines and the end of the rink on either side is known as the "attacking zone" or the "defense zone," depending on which team is on offense.

The remaining markings on the ice consist of five large red circles each with a red dot in its center, and four red dots in the neutral zone. The circle in the center of the ice is known as the "center circle"; the remaining circles are just in front of and to either side of the goals. All the circles are called "face-off circles."

Ice hockey is played between two teams of six men each. Those who do the most skating are the three forwards, who are primarily concerned with offense, and two defensemen. The remaining man is the goalkeeper, also called the goaltender or goalie, who is stationed in the crease and whose sole job is to keep the puck from going into his team's goal.

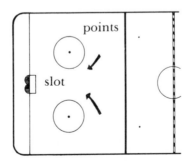

The game begins when the referee, one of three officials skating on the ice, drops the puck between two opposing players who are standing at the center face-off circle. Around that circle are deployed the remaining skating members of both teams. The object of this "face-off" is for one of the men to gain control of the puck and direct it with his stick to a teammate.

Whichever team takes control of the puck is now on the attack. They will try to skate with the puck, all the while using their sticks, into the other team's defense zone, and shoot it into the goal past the goalie. At the same time the defending team tries to break up the attack, take the puck away, and shoot it into the other team's goal.

From this point on, the teams skate from one end of the ice to the other, possession of the puck changing frequently. (Occasionally one team will gain control of the puck early and tend to keep it.) Offense and defense in hockey are determined solely by possession of the puck, and thus a major part of the action is aimed at getting or maintaining that control.

From time to time the action is stopped by an official's whistle. The principal reasons for this are that the referee has lost sight of the puck; the puck has been deflected up and out of the rink; a goal has been scored; or a violation—especially of the restrictions on player or puck movement—has been committed.

Whatever the reason for stoppage of play, it is quickly restarted with a face-off as at the beginning of the game, usually in the nearest face-off circle.

THE RULES OF HOCKEY

PUCK CONTROL   There are strict limitations on the ways in which the team in possession of the puck may move the puck toward the opposition goal. First, no player but the goalie may manipulate the puck with his hands (although if the puck is sent flying through the air a player is allowed to stop its motion with a hand, though not to hold on to it). Second, no player may kick the puck, although the puck may be accidentally deflected off a skate.

The only way the puck may be legally moved, then, is by being *passed, shot,* or *carried* with the hockey stick.

A pass in hockey is made by hitting the puck with the blade of the stick, sending it skimming along the ice (or occasionally through the air) to another player. A shot is similarly hit, but in this case it is aimed at the opposition goal or at an unoccupied part of the ice. The puck is carried when a player manipulates it with his stick while he skates, keeping the puck under control by short little taps from one side to the other. This maneuver is known as "stick-handling."

There are further limitations on the ways in which the puck may be advanced, having to do with the position of the players in relation to the puck. Violations of these restrictions are known as "offside" and "icing," and are among the most frequent reasons for stoppage of play.

OFFSIDE   When a player has received the puck in his own zone, his aim is to move it as quickly as possible toward the opposition goal. If he does not do so according to strict rules, however, he may commit an offside violation, which not only breaks up the attack but costs his team possession of the puck.

There are two kinds of offside called in hockey: offside on a player, and an offside pass. Offside is based on the rule that *no member of the attacking team is permitted to cross the defensive blue line ahead of the puck.* (A player is considered to have crossed the blue line if both of his skates are completely across it.)

If no man on the team may cross the blue line before the puck does, then obviously the puck may not be passed across the blue line, and this, in fact, is the reason for the offside rule: to prevent one team from stationing one or more players deep in the opposition zone to receive the puck. There are only two ways in which the puck may legally cross the blue line: It may be carried across (the blade of the stick is in front of a player when he is stick-handling, so the puck is always in front of him); or it may be shot across. This shot may be aimed at the goal (although it is unlikely to succeed from such a distance), or it may be a shot taken at an empty part of the ice, usually the corners behind the enemy goal line. A puck sent into the enemy zone by such a shot is said to have been "dumped" in.

Now let's see how the offside rule works. Suppose a forward of the attacking team has control of the puck and is skating toward the opposition goal. He and the other two forwards are all in the neutral zone (between the two blue lines). One of the forwards, in his excitement, overestimates the speed at which the man with the puck is skating, and finds himself across the blue line, in the opponent's defense zone. The whistle blows and offside is called.

An offside pass is made by a player from his defense zone across the *red* line to a teammate who is standing in the neutral zone. In effect, this means that players may not *pass* across two consecutive lines (blue and then red).

The penalty for either type of offside violation is loss of the puck and a face-off at the circle in the neutral zone.

In practice, it is not always easy to see when an offside has occurred because the game moves so quickly. It is this very fast pace, in fact, that causes most offside violations: often the players themselves are unsure of just where the puck will be at any given moment, and a wrong estimate can easily lead to an offside call.

ICING   The rule prohibiting icing states that a player who is standing on his own side of the *red line* may not shoot the puck across the *goal line* of the opposing team. This rule was introduced in 1931 to speed up the game. Before icing became a violation, a player could send the puck deep into enemy territory simply to get it out of his defense zone (as long as no teammate was standing across the enemy blue line). The icing rule was instituted because games sometimes became boring exercises in shoving the puck from one end of the ice to the other, with very little skating, either defensive or attacking, and few shots on the goals.

The penalty for icing is a face-off in the offending team's zone.

Icing does occur from time to time in most games, usually as a desperation measure to clear the puck from a team's own zone. Sometimes when it happens you will see a teammate of the offending player racing desperately down the ice to get to the puck before a member of the opposing team does. If he can do so, icing is not called; this has merely become a long pass. Similarly, if the opposing goalie is the first player to touch the puck, icing is not called, because the action is now considered a "shot on goal."

PENALTIES AND POWER PLAYS

It becomes quickly apparent to a new viewer of hockey that the means that both teams use to take control of the puck include not only interception and maneuvering with the hockey stick, but also sometimes violent body contact, known as "checking." There are limits on this contact, however, and any man who violates them is penalized by being removed from the ice and sitting in the "penalty box," an enclosed bench on one side of the rink.

We will go into the violations that lead to penalties of this sort in the next chapter. The important thing to know is that the penalized player must remain "in the box" for a certain period of time, usually two minutes, and during that time his team is not permitted to substitute another player. Thus, the players on the ice (excluding the goalies) will be skating five men against four. This imbalance of players is known as a "power play" and is one of the most exciting aspects of any hockey game. (If, as sometimes happens, players from each team are sent to the penalty box at the same time, there is no power play because the teams remain evenly matched.)

During a power play, the team with the man advantage—which is said to "have the power play"—tries to score goals, while the shorthanded team tries any defensive measures it can think of to stop them (or, rarely, tries to score itself).

Usually the shorthanded team puts certain players on the ice who are known as "penalty killers"; these players try, in effect, to "kill the penalty," to survive the power play without a goal being scored against their team.

There are two common ways for a shorthanded team to accomplish this. The first is to continually clear the puck out of their own zone: a shorthanded team is allowed to send the puck all the way down the ice without being called for icing. This maneuver quite effectively uses up penalty seconds because the opposing players cannot send it directly back, which for them would be icing. Furthermore, because of the offside rule, all members of the attacking team must move back to center ice out of the attacking zone to avoid being offside while the puck is brought back. One or two "dumps" into the attacking team's goal area usually disorganizes the power-play team sufficiently to prevent it from scoring.

The other way to handle penalty minutes, which is more exciting to watch than continual clearing of the puck, is for the shorthanded team to try to keep possession of the puck themselves through intricate passing and skatework. The point of this strategy is not necessarily to score, but rather to prevent the opposition from setting up an effective attack. However, a shorthanded team that does manage to keep possession will occasionally score a goal for themselves. This relatively rare event is known as a "shorthanded goal."

Power plays result in goals 20 to 25 percent of the time. As soon as a goal is scored, no matter how much time has elapsed in the penalty, the man in the penalty box returns to the ice (unless the penalty was a major one, as will be explained in the next chapter).

THE PLAYERS

Because a hockey game moves so quickly, with possession of the puck changing hands sometimes from moment to moment, all players must be ready to play both offensively and defensively. Each position carries certain special responsibilities, however.

The three forwards are considered primarily offensive players, and each is responsible for his own area of the ice. The forwards are the center, who skates in the middle of the ice, and a left and a right wing, who flank him. The main responsibilities of all forwards are to lead an attack, to move the puck toward the opponents' goal, and to shoot it into the goal with their sticks. They are also expected to help the defense by blocking shots taken at their own goal or by taking the puck away from the opposition when the action is in their own end of the rink. The same three forwards customarily skate together and are known collectively as a "line."*

The two defensemen are called the right and left defensemen. Their primary responsibilities are to prevent opponents from taking shots at their goal, to assist the goalie in deflecting any such shots, and to take the puck away from the opposition. They also assist in the attack when the action is at the other end of the ice, and of course if they have a chance to shoot the puck into the opposition goal, they will take it.

It is very difficult when watching your first few hockey games to be certain whether you are watching a forward or a defenseman, because the action is so fast and changes direction so often. The team on the attack will usually station the forwards closest to the opposition goal while the defensemen tend to hang back near center ice, ready at a moment's notice to rush back and defend their goal.

Because of its nonstop action, hockey is an exhausting game to play. Except for the goalkeepers, who usually play an entire game, players—especially forwards—generally don't stay on the ice for much longer than two minutes at a time. Substitutions are freely allowed: A man going out may come back into the game at any time. Often substitutions are made while play is stopped, but sometimes when the action has been fast and furious and there isn't any stoppage, the coach may decide to "change on the fly," or substitute players during the action. This most often occurs when a team has just lost possession of the puck deep in opposition territory and has time to change before play reaches its own goal area.

Changes are usually made in groups: The three forwards are

---

*Very good lines come to be known by nicknames—usually the name of one of the stars on the line, such as the Lafleur Line of the Montreal Canadiens. Occasionally the lines are given more colorful names—the "Kraut Line," "Production Line," and "Punch Line" played respectively for the Boston Bruins, Detroit Red Wings, and Montreal Canadiens. The New York Rangers' starring line in the 1978–79 season included the two Swedish players Ulf Nilsson and Anders Hedberg, who skated with Pat Hickey, number 16. This line was referred to as the "Swede-16 Line."

usually changed as a unit for another line, and the defensemen change in pairs.

If you are watching hockey on television, you won't often see the actual mechanics of changing, because it will happen off-camera, but the announcers will alert you with, "Team A is changing now," or "The offensive team changes on the fly." If you are at a live game it can sometimes appear as if there are several dozen people on the ice at once. In fact, in the confusion of the game sometimes more than six men may actually be playing for the same team at the same time. If this is discovered, it is considered a violation and is penalized.

The one player who stays on the ice throughout the entire game is the goalie, who is the most important man on the team. His "territory" is the crease and the area adjacent to the goal, and his responsibilities are awesome. While it might seem that preventing a goal from scoring is a simple matter, in reality the mouth of the goal is a rectangle four feet high by six feet wide; furthermore, the puck may be traveling toward it on the ice or through the air, from any direction and at speeds of up to 120 miles an hour. When you add the fact that most shots on goal are taken while there is a crowd of moving players around the net who often block the goalie's view, it seems miraculous that any goals are ever prevented.

Because of the speed of the puck and the concentrated action that tends to take place at the goal ends of the rink, the goalies wear very heavily padded clothing and special protective masks, which may be made of molded plastic and painted in bright designs, or which may look something like a catcher's mask in baseball. All this equipment can weigh as much as 40 pounds.

The way the goalkeeper prevents a goal from being scored varies with the individual style of the man, but he is allowed to catch (but not hold) the puck, hit it with his stick, fall on it (but only when it is in the crease), or throw his body across the goal mouth to deflect it, among other stratagems. Watching a good goalie in action is one of the most exciting aspects of hockey; it can be like watching an acrobat with lightning-quick reflexes. While you're still trying to sort things out in your first games, it's a good idea to keep an eye on the goalie whenever the action has moved to his end of the ice.

SCORING

It is quite likely that the first hockey game you see will have very few goals scored. This does not mean that it will be a dull game; the fact is that hockey is by nature a low-scoring game. A score of 3–2 is much more common in hockey than, say, 9–5, and a score of 1–0 is not uncommon.

Hockey games often end in ties, and unlike most other major team sports, there is no sudden-death overtime, except in the playoffs. Even a game tied at 0–0 will end when the third 20-minute period is up.

CHAPTER 23 HOW THE GAME IS PLAYED

There are over 80 official rules of hockey. Most of these contain several subrules, covering everything from standards of equipment to any possible infractions and situations that may come up. It's not my intention here to go into every nuance of the rules of hockey. Still, after you have been watching for a while, it is natural to want to know more about the game, particularly in the matter of violations. Following are some of the more than basic aspects of hockey, which will increase your understanding and enjoyment as a fan.

HOCKEY OFFICIALS

The life of an official in the NHL is not an easy one, with so much fast, continuous action to oversee. At each game the officials are called upon to make many judgment calls, and the wonder is that they perform their duties so well. From the spectator's point of view, the three most important officials are the referee and two linesmen.

The referee is easily identifiable: he wears a black-and-white-striped shirt and red armbands. His main function is, essentially, to control the game. In a disputed call he makes all final decisions.

The referee is responsible for starting the game (with a face-off in the center circle) and calls most of the penalties. He keeps his eye on the puck at all times, and when he cannot see it for any reason—if it has gone into the stands or a player has fallen on it—he immediately stops the play by blowing his whistle. If there is a fight, especially one involving several players, the referee is responsible for watching closely to determine, if possible, who started the fight and what the penalties should be.

The character of the game depends to a large extent on the referee and the amount of control (or lack of it) that he asserts early on. If he calls infractions readily and consistently from the outset, for example, the game is a good deal less likely to become extremely violent, no matter what the level of rivalry or the importance of the game.

The referee is assisted in his duties by the two linesmen, who also wear striped shirts but no red armbands. Their three main duties are to call icing, to call offsides violations, and, perhaps most important, to prevent or to break up fights. (The referee never interferes in fights because of his obligation to determine responsibility.) I've often thought that to be a hockey linesman must take a great deal of physical courage, since they are so often called on to wade into a melee of flying fists and sometimes sticks.

There are also several officials in every hockey game who you don't see but who are essential to the smooth running of the game. Among these are two goal judges, one at each goal. They sit in specially protected areas just behind the goals, and their sole responsibility is to determine if the puck has gone completely across the goal line between the goalposts. If a goal judge is certain that has happened, he presses a switch that lights up the red goal light atop the cage.

After you have been watching hockey for some time, you will notice that sometimes the red light goes on, but the referee declares that no goal has been scored. Usually this happens because some infraction occurred prior to the goal, and the referee had already blown his whistle to stop play but the goal judge didn't hear it (which is hardly suprising considering the usual level of noise in an arena when action is heavy around the goal area). Sometimes no goal is declared because the puck went into the net illegally. (It was kicked in, for example, or deflected off an official, or the net was knocked off its moorings.) In any of these cases the referee has the final say; the goal judge's only responsibility is to determine that the puck went completely across the line.

It says a great deal about the nature of hockey that there is an official whose sole duty it is to keep track of penalties. Besides listing the penalties called and whom they were against, how long they lasted, and so forth for each player for the official records, the penalty timekeeper is also responsible for seeing that each penalized player serves the full amount of time he has been charged with and does not reenter the ice until his time is up.

Other officials include the official scorer, who keeps a record of the players on each team as well as of who is on the ice at any given minute; the game timekeeper, who keeps track of the actual time of the game and gives a one-minute warning before the end of each period; and the statistician, who is responsible for recording all statistical information about the teams and the players.

THE PUCK

The puck is the focus of every game of hockey. All arenas keep a large stock of frozen pucks for each game: a cold puck moves more easily on the ice than a warm one.

It may seem too obvious to mention, but when you are first getting to know hockey, the best way to understand what is happening is to follow the puck—see who has it and what he is doing with it.

The official rules of hockey state that *the puck must at all times be kept in motion*. We have already seen that no player other than the goalie can handle the puck or deliberately fall on the puck.

It is also against the rules to deliberately hit the puck out of the rink. (Although this does happen often, *intent* is hard to prove, and this infraction is seldom called.)

"Freezing the puck" means stopping its motion in the course of play, and if done intentionally, it is a violation. Often two or more players are competing for the puck against the boards, and the puck becomes trapped between their skates and the boards or between their two pairs of skates. In this situation one of the players may be *trying* to freeze the puck, usually because his opponents have a strong attack going, and he feels that it is safer to stop the attack and risk a face-off than to let their momentum continue. When players are simply competing for the puck you will often hear TV announcers say something like "Roberts and Humphrey battling along the boards, Slater trying to dig the puck out." (Meaning that Slater has joined the fray and is trying with his stick or skate to get possession of the puck.) At some point the puck will be knocked loose, will stop altogether, or will be lost to the sight of the referee, in which case the whistle blows and there is a face-off at the nearest face-off circle.

Which brings us to face-offs, or, in hockey jargon, the "draw." When I first began watching hockey I was convinced that the positioning of a face-off is arbitrarily decided. I have since learned that the majority of face-off situations have quite clear-cut guidelines for positioning of the puck, although in some cases the rules are quite complex.

As a rule, you can assume that a face-off will take place in the circle nearest to where the infraction occurred. For example, if play is stopped because of an infraction by the defending team in their own zone, face-off occurs in a face-off circle near their goal. This most commonly occurs during icing.

However, if play is stopped because of something done by an attacking player in the attacking zone, the face-off takes place in the face-off circle in the *neutral* zone.

If play is stopped anywhere on the ice because of an infraction by members of both teams, the face-off takes place where the infringement occurred, and this does not necessarily have to be a circle.

CHECKING

When you first begin watching hockey you will notice that the players often knock each other down, skate directly into one another, and frequently and with great relish throw each other into the boards. At first you may be shocked by the extent of this violence and wonder why the officials don't do anything about it. You will discover, however, that it is an integral part of the game, and that the officials do something about it only if it is not kept within certain prescribed bounds.

This violence is all a part of checking, which is the most potent defensive tactic in hockey. Checking takes many forms, but in general a defending man checks his opposite member on the other team by covering his movements and trying to prevent him from receiving the puck, or from passing or shooting it if he has it.

You will often hear the announcers speak of "fore-checking" and "back-checking." These terms refer to where the checking is taking place. Back-checking occurs in the checking team's defensive zone and is usually done by the forwards, skating backward. Back-checking is designed primarily to keep the puck out of the net and is thus an extremely important defensive tactic. Fore-checking, while also a potent defensive weapon, takes place at the end of the ice *away* from the defenders' goal. It usually begins when a team on the attack loses control of the puck and suddenly becomes the defending team. The new defenders now begin to check the other team to keep them in their own zone or force back into it. Effective fore-checking, if it results in regaining control of the puck, can thus eliminate the need for back-checking. Since the best offense is often a good defense, and because the puck changes possession quickly and often, checking can also be considered an offensive weapon.

The means of checking, no matter where it takes place, are what make hockey a hard contact sport. Checks may be delivered with the body or the stick. In many cases the aims of checking are accomplished without any physical contact at all—just the threat of contact is enough. To be successful any hockey player, regardless of his skills, must be willing to give and to receive checks when the occasion requires. As we shall see, some players specialize in the more violent forms of checking.

The basic types of checks in hockey are as follows:

BODY CHECKS   The purpose of a body check is to stop an opponent or force him to skate in another direction; to keep him from getting in position to receive a pass; or sometimes simply to harass and disorganize the attack—as, for example, during a power play. Body checks are given with the hips or shoulders. It is illegal for the checker to use any other part of the body—such as the elbow—and he is not allowed to take more than two steps before throwing a shoulder or hip at his opponent. Moreover, checks may not be delivered from the back—only from the front or side.

When you consider that this contact is going on while the men are skating as fast as they can, you can recognize the devastating impact of a well-delivered check. On the other hand, a check that misses usually takes the checker himself out of the action; further-more, hockey players are taught to meet a check with a counterthrust of their own, forcing the checker to absorb some of the punishment.

A variant of the body check is the *body block*. Here again the defensive player uses his body to stop or deflect an opponent, but he does it without delivering a violent blow; rather he skates into his target or against him and forces him out of position.

Often a body check or a body block is designed to drive the opponent against the boards; this tactic is used most frequently against the player who has control of the puck in the checker's defensive zone. (Legally, any member of the attacking team except the goalie may be driven into the boards.) Checking into the boards is a common and spectacular feature of most hockey games. Though the attacker is often simply skated or nudged against the boards, sometimes he is thrown there with a strong body check. When this happens you can hear the boards rattle up in the top row of the stands. A game I watched on TV between the N.Y. Rangers and the Atlanta Flames, who are known as a "hard checking" team, resulted in three time-outs to replace the broken Plexiglas along the boards!

There is a narrow line between so-called hard checking and gratuitously violent checking; one is employed as a potent tactic to gain control of the puck, while the other is designed primarily to intimidate the opposition. Although capable of good hard checking, the Montreal Canadiens, considered for many years one of the best teams in the NHL, rely primarily on spectacular skating, passing, and shooting. The corollary of this is the belief that many other teams rely on brute force because they lack the finesse and skill to shoot well, pass well, skate well.

While there may be some truth in this charge, some teams with excellent hockey skills, such as the Boston Bruins, are also known as "dirty" teams—checking more violently and more often than necessary. This kind of gratuitous hard checking is sometimes used as a retaliatory weapon and can often escalate into a fistfight or even a brawl.

During the Stanley Cup play-offs in 1978, my team, the New York Islanders, were playing the Toronto Maple Leafs, an especially physical team. Early in the game, my favorite player, the rookie Mike Bossy, was checked violently and unnecessarily into the boards. For ten heart-stopping minutes Bossy lay unmoving on the ice. Everyone watching was sure that he was dead or had a broken neck. Miraculously, Bossy recovered with only a sprained neck and played in the next game.

Partly because of the intimidation by the Maple Leafs, the Islanders lost the play-off series. However, at their first meeting of the 1978–79 season, the Islanders, normally a very clean, classy skating team, retaliated against the Maple Leafs with some of the heaviest checking I have ever seen. Even though as a rule I find gratuitous violence a turnoff, I have to admit I was cheering as loudly as all the other Islanders fans, even at the fistfights!

STICK CHECKS The purpose of stick checking is to take the puck away from the player who has it. There are a variety of stick checks, which are not easy for the spectator to distinguish from one another. These include the *poke, sweep, hook,* and *lift* checks. For all practical purposes you do not really need to know the fine points of these checks; their names are descriptive. Announcers frequently refer to them in a sort of shorthand: "Poked away by McGillicuddy"; "Good sweep by LaMaire and passed to . . ."

Stick checks are used *only* on the puck: it's a serious violation to use a stick against a man.

PENALTIES

An old Charles Addams cartoon shows a penalized hockey player sitting on the sidelines, chained in the stocks. While the penalty box is much less intimidating than the stocks, the purpose of the penalty is pretty much the same—exhibition and restriction. It is a penalty to the individual player, denying him the chance to play for a specified time; and it is a punishment to the team, who must skate shorthanded for the duration of the penalty.

Most offenses that cost penalty minutes occur simply because of the hard contact nature of the game of hockey. Some offenses result from checks that are applied incorrectly or too roughly, others because of various forms of fighting inspired by hard checking. The variety of penalties given and how long each lasts may seem puzzling and even arbitrary. This is so because they often are, in fact, arbitrary.

Some players, for example, will do plainly illegal things such as tripping an opponent if they are sure that no official is watching, or if they're desperate. Because there are only one referee and two linesmen, and because the action is taking place all over the ice, players get away with this sort of thing quite often. Penalties may also seem arbitrarily dispensed when a large fight has erupted. After the fight has been stopped and the officials confer to sort things out, the resulting penalties may not seem fair in proportion to what happened and individual responsibility. No amount of booing by the fans will change things, however.

Another seemingly unfair situation often occurs when a game is very close and time is running out. Two players will fight or start to fight (in announcer jargon, "start to go"); while the officials look on tolerantly the players finish their business or are separated and play resumes as if nothing had happened, with no penalties awarded.

This can happen when the officials hesitate to make an already uneven or lopsided game more so; it can also happen as a kind of balance for penalties called too harshly earlier in the game. Sometimes if a game has already been dragged out because of a great many penalties, the officials choose to overlook a minor fight. The players are aware of all this, of course, and take advantage of it. With six minutes to go, a fight broke out during a closely contested 1978 game between the Philadelphia Flyers and the Islanders. The game had been marked by a lot of illegal checking and fighting, and the officials decided to ignore the fight. One of the announcers remarked, "I've got a feeling from this point on it will take maiming before the referee will call a penalty." Thankfully, there was no maiming in the remaining minutes—nor were any further penalties called.

One final note: sometimes a referee sees an infraction committed but does not call the penalty right away. This happens if the infraction was committed against the team in possession of the puck. So that they can maintain their attack the referee delays the whistle until they score a goal or lose possession. (He raises his hand to indicate the delay.) If they score, the penalty is forgotten (unless it's a major penalty); if they lose possession play is stopped and the penalty is awarded.

MINOR PENALTIES   A player who is given a minor penalty must leave the ice and spend two minutes sitting in the penalty box while his teammates skate shorthanded. As soon as a goal is scored by the other team, the player may return to the ice. The principal offenses that call for a minor penalty are:

Boarding   When a player checks another into the boards with "unnecessary violence," he draws a two-minute penalty. As with many hockey calls, violence is in the eye of the beholder, and an action that might call for a penalty on one play won't necessarily do so on another. As a rule, a player is more likely to be penalized for boarding an offensive player who does *not* have possession of the puck.

Charging   Like boarding, this penalty is called for an incorrectly delivered check. A player is charging if he takes more than two steps before delivering a body check to his opponent. Charging can also be called on a player who checks a goalkeeper in the crease, although goalies are exempt from checking even outside the crease.

Delay of Game   This penalty, which is seldom called, penalizes a player who deliberately stalls the game by taking too long getting onto the ice, for example, or deliberately shifting the goalposts or, as an act of desperation, deliberately shooting the puck off the ice and into the stands. It can also be called on a player who falls on the puck or freezes it when he is not being checked. As with many minor penalties, delay is mostly a judgment call on the part of the referee. In most games several pucks are shot up into the stands, and usually the shot is assumed to be accidental.

Elbowing   Just what it sounds like. This is most often called when a player delivers a body check using the elbow instead of the shoulder.

Fighting   A variety of penalties can be given for fighting ("fisticuffs" in the rule book). Officially, fighting draws at least five minutes, but if it doesn't look serious to the referee, he often gives a minor penalty to both players involved in a fistfight, calling the violation "unnecessary roughness."

High Sticking   Anytime a player lifts his stick above shoulder level he is in trouble. If he attempts to pass the puck by "batting" it with the high stick, play is stopped and a face-off is held in his team's defensive zone. If he makes a goal by batting with his stick high, the goal is disallowed. And if he hits another player—or even threatens to—with his stick, he is given a two-minute penalty.

Holding   Just what it sounds like. No player is allowed to impede another's progress by holding him with hands or stick.

Hooking   Using the curved end of the stick to trip or hold back an opposing player.

Roughing   This penalty is often used as a sort of catchall by the referee, especially when several players have been involved in a fight. The official term for it is "unnecessary roughness," though what is necessary and what isn't is a matter of interpretation.

Slashing or *spearing*   an opponent with a stick are both extremely dangerous, and are considered major violations if they result in injury.

Tripping This violation is a difficult penalty to call, because throughout the game one or more players are constantly sprawling on the ice, and sometimes the tripping or loss of balance is quite accidental, or made to look so. If a man is tripped while he has the puck near the goal, this is a more obvious infraction and instead of drawing a two-minute penalty, can result in a penalty shot (see page 260).

In addition to the above minor penalties, the following two special categories may be handled as minor penalties:

Bench Minor Penalty Every sport has some sort of penalty system to deal with interference by players on the bench or by the coach. In hockey the bench minor penalty serves this purpose. It is imposed if anyone on the bench, including the trainer, does anything to interfere with the game, such as throwing something on the ice, using foul language, or strenuously arguing with an official. The bench minor penalty is the same as for a minor penalty committed on the ice: a designated player is put in the box and his team plays one man short.

Interference A minor penalty is called on any player who deliberately impedes the progress of an opponent, or who knocks his stick out of his hand, or prevents him from picking up a dropped stick. More serious forms of interference—especially interfering with a player in possession of the puck—can draw severe penalties, including awarding of a goal to the offended team.

MAJOR PENALTIES The whole purpose of the penalty system is to punish a team for doing something that makes the game unfair. Taking one player off the ice and leaving his team shorthanded increases the chances for the opposing team to score. A major penalty makes that chance a near certainty, because a player who is put in the box for a major penalty is made to stay there for five minutes while his team skates shorthanded. In hockey, five minutes is a very long time. Even more seriously, a player serving a major penalty may not return to the ice until his time is up, no matter how many goals are scored against his team.

In addition to being put in the box, the player may be fined, depending on the nature of the violation.

The principal offenses that call for a major penalty are actual injury to an opponent's head and face resulting from any of the actions that would otherwise call for a minor penalty (roughing, hooking, high sticking, etc.); or, in the officials' judgment, deliberate intent to injure an opponent. Another important offense that *may* call for a major penalty is fighting.

Because fighting breaks out so often in hockey, a number of special rules have been devised to keep any fight from widening. One of these is the so-called third-man rule, which provides automatic penalties including a fine, a double minor penalty (two minor penalties served consecutively), and suspension for the rest of the game ("game misconduct penalty") for any player who joins an existing fight between two players. (His team, however, is allowed to substitute for him after the double minor is served.) The penalties for players who leave their bench or the penalty box to join an existing fight are likewise severe, and may include large fines.

A measure of how serious fighting can be is the outcome of a fight that occurred between Wayne Maki of the St. Louis Blues and Teddy Green of the Boston Bruins. Green, after spearing Maki, was hit over the head by Maki's stick and rendered senseless and near death. After two brain operations, he recovered enough to once again play hockey. (Ironically, Maki died of a brain tumor some five years later.)

That fighting is dangerous is well recognized by all players. When a fight breaks out usually the players involved will drop their sticks and gloves: fighting with sticks brings especially severe penalties. As soon as an altercation starts between two players, quite often the remaining players on the ice will "pair off," or form pairs made up of one man from each team. This looks like nothing so much as a group of skaters in heavily padded uniforms waiting around for the band to strike up a waltz. They stand face-to-face, grasping each other's jerseys to steady themselves, often talking or laughing. The idea is to get players who at the moment have nothing against each other away from the action; with any luck tempers will remain calm and there will be little temptation to help out a teammate who is already at blows.

Revenge for injury to a teammate is one of the main motivations for serious fights. Or fights may break out because one team is losing and the players feel frustrated; a team may feel it has been treated unfairly by the officials; or it is a game between long-standing rivals.

It is the linesmen's responsibility to break up fights, but often teammates will help, or will at least restrain their more hotheaded members from joining a fight. Sometimes it takes a long time to break up a fight; the linesmen finally get the feuders apart and the second they let them go, they're back at it again.

MISCONDUCT PENALTY This penalty is generally imposed on players who argue too much with the officials or use foul or obscene language. (The question of arguing with officials comes up often in all sports; hockey has solved this by means of a rule whereby only the team captain or his designated alternate is allowed to question officials about their decisions.)

The penalty for misconduct is removal from the game for ten minutes (a substitute is allowed) and an automatic fine. In especially serious cases, a player may be charged with a game misconduct penalty and removed for the rest of the game. A game misconduct penalty is also given for deliberate injury of an official. If the goalie is given a misconduct penalty, he is allowed to remain on the ice, but another player from his team must serve time in the penalty box in his stead.

MATCH PENALTY This is one of the most severe penalties of all, and is given to any player who has *deliberately* injured an opponent. Again the question of intent is left up to the referee. Match penalties are never given lightly: a player who draws one is automatically suspended for the rest of the game; he is ordered off the ice and to the dressing room, and is given an automatic fine. In addition he may be assessed further fines or even suspension by the president of the league, who investigates all match penalties.

Not only is the player himself punished for his infraction, but his team is also severely penalized. Depending on the nature and severity of the injury he caused, another member of the team is sent to the penalty box for either five or ten minutes while the team skates shorthanded. He may not return to the ice until the time is up, no matter how many goals are scored.

PENALTY SHOT   A penalty shot is given to a player who is illegally checked while he is in the goal area, in possession of the puck, and seemingly about to score.

You won't see a penalty shot often, but when you do, it's very exciting. First, all members of both teams, except for the player who is to take the shot and the goalie, must stand to the side of the ice. Then the offended player starts skating with the puck from center ice toward the opposing goalie. When he is in range, he shoots. About one third of all penalty shots result in goals.

Because the penalty shot is called so rarely, defending players will fairly often trip an opponent who seems about to score. The most likely consequence of this action is a power play by the offended team, which is surely preferable to an almost certain goal.

DELAYED PENALTY   You will sometimes hear a "delayed penalty" called. This occurs most often when there have been one or more fights involving several players, or when there is an unusual amount of illegal checking.

The rules state that no team ever has to play with fewer than three players on the ice (four, counting the goalie). So if a team has two players already sitting in the penalty box and a penalty is called on a third player, his penalty time is delayed until one of the players already there has gone back to the ice. Now the third player begins his penalty time and the team is once again skating with three. This can get very confusing when there has been a large brawl and numerous players from both teams are penalized.

If you're watching hockey on TV or listening to the radio, the announcers will keep you informed as to who is serving time and how much penalty time remains for each team. In person it's a little harder to tell, but the scoreboard will list the penalties in progress and time remaining for each player.

GOONS, ETC.

When you are reading about hockey or listening to the pre-game show you will sometimes hear about so-called goons or enforcers. These are players whose main purpose is to get even for assaults on their teammates, or to intimidate important members of the opposition by checking them violently or by involving them in fistfights.

You can usually tell who these players are by looking at the team's statistics: generally the player with the highest overall average of penalty minutes is the enforcer. Almost all teams, even the most skilled, have one or more players whose primary job is to beat other players up; it's a bonus if he's also skillful at skating and shooting.

As Shirley Walton, a hockey writer, points out, the trend in the NHL has been to increasing reliance on physical violence and less on finesse in skating and passing. Even the concept of the "enforcer" has changed; in earlier days such men were more often called "policemen." Their primary duty was to use violence as a last resort to *stop* harassment of their teammates. Today, unfortunately, such players are often sent onto the ice to instigate violence.

An example of the kind of game this sort of dirty play can lead to was provided by the N.Y. Rangers and the St. Louis Blues early in 1979. The Blues, not a particularly good team, were outplaying the Rangers and held a tie into the third period. The Rangers, who had been much better that season than anyone expected, were apparently frustrated, and their prime enforcer, a native New Yorker named Nick Fotiu, got into a fistfight with the St. Louis enforcer Steve Durbano. Sticks went up and at that point the benches emptied and a general brawl broke out. Before it was over, Durbano had made an obscene gesture to the crowd, and Fotiu tried to follow him into the dressing room, swinging all the way. Durbano's total of 45 penalty minutes was the second highest ever meted out in a game. Fotiu received a total of 22 minutes, and altogether the game was delayed more than 15 minutes.

Because of episodes like the above, there is increasing concern within the NHL about violence in the game, particularly the sort that leads to near riots. Solutions that have been discussed include the outlawing of fighting altogether, as it is outlawed in other sports: a player who resorted to "fisticuffs" could thus find himself not only ejected from the game but heavily fined and perhaps suspended from the next game as well. Such severe penalties, if applied evenly, might well reduce the incidence of violence; certainly the present rules do little to discourage it.

As Durbano, discussing his role in the Rangers-Blues brawl, explained to the *New York Times*: "I was out of the game. I just wanted to get my money's worth if that's the way it was going to be."

CHAPTER
24 BEHIND THE ACTION

One of the most thrilling sights in hockey is a series of well-executed passes among members of an attacking team skating toward the opponents' goal. Teams that excel in passing can seem to possess an almost extrasensory ability, as the puck skims just past a defender to be picked up by another player and then perhaps sent to yet a third. (Interception of passes is also exciting—if it's your team that takes the puck away.)

There are several types of passes in hockey. The ones you are most likely to notice and to hear mentioned by the announcers are the following:

Drop pass Instead of sending the puck across the ice to a receiver, the passer skates ahead, stick-handling, and then abruptly leaves the puck behind to be picked up by another player who is following him. This pass, which is hard to see on TV, is spectacular to watch in person.

Other types of passes include the *sweep pass,* in which the stick is directed at the puck in a sweeping motion; and the *flip pass,* in which the puck is "scooped" up with the blade of the stick and directed above the surface of the ice. Passes are sometimes made off the boards as well: in this case the passer aims the puck at the boards at such an angle that it will bounce off in range of the man he is passing to. This is usually done most effectively by the home team, who are familiar with their own rink and the idiosyncrasies of its boards.

The above terms refer to the mechanics of passing. Just as important is the purpose of a pass. For example, a *clearing pass* is made when a defender passes to clear the puck from his own goal area. A *centering pass* is used when shots are being taken on goal: One of the attackers shoots to the center of the attacking zone, hoping to set up a good shot for the receiver.

Teams that use a great deal of passing are also likely to use the tactic known as "headmanning" the puck. This means continually and quickly passing the puck to the man who is farthest ahead on the attack, in order to avoid offsides. This can result in extremely swift movement down the ice. The Montreal Canadiens have perfected headmanning, and their almost choreographed skating and passing are thrilling to watch. When they are playing well, the team becomes an entity in itself, transcending the skills of any one man.

Just as there are different types of passes, so there are different types of shots on goal. These include the *forehand* and *backhand* shots. As in tennis, the former is delivered by a player from the side that corresponds to his "handedness"; the backhand, considered one of the most difficult in all of hockey, is delivered from the "wrong" side, with the player's arms crossed in front of him. Others are the *wrist shot*, delivered with the snap of the wrists, and the spectacular and relatively recent *slap shot*. The slap shot was made possible by the introduction of a slight curve to the blade of the hockey stick, and is delivered by swinging the stick back, then bringing it down against the puck with a forceful slap. It is the most powerful of all shots—traveling at speeds of up to 120 mph—but is also more difficult to control than other shots. The slap shot is most often used when the player is relatively far from the goal.

You may hear announcers speak of a "screen" or "screen shot"; this is a shot of any type taken while the goalie's vision is blocked by another attacking man.

Another tactic used in passing, shooting, and sometimes in checking is one you will hear referred to as "deking." Deking simply means faking out the opposition: pretending to pass in one direction but actually passing in another; pretending to move to the right but at the last minute switching to the left, and so on.

There are several styles of games in hockey; these depend not only on the strategic decisions of the coach on a given night, but also on the skills of the individual players on both teams. Most exciting to watch is a so-called rushing or fast-breaking game (also called "breakaway"). The idea is to get one man out front with the puck with nobody between him and the opposing goalie. This ideal seldom works in practice, but a one-man advantage can, as we have seen, make quite a difference. In a fast-breaking game you will often hear the announcers speak of "two-on-one" or "three-on-two." They mean that two (or three) attacking players have reached the opposition area with one (or two) defenders between them and the goal.

Another type of game that may or may not include fast-breaking is the so-called pattern game, which involves a lot of fancy skating and passing down the ice. A pattern game is so called because the passing and skating are for the most part well-rehearsed maneuvers, with the relationship of the players to each other part of a pattern.

When announcers refer to a "tight" game, they mean there is an emphasis on defense, usually with a lot of heavy checking by both sides.

The type of game is usually determined by the coach, who takes into account such factors as his own team's abilities as well as those of the opposition. While the players on the ice have quite a bit of freedom to respond to the changing conditions of the game, the coach determines who is on the ice at any given time.

Not only do coaches customarily employ certain players as penalty killers—or power-play specialists—they try to balance the skills of an opposition line with strategic line changes. Sometimes just before a face-off you will see the players of one team change, then the other team change, as the coaches try to outwit each other by "matching lines." In these switching contests, the home team is always allowed to make the final line change.

SCORING GOALS

To the uninitiated observer, the action at the goal areas may appear to be a randomly organized sort of a brawl. Actually, most of what happens does so according to plan. To get a better idea of what is going on at the goals, we'll need to take a closer look at the rink.

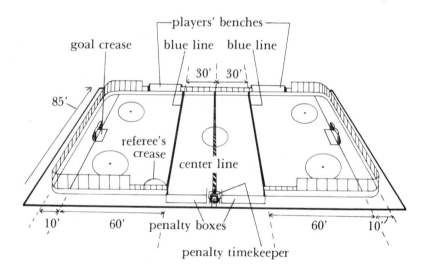

The most important areas in terms of scoring, apart from the goaltender's crease, are the *slot* and the *points*. The slot is the area just in front of the crease, between the two face-off circles, while the points are imaginary areas between the face-off circles and the blue line.

Most goals are scored from the slot; therefore, a prime tactic for all attacking teams is to station one or more players there. The obvious countertactic is to cover the man in the slot and take him out of action if possible (by back-checking).

An added complication is that it is illegal for an attacking man to stand in the crease or harass the goalie; attackers may enter the crease area only if the puck is already there. They usually do this to get a rebound, which occurs when the puck bounces off the goalie or his equipment, another player, or the goalposts. A player with good reflexes can quickly shoot the rebound at the goal.

The man who stands in the slot is usually the center, though often one of the wings has this job; the other two forwards then usually cover the sides of the rink while the defensemen stay at the points—far enough back that they can quickly skate back to defend their own goal if necessary.

Ideally, then, the attack on the goal will begin with the men on the points passing ("feeding") the puck to the man in the slot while the wings are ready to skate in and shoot any rebounds off the goalposts. Of course the defending team is trying strenuously to thwart these efforts. They are furiously back-checking, trying to force the action to the sides of the rink, where it is difficult to shoot, or to the corners, where they can battle for possession of the puck, or behind the net.

Regardless of the action by the skaters, the drama at the goal finally focuses on one man: the goalie. You will probably find that you, like members of the team, quickly become protective of your own goalie. The ways in which he can stop the puck are many: he can catch it and then drop it for a teammate; he can fall on it or catch it and "hold on" for a face-off; or he can clear it himself with his stick. Technically, the goalie is not allowed to freeze the puck anywhere but in the crease, although this rule was seldom enforced until the 1978–79 season, when referees began calling a minor penalty for delay of game by goalies. This rule was designed to make the game more "exciting"—that is, higher scoring—to attract a bigger TV audience. It may very well lead to more scoring, but whether or not this will improve the game of hockey remains to be seen.

One of the most harrowing actions in hockey sometimes occurs near the end of a game where the score is tied or the opposition leads by one goal. When this happens you will often see the losing team, or the team that most needs a win or a tie, do something almost unthinkable: while action is going on at the other end of the rink, the desperate team's goaltender will skate off the ice and an extra attacking man will come in. There is no more chilling sight in sports than the wide-open, untended goal cage of your own team.

This maneuver is not really as dangerous as it appears, however. Your team has probably lost anyway, and one more goal won't make all that much difference overall. Besides, with an extra man skating on the ice you now have the equivalent of a power play, giving your team a good chance to score and tie the game up. Still, there's that empty net . . .

A high-scoring hockey game is usually no more interesting than a high-scoring baseball game, and indicates either a great imbalance in the levels of skill between the two teams (a common occurrence in the NHL) or simply sloppy play on one or both sides. Sometimes, particularly in high-scoring games, the players and crowd go bananas because one player has just got a "hat trick," that is, he has scored three goals in one game. (Traditionally, the crowd threw their hats on the ice when this occurred.)

CHAPTER 25 FOLLOWING THE GAME

READING ABOUT HOCKEY

Anyone who has watched hockey for any length of time quickly learns that one of the most important criteria for judging a player is the number of "points" he has accumulated.

Points are assigned by the official scorer whenever a goal is made, depending on who actually made the goal and who assisted him with it. Assisting might mean setting up a goal by passing the puck to a man in the slot, or rebounding the puck into the goal. Each goal and each assist is worth one point, but no more than two assists are given for the same goal, and no player receives more than one point on a play.

A player's statistics usually give not only his total number of points, but also the (cumulative) number of goals he has scored in the season. Anything over 25 goals for the season is considered good. Fifty goals is the mark of a superstar. Although forwards have the most chances to score goals, defensemen can score points for goals as well as assists.The exceptionally brilliant defensemen Bobby Orr and Denis Potvin each accumulated over 100 points for a season—a number considered outstanding for a man in any position.

The statistic used to determine a goaltender's effectiveness is the "goals-against" figure, or the average number of goals scored on him per game. Since an average of 3.5 goals is scored by each team per game, a 3.5 goals-against average would be expected. Anything under a 3.0 goals-against average is considered very good, while under 2 would be phenomenal.

Assuming your local newspaper prints hockey statistics (and not all do yet), you will see that statistics are kept for teams as well as players. To get an idea how to read these, look at the final standings of the teams in the NHL on April 10, 1978, as they appeared in the *New York Times* (opposite page).

You read these numbers as follows: G.P.—games played; W— number of games won; L—number of games lost; T—number of games tied; Pts—number of team points.

Team points, which are compiled to determine the relative positions of teams in the league, are figured by doubling the number of wins and adding one point for each tie. These numbers are used in deciding which teams will compete in the play-offs, and in what order. The "goals for and against" figure is used to determine "wild-card" entries in the play-offs, home ice advantage in the games, and to break ties for total number of team points. As you can see from the above ranking, there is quite a variation among the abilities of the teams in the NHL.

If your town has a hockey team the paper will undoubtedly print stories on each game, which you can easily follow once you know the basic terminology; a little more difficult to read is the tabular report of the game. Once interpreted, these reports can give you a pretty good idea of what happened during a game you missed, or clear up any confusion you may have about a game you watched. For example, looking at the report of the April 9 game between Minnesota and Chicago, we can reconstruct a suprising amount of information (see page 272).

The first three numbers show the goals scored in each period by each team; the fourth shows the total for the game. Thus we learn that Chicago, which won 4–2, led in the game throughout the three periods.

FINAL STANDINGS
CAMPBELL CONFERENCE
Patrick Division

	G.P.	W.	L.	T.	Pts.	Goals For	Agst.
*Islanders	80	48	17	15	111	334	210
†Philadelphia	80	45	20	15	105	296	200
†Atlanta	80	34	27	19	87	273	252
†Rangers	80	30	37	13	73	279	280

Smythe Division

*Chicago	80	32	29	19	83	230	220
†Colorado ...	80	19	40	21	59	257	305
Vancouver ...	80	20	43	17	57	239	320
St. Louis	80	20	47	13	53	195	304
Minnesota ...	80	18	53	9	45	218	325

WALES CONFERENCE
Norris Division

*Montreal ...	80	59	10	11	129	359	183
†Detroit	80	32	34	14	78	252	266
†Los Angeles .	80	31	34	15	77	243	245
Pittsburgh ...	80	25	37	18	68	254	321
Washington ..	80	17	49	14	48	195	320

Adams Division

*Boston	80	51	18	11	113	333	218
†Buffalo	80	44	19	17	105	288	215
†Toronto	80	41	29	10	92	271	237
Cleveland	80	22	45	13	57	230	325

*Clinched division title.
†Clinched one-of-eight playoff positions.

The material below the score tells in more detail how the goals were scored and what penalties were given throughout the game. From this information it appears that the third period, although it may not have been well played, was certainly action-packed. The

AT CHICAGO

Minnesota .... 1 0 1—2
Chicago .... 2 1 1—4

First Period—1, Chicago, Marks 14 (Mikita, :19. 2, Minnesota, Younghans 9 (Sharpley, Barrett, 7:14. 3, Chicago, Marks 15, 16:11. Penalties—Boo, Min, major—misconduct; 1:51; Bulley, Chi, major, 1:51; Mc-Gee, Min, 9:43; Rota, Chi, double minor, 15:57, Engele, Min, minor-major, 15:57.

Second Period—4, Chicago, Bulley 23 (Mikita, Boldirev), :57. Penalties—Rota, Chi, 2:25; Logan, Chi, major, 5:01; Younghans, Min, major, 5:01; Rota, Chi, 15:24; Boo, Min, 15:24; Boldirev. Chi, 16:23.

Third Period—5, Minnesota, Butters 1 (Maxwell, Young, 3:03. 6, Chicago, Rota 17 (Boldirev, Hicks), 16:10. Penalties—Bulley, Chi, major, 10:36; Barrett, Min, major, 10:36; Boldirev, Chi, major, 17:18; Bulley, Chi, major, 17:18; Mulvey, Chi, game misconduct, 17:18; Engele, Min, major, 17:18; Boo, Min, 17:18; Bennett, Min, major-misconduct, 17:18.

Shots on goal—Minnesota 13-5-6-24. Chicago 10-11-7-28.

Goalies—Minnesota, LoPresti. Chicago, Esposito. A—10,021.

first significant action was the fifth goal of the game, scored by Butters of Minnesota. The number *1* following his name tells us that this was his first goal of the season. He was assisted in the goal, which occurred three minutes and three seconds into the period, by Maxwell and Young. (The exact time at which a goal is scored is considered important in hockey because many fans, especially in French Canada, bet on this basis.) The sixth and final goal of the game was scored nearly 15 minutes later by Rota, his seventeenth for the year.

Following the information on goals is a listing of penalties and the times at which they were awarded. If there is no explanation, a penalty was a minor one that occurred on the ice. In this particular case it appears that a fight broke out between Bulley and Barrett at 10:36 into the period. Scarcely had Bulley returned to the ice when he got into another fight, this time with Boldirev. Mulvey apparently couldn't resist the temptation to join in and received an automatic game misconduct penalty for being third man into a fight. At this point the altercation turned into a general brawl, resulting in three more major penalties.

By the shots on goal statistics, which are broken down by periods and totals, we see that the most attempts occurred in the first period, the least in the third (presumably everyone was too busy fighting to try to score).

Finally, we read that 10,021 fans watched LoPresti and Esposito defend their respective goals.

IN PERSON OR ON THE TUBE?

There is no doubt that seeing any event in person is more immediately exciting than watching it on TV, whether you understand the sport or not, because a crowd's enthusiasm is contagious. Some people, however, myself included, find the noise of an exciting crowd overpowering—and there is *nothing* noisier than an excited hockey crowd.

Most of the hockey fans I have canvassed agree that the best way to begin watching hockey is to go to games in person with a knowledgeable friend. If this is not possible, you will probably find it easier to follow the game on TV, because the announcers will explain much of the action, and because the instant replay really helps, especially when goals are scored. Unfortunately, the TV camera usually stays with the puck-carrier in a close shot, limiting your view to a portion of the ice and the players in that area.

The rink also tends to look much smaller on TV, which can give a distorted impression of how much action is going on. Furthermore, since many infractions occur away from the immediate vicinity of the puck (and the officials), you won't have any idea how most fights got started.

When you attend a game in person it's a good idea to sit high up in the stands so you can follow the flow of the game. I like to sit in the central part of the sidestands, though many fans prefer to sit behind the goals.

The scoreboard information will vary from arena to arena, but it should tell you the score, the time remaining in the period, which period it is, and the current penalty situation (who is serving, how much time remains on the penalty or penalties). The public-address system will often announce referee calls, but not always, and not all calls. Many knowledgeable fans watch the referee and linesmen signals, although I generally find these difficult to follow. By the time I've found the official and interpreted his sign, the action has moved on and I've missed something.

If you want to try it, the main signals are as follows:

CHARGING
Rotating clenched
fists around one
another in front
of chest.

HOLDING
Clasping either
wrist with the other
hand well in front
of the chest.

DELAYED CALLING OF PENALTY
Referee repeatedly points with free hand (without whistle) to player to be penalized until play is stopped.

SLOW WHISTLE
Either arm, in which whistle is held, extended above head. If play returns to Neutral Zone without stoppage, arm is drawn down the instant the puck crosses with line.

ELBOWING
Tapping either elbow with the opposite hand.

ICING
Arms folded across the chest.

SLASHING
A series of chopping
motions with the
edge of one hand
across the opposite
forearm.

MISCONDUCT
Placing of both
hands on hips
several times and
pointing to
penalized player.

HOOKING
A series of tugging
motions with arms,
as if pulling
something toward
the stomach.

HIGH STICKING
Holding both fists,
clenched, one
immediately above
the other, at the
height of the
forehead.

"WASH OUT"
Both arms swung laterally across the body with palms down:
1. When used by the Referee it means goal disallowed
2. When used by Linesman it means there is no icing or no off-side.

TRIPPING
Extending right leg forward, clear of the ice, and striking it with right hand below the knee.

CROSS-CHECKING
A series of forward and backward motions with both fists clenched extending from the chest.

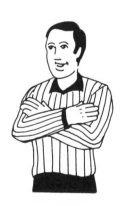

INTERFERENCE
Crossed arms stationary in front of chest.

Listening to hockey on the radio is not as satisfactory as with some sports, but if you have been following the game for a while you won't be thrown by descriptive but jargon-heavy commentary such as, "McGillicuddy deking to the left and feeds to Crumpet; slapped wide and cleared by Cornwall." It takes only a little imagination to transfer these words to a picture of the rink in which McGillicuddy is racing for the net, being vigorously back-checked; he passes the puck to Crumpet for a shot; Crumpet tries a slap shot on goal, which misses wide of the net; the defending player Cornwall now clears the puck out of his own zone. Of course most of the time you won't have any idea where all the players are in relation to each other, but late in the season, especially if your team is a candidate for the play-offs, you can get a lot of hockey excitement on the radio.

So far I've talked about following hockey on TV and radio. But what about the effect these media have on the game itself? As with all other sports, this influence is strong and growing, affecting strategy and tactics and even the rules. For example, although the clock stops briefly whenever the action does and is restarted only at the face-off, hockey has no time-outs as such. Or rather there *were* no time-outs until the 1978–79 season, when the NHL decided to allow one 30-second time-out per game, per team (to be initiated only when the action has stopped for other reasons). Although it was not announced, it is obvious that the purpose of this rule is to make more time for TV and radio commercials, which are now inserted any time there is a "break in the action," and which last for the full 30 or 60 seconds, often slowing the tempo of a game and extending the interruption of the action. Like the new rule forbidding a goalie to freeze the puck, this rule is designed to increase hockey's share of the TV market, and is therefore probably a good thing overall for hockey fans because it will make hockey more widely available. But it will also slow down the game and change it in ways we can't predict. I wouldn't be surprised if a few years from now there are several regular time-outs throughout hockey games.

THE PLAY-OFFS

The National Hockey League is divided into two conferences, the Campbell and the Prince of Wales; these conferences are further subdivided into two divisions: Patrick and Smythe for the Campbell Conference, and Norris and Adams for the Wales. Theoretically these groupings are arranged in such a way that there is an even balance of skill among teams in each division, although in practice it doesn't work out that way.

The ultimate goal for any hockey team is the celebrated Stanley Cup, which is won after a series of games played by the two survivors of the preliminary play-off rounds. The first round, which is set up so that almost every team in the league has a chance to play, is a best two-out-of-three-game contest. The four division winners, plus the next 12 teams with the highest point totals regardless of conference or division, compete in this round. Because each game must be decisive, tied games go into sudden-death overtime, meaning that whichever team scores first in the 20-minute overtime period (or as many subsequent overtimes as necessary) wins the game. If no one scores, another overtime period is played. The winners of the preliminary series now move on to the next round, the quarterfinals (where there are eight teams competing). In this contest, the team with the most team points plays the eighth-ranked team; the team second in points plays the team ranked seventh, and so on. This pairing helps ensure that the good teams don't eliminate each other before the semifinal and final rounds. The semifinals repeat this process, leaving two teams, presumably the two best in the league, victorious and ready to compete for hockey's most valued prize.

AWARDS

Not every team can win the Stanley Cup or even make the play-offs, but outstanding players from any team are eligible for the many awards that are given out at the end of the season. Most of these awards are in the form of a trophy and a cash prize as well. Among the most important of these are:

Art Ross Trophy—given to the player with the highest number of points
Calder Trophy—rookie of the year
Conn Smythe Trophy—most valuable player in the play-offs
Hart Trophy—most valuable player to his team (often the highest scorer)
James Norris Trophy—best defenseman in the league
Lady Byng Trophy—best sportsmanship
Vezina Trophy—best goaltending (given to the team with the fewest goals scored against, and often shared by goalies on the team).

PART 6
SOCCER

SOCCER FACT SHEET

Where played: large grassy field.

Game divisions: two 45-minute halves. No time-outs. Sudden-death overtime in case of tie.

Average duration: one hour and forty-five minutes.

Offense/defense consideration: winner of coin toss chooses either to start on offense or which goal to defend.

Governing body: North American Soccer League (NASL).*

Number of men on the roster: 30.

Equipment: one soccer ball.

Regular season: end of March to early August (followed by play-offs).

TEAMS

NATIONAL CONFERENCE

Eastern Division
New York Cosmos
Rochester Lancers
Toronto Blizzard
Washington Diplomats

Central Division
Atlanta Chiefs
Dallas Tornado
Minnesota Kicks
Tulsa Roughnecks

Western Division
Angeles Aztecs
Portland Timbers
Seattle Sounders
Vancouver Whitecaps

AMERICAN CONFERENCE

Eastern Division
Ft. Lauderdale Strikers
New England Tea Men
Philadelphia Fury
Tampa Bay Rowdies

Central Division
Chicago Sting
Detroit Express
Houston Hurricane
Memphis Rogues

Western Division
California Surf
Edmonton Drillers
San Diego Sockers
San Jose Earthquakes

*Also American Soccer League (ASL). See Part One, page 17.

CHAPTER
26 THE INTERNATIONAL SPORT

In ten years soccer will be the number-one sport in the country.
—PHIL WOOSNAM, commissioner of
the North American Soccer League

Mention soccer almost anywhere in the world and you will likely receive a puzzled look. Mention football, however, and you will undoubtedly be met with enthusiastic smiles and perhaps vigorous discussion of the merits of one country's national football team over another's. This excited reaction won't have anything to do with the game you think of as football, however, but with the most widely played and watched game in the world, known here as soccer.

The fact is that "football" (or futbol) anywhere but in North America means the game that we call soccer. The reason for this has to do with the historical roots of the game. Two centuries ago soccer was played in the British Isles with very much the same rules as the modern game today; that is, by moving a ball with the feet, with no use of hands allowed. In 1823 at the school of Rugby, a dissident player picked up the ball and ran with it. This heresy led to a change in the rules and resulted in the game known today as rugby, and with further modifications in the games of American and Canadian football. Purists continued to play the original game under its original name of football. (The name "soccer," by the way, is a corruption of the abbreviation Assoc., as in the British Football Association.)

During the late nineteenth century and into the twentieth, the original game of soccer began to spread throughout the world until it had become the national sport of nearly 150 nations. The world championship of soccer, the World Cup, is played every four years and creates worldwide nationalistic frenzies that cannot be imagined in this country. Dedicated soccer fans, which means nearly everyone outside of North America, are true fanatics (from which, in fact, the word "fan" derives).

The appeal of soccer is so evident that it's difficult to imagine why it's only now catching on in America, which is surely the most sports-minded country in the world. And catching on it is; in parks and playgrounds everywhere people of all ages are running and kicking that white-and-black soccer ball. Increasingly soccer is being played in high schools and colleges—sometimes as an addition to the athletic curriculum, sometimes as a replacement for more expensive and dangerous sports such as football.

Why are all these people playing soccer? Because it's fun, and simple, and exciting. It requires no equipment beyond a ball and a place to run and kick it. The great Brazilian player Pelé, who is said to be the most widely known person in the world, began playing soccer by kicking an old stuffed sock with his bare feet.

Soccer is easy to learn—it has the least complicated rules of any team sport. There is little violence or physical danger in soccer, yet soccer is ideal for anyone who likes an action-packed game because its very essence is nonstop action. Soccer places no premium on strength and size, rewarding rather agility and endurance—areas in which, by the way, women excel.

As a spectator sport, soccer is unbeatable. There have been professional and semipro teams in the United States throughout this century, but until the last few years they have not been widely popular. In the next pages we'll examine the reasons for pro soccer's slow growth and take a closer look at this remarkable sport, which has finally come to America.

CHAPTER
27 THE BASICS

Soccer is played on a big grassy (or Astroturfed) rectangular field, marked off with horizontal lines, circles, and semicircles. The two short sides of the rectangle, which may be 50 to 100 yards in length, are called the "goal lines"; while the long sides, from 100 to 130 yards, are called "touchlines." At either end of the field is a large cagelike goal, which is made of two upright bars with a bar across the top, and netting covering the back of the goal. In front of the goal a large rectangle, called the "penalty area," is marked off; within it is a smaller rectangle called the "goal area." A semicircle, known as the "penalty arc," extends from the large rectangle toward the middle of the field.

Following is a diagram of a soccer field showing the names given to all the field markings.

Soccer is played between two teams of 11 men each who come onto the field dressed in shorts, jerseys, running shoes, and knee socks. One man from each team, who positions himself in the goal area, is dressed in a uniform colored differently from those of his teammates, and he may be wearing a cap and gloves as well. This man is, not surprisingly, called the goalkeeper or goaltender.

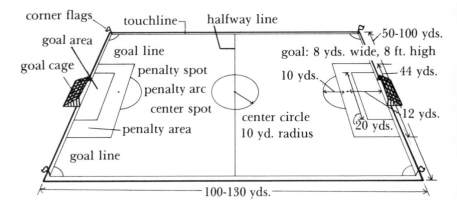

When play is ready to begin the players spread out, each team occupying one half of the field. One man from the team that earlier won the toss of a coin enters the center circle for the "kick off," a short kick of the ball from the center spot to one of his teammates who is just across the halfway line. For the next 45 minutes, the members of both teams will run from one end of the field to the other, kicking the ball as they do, with virtually no stoppage of play.

It will be quickly apparent that each team is trying to propel the ball into the goal of the other team, but the first thing you will probably notice at your first soccer match is that while the players move the ball very effectively from one part of the field to another, they never use their hands. Instead, they kick the ball or run with it, directing its motion with their feet as they run. The first time you see a player do this you will wonder how he can keep the ball going without tripping himself. Even more bizarre, the players bounce the ball off their head. At first this may appear to be accidental, but soon it becomes apparent that use of the head is not only deliberate, but gives a player a great deal of control over where the ball goes. Other parts of the body that are used to control the ball include the thighs and chest.

When the ball goes out of bounds, there is no stoppage of play, but a player from the team that was not responsible for the ball going out of bounds crosses the touchline and, solidly planting both feet, holds the ball high over his head with both hands and throws it in to a teammate, who takes possession of the ball using his feet, head, or chest, and the action immediately begins again, sweeping in the direction of that team's goal.

As play approaches the area of either goal, it generally becomes even faster paced. From time to time play will stop momentarily, then start again with another throw-in from out of bounds or with one of a variety of kicks in the goal area, or from the small semicircles marked just inside each of the four corners of the field. When the ball is kicked directly toward the goal, the goalkeeper springs into action, stopping the ball in any way he can, with legs, body, head— or hands, for the goaltenders are the only ones who are allowed to use their hands in the game, and only when they are in the area of the goal.

Occasionally the ball is placed by an official in front of the goal and an attacking player prepares to kick it in without active opposition. Before he does so, four or more players of the defending team line up, side by side like a kind of human barricade, and face the player, who is about to kick the ball from ten yards away. After the kick, the men instantly spring back into action.

Throughout all of this there will be some body contact, resulting often in players being knocked down, only to be helped up moments later by another player while the action continues. Whenever a goal is scored, which is rarely, the members of the scoring team normally leap into the air and hug one another, then play quickly resumes with a kick by the other team from the center circle. Even if few or no goals score, however, you will probably find yourself caught up in the excitement of the game.

Although the main principles of soccer are immediately clear, you may find yourself puzzled by some aspects of it. Why do those men form a human barricade, for example? And why are they hitting the ball with their head? What is the meaning of those kicks from the corners and goal area?

THE RULES

The rules of soccer are for the most part simple, based on two principles: the aim of the sport is to get the ball into the goal, and there is to be as little physical contact as possible.

I have already mentioned that players (except the goalkeepers) are not allowed to use their hands or arms to maneuver the ball or to restrict their opponents, but they may use any other part of their body as long as they do not make contact with an opponent (with one exception).

The ball may be moved down the field only with the feet or other parts of the body. If a player is running with the ball, keeping close control of it by short kicks from side to side, he is said to be "dribbling" it. He may pass the ball to another player with a kick or with his head, which is known as "heading" the ball. This maneuver is far less dangerous than it looks: not only is the forehead, the area of contact, one of the thickest and strongest bones of the body, but many soccer players work out with weights to develop very strong neck muscles. A shot or a pass made off the forehead is called a "header," and a player who heads well is said to be "strong in the air."

When receiving a pass, a player will often control the ball by first bouncing it up to his chest and then back to his feet where he can begin to dribble, pass, or shoot. Any such action to control a pass is known as "trapping" the ball, and it may be performed with the feet or thighs.

One of the most striking things about soccer is that for all the nonstop action there is remarkably little player contact. The only deliberate contact permitted, in fact, is known as "charging," which is legal only when two players are fighting for possession of the ball. Charging is a shoulder-to-shoulder check from the side.

In addition, players may attempt to steal the ball from another player by using their feet: this maneuver is known as "tackling," and must be done very carefully to avoid kicking or tripping the opponent, which are considered fouls. A player is permitted to tackle from the front, the side, or the rear. Tackling from the rear is a very tricky maneuver, usually used as a desperation measure, because the danger of fouling is so great. In addition, there is a "sliding" tackle, which is usually a last-ditch attempt to take the ball from an offensive player who is running with it toward the goal. In a sliding tackle, the defender judges where the ball will go, then slides into it, generally hoping to knock it out of bounds. If his timing is wrong, he is usually left sprawling on the grass while his opponent dribbles on, unhindered.

Anytime a player causes the ball to go out of bounds, the other team gets possession of the ball. If the out of bounds occurs anywhere *between* the goal lines, the ball is put back into play by a "throw-in," in which a player of the team gaining possession takes the ball in both hands behind his head, then brings it high over his head and, keeping his feet stationary, throws it inbounds to a teammate.

Very rarely, when the referee has to stop the action because of an unusual occurrence such as a serious injury, the ball is put back into play by a "drop ball," in which he simply drops the ball between two opponents. As soon as the ball touches the ground, the players vie for control of it.

KICKING

There are a variety of special kicks used in certain situations. Many of them are used to give possession to the nonoffending team after a violation has been committed. These kicks are as follows:

KICKOFF This is used to begin each half, as well as to award the ball to a nonscoring team after a goal is scored. As with almost all kicks, all players must stand ten yards away from the kicker.

FREE KICK A free kick is a term covering a variety of kicks that may be awarded to a team that has been fouled against. There are two types of free kicks, direct and indirect. A *direct kick* is so named because a goal may be scored directly from this sort of kick; a goal may be scored from an *indirect kick* only if the ball has first been touched by a player (on either team) other than the kicker. Either sort of free kick is taken with the ball lying in a stationary position on the ground, and other players may not touch the ball until it has traveled the length of its own circumference.

During any free kick that is taken within scoring range, the defending players, although they may not interfere with the kicker or the kick, may form a "wall" by linking arms and standing very close to one another in hopes of blocking the kick or reducing the angle of vision of the kicker.

CORNER KICK   A corner kick is a direct free kick awarded to the attacking team when a member of the defense has caused the ball to go out of bounds over the goal lines (but not into the goal). The kick is taken from one of the semicircles at the corners of the field and is usually shot toward the goal mouth. While a goal may be scored directly from a corner kick, usually it is kicked to one of the members of the kicker's team, who must stay at least ten yards away.

GOAL KICK (also called "defense kick")   If a member of the attacking team causes the ball to go out of bounds behind the goal lines, the defense is awarded a goal kick, which is an indirect free kick to clear the ball out of the penalty area.

PENALTY KICK   This is a kick awarded to the offended team for serious infractions. It is a direct free kick taken from the penalty spot, a mark 12 yards in front of the goal. In essence, it is a shot at the goal unimpeded by any defender except the goaltender, who must remain motionless until the kick has been made. A successful penalty kick is known as a "conversion."

Since nearly 50 percent of all goals scored in soccer come from direct and indirect free kicks, penalty kicks, and corner kicks, it is obviously to a team's advantage to commit as few infractions as possible. Following is a summary of the few violations and fouls in soccer and the punishments for each.

VIOLATIONS

There are nine fouls in soccer. Each of them is penalized by the award of a direct free kick to the other side; any of these offenses, if committed *deliberately* within the penalty area by a member of the defending team, is penalized by a penalty kick to the offense. The nine fouls are kicking or attempting to kick an opponent; tripping an opponent; jumping at an opponent; charging an opponent violently; charging an opponent from behind; hitting an opponent; holding an opponent; pushing an opponent; or handling the ball (except for the goalkeeper).

The following offenses are considered somewhat less serious and are punished by the award of an indirect free kick to the offended side. They are: playing in an unfair or dangerous manner— for example, trying to kick at a ball while it is being held by the goalkeeper; charging a player who does not have possession of the ball; intentionally obstructing an opponent (standing in front of an opponent to physically prevent his forward movement); and charging the goalkeeper, unless he is holding the ball or is outside the goal area.

For "serious misconduct," such as leaving the field while the game is in progress; repeatedly committing violations; arguing with the referee; or committing "ungentlemanly conduct," the offending player is given a "yellow card" by the referee and the other team may be awarded a free kick as well. A yellow card is a warning; upon the next such offense, the player is given a "red card" and ejected from the game, and his team may not make a substitution for him.

A player is ejected immediately without a warning if he plays violently or uses foul language, or commits a second misconduct offense. When a player has been ejected from the game, play resumes with an indirect free kick to the other side.

Except for serious misconduct, penalties are not enforced rigidly in soccer, because of something known as the "advantage rule." This rule gives the referee leeway, allowing him to ignore a violation if its enforcement would be to the advantage of the offending team. For example, suppose a member of the Bumblebees kicks the ball into the Grasshoppers' goal mouth, and a Grasshopper player (not the goalie) tries unsuccessfully to deflect the ball with his hands. Instead of disallowing the goal and awarding a free kick to the Bumblebees, the referee would ignore the illegal use of hands and allow the goal to stand. If the advantage rule does not apply, all penalties are enforced.

ACTION NEAR THE GOAL

The only other important rules in soccer concern play near the goal area. They have to do with player position and actions by the goalkeeper.

OFFSIDE   One of the few restrictions on player movement within the field is known as the "offside" rule, which is different under international and NASL rules (see page 313, Chapter Twenty-nine). The offside rule in American soccer is that a player is not allowed to receive a pass from a teammate inside the opposition's 35-yard line *unless* there are two defenders between him and the goal (one of these defenders is the goalkeeper). If he receives the ball here by any other means, the offside rule does not apply. When a team commits offsides, the opposition is awarded an indirect free kick.

The offside rule seems very simple and it is—except to a player in the heat of a game. As Jack Feuer, a writer specializing in soccer, explains, "It usually happens on a fast breakaway down to the goal area, when it's hard to keep in mind who is where all the time. Here you are racing toward the goal, and all of a sudden the whistle blows and everything comes to a dead stop. Then the other team gets the ball and you have to start all over. I'll tell you what offside is, it's the destruction of a golden opportunity."

ACTIONS BY GOALKEEPER   Whenever the goalkeeper stops the ball in his own penalty area, he has the option of kicking the ball from there deep into enemy territory (downfield), or of throwing or kicking it to a teammate. The only restriction is that once he has taken possession of the ball he is allowed to take only *four* steps; if he takes more, the opposition is awarded an indirect free kick. Sometimes you will see a goalie get around this rule by setting the ball on the ground while he surveys the situation, then picking it up again; or he may quickly pass the ball to a teammate and then take it back again before his kick.

On the following pages are some of the more common referee signals in soccer.

INDIRECT FREE KICK

DIRECT FREE KICK

PENALTY KICK
The referee indicates
the penalty mark.

GOAL KICK

CORNER KICK

CAUTION OR EXPULSION

A yellow card serves as
a warning to the player;
a red card indicates expulsion.

OFFSIDE

THROW-IN

PLAY ON—ADVANTAGE

If the referee invokes
the advantage rule, he indicates that
play is to continue.

SCORING

Each goal scored in soccer is worth one point. As a rule soccer is a very low-scoring game, and in international matches ties of 0-0 are common. In the NASL, because it is believed that fans do not enjoy seeing tied games, an elaborate tie-breaking system has been devised that works like this: If a match ends tied there is a sudden-death overtime period of seven and a half minutes; whenever either team scores, the game is over. If no goals are scored by the end of the overtime period, it is followed by another such overtime. If no goal has been scored at the end of this, play proceeds to the "shoot-out," which is wholly an NASL invention. The shoot-out is a little silly in conception but rather exciting to watch. Five players from each team are chosen to challenge the opposing goalkeeper without any intervening players. The players are given the ball at the 35-yard line and then have five seconds each to take a shot, which the goalie tries to block. The side that scores the most goals wins. If the score is still tied after a shoot-out, further shoot-outs are held until one side or the other has won.

THE MEN ON THE FIELD

Player positions are less rigid in soccer than in the other team sports, and can best be described by reference to the three areas of the field where the players' primary responsibilities lie—backfield, or the area nearest the team's own goal; midfield; and front field, the area nearest the opponents' goal. Although all players are responsible for both offense and defense, depending on possession of the ball, the three groups of players are loosely divided into defensive and offensive categories. These groups are the backfield men (defensive); the front field men (offensive); and the midfield men (overlapping responsibilities).

The players in the backfield are referred to as fullbacks or simply "backs," and there are usually four of them (though there may be more or fewer, depending on the philosophy of the team's coach). If there are four backs, they are usually called right back, right center back, left center back, and left back. On some teams an extra backfield man called a "sweeper" plays behind the line of fullbacks close to the goalie.

The backfield men try to keep the ball and the opposition players from getting close to their goal area, and to prevent scoring when the other team does break through.

The men on the front line, of whom there are usually three, are called forwards or strikers. The two men on the ends of the line are sometimes called left and right winger or flanker, while the man in the middle may be called the central striker or targetman. These players are primarily concerned with attempting to score goals, and they are usually the fastest men on the team.

Between these two lines of men are the midfield men, who serve as a link between the offensive and defensive lines, and who are ready to help their teammates on either offense or defense. They are known variously as halfbacks, midfielders, and linkmen, and since there are usually three of them they are further subdivided into right, central, and left. The midfield men generally cover the area of the field from their own 18-yard line to the opposing 18-yard line.

There are three substitutions per team allowed in the North American Soccer League; once a man has left the game, however, he may not reenter. If a player is expelled from the game for unsportsmanlike conduct his team is not allowed to replace him and must play one man short.

Because a soccer match is played in two 45-minute periods, with no time-outs, and since so few substitutions are allowed, a soccer player must be in top-notch condition. Sometimes the team with better endurance will win the match through a kind of attrition.

The 22 players on the field are controlled by three officials: a referee and two linesmen. The referee in soccer has a great deal more responsibility than referees in most sports; in addition to controlling the game and serving as final arbiter in disputes, he is also responsible for keeping time during the game (and deciding whether to stop the clock on the very few occasions that warrant it in soccer). He is assisted in his duties by the two linesmen, and will take their word in any plays that he did not see clearly. The linesmen are primarily responsible for indicating which side is responsible when the ball goes out of bounds; they do this by raising a small flag that they carry.

Officiating a soccer game may sound like an almost impossible job—after all, football, with the same number of men on the field as soccer, has no fewer than seven officials—but in fact, because there is so little contact in soccer and because the rules are essentially simple, there are seldom disputes or plays requiring a complicated decision.

There is very little else to know about soccer. In the next chapter we'll take a look at the skills and strategy that make it such an exciting sport to watch.

CHAPTER
28 BEHIND THE ACTION

To a first-time American soccer observer, the fact that the players don't use their hands may seem not only strange but inefficient. And yet good soccer players are able to control the ball with every bit as much skill and accuracy as other athletes can be using their hands. One of the most thrilling aspects of watching soccer, in fact, is observing the pinpoint control the players have over the ball. A truly great player can not only propel the ball exactly where he wants it to go, either over the heads of the defenders or through a running group of them, but can also sometimes anticipate where a teammate will be to receive a pass. When you are watching this sort of play it seems unbelievable: the player will kick toward a knot of defenders, and then mysteriously a "hole" will open up in the line of defense, allowing the ball to pass through just in time for the player's teammate to trap it and begin running. Players who are able to consistently anticipate the movement of the players around them, as well as to control the ball accurately, seem to possess an almost extrasensory ability, which is sometimes called "soccer sense." The greatest soccer players do not really possess superhuman abilities, of course, but rather a combination of unusual talent and years of hard work in perfecting basic soccer skills.

We have already seen that the ball can be controlled by use of the thighs, chest, and head. It is with the feet, however, that soccer players maneuver the ball most of the time.

The basic soccer kick is delivered with the instep of the foot rather than with the toe, as in American football, because an instep kick is easier to control and aim. In this sort of kick the ball is propelled from the area of the shoe where the shoelaces cross. The other two basic techniques used in kicking are the "outside kick," which comes off the outside edge of the foot, and the "inside kick," which is delivered from the inside of the foot. The instep and outside kicks are most powerful and are used for long passes and shots at goal; the inside kick is considered most accurate, and is usually used for short passes.

Using these and some other techniques, players can deliver a variety of kicks adapted to the rapidly changing game situation.

Among these are the "chip," a short pass, which goes up and over a defender or defenders, and a "volley" kick, which is any kick delivered while the ball is still in midair.

The most exciting kicks in soccer, however, are specialty kicks, which are used in specific situations, and which may be referred to by announcers under a variety of names.

The "banana kick," for example, is so called because it curves in midair. It is usually used when a player is taking a direct free kick at the goal. The idea is to get the ball to curve in toward the goal mouth from a corner kick, or around the "wall" of players stationed in front of the kicker. Even if the ball doesn't go into the goal from such a kick, its curving motion can draw the goalie away from the goal mouth, allowing a teammate of the kicker to then take a shot at goal.

The most spectacular kick you are likely to see is known variously as a "scissors kick," "bicycle kick," or "overhead volley." It is made when a player receives a pass at about chest or shoulder height. Leaping up, he kicks the ball backward over his own head, and usually ends up on his back on the ground. This is one of the most powerful kicks and is usually used either to take a shot at goal (the player is facing away from the goal in the goal area), or to clear the ball quickly from his own goal area.

An exciting variant of an overhead kick, which is sometimes seen in top international play, occurs when a player is being guarded ("marked") very closely by an opponent and kicks the ball over his own head, whirls, controls his own pass, then runs on leaving the bewildered defender behind.

SYSTEMS OF PLAY

Because soccer is such a fluid game, it has very few set plays. For the same reason, it has fewer set formations than does its American cousin, football. Instead, soccer strategy relies on a number of "systems," or loose formations.

Soccer has only been played internationally in the last century, but in that time its general strategy has undergone vast transformations (although there have been very few changes in the rules). In the early days of soccer, most of the emphasis was put on offense, and the front field line might consist of as many as eight forwards, leaving only two men to guard the midfield and rear. Gradually the balance of the game shifted, the style becoming ever more defensive. Then there were formations described as 5-3-2 (the backfield number is always given first; thus this formation would consist of five backs, three midfield men, and two forwards). Such a defensive setup made penetration into the goal area very difficult, and it also tended to lead to a very low scoring, stalemated type of game. In modern soccer there is growing reliance on "total" soccer. The idea is that each player is theoretically capable of playing any position on the field, so offensive and defensive assignments are not as clear-cut as in the old days. The concept of total soccer allows men to switch positions when necessary, and because of this any player can score, just as any player can defend.

Although many formations are used by the top teams today, one of the most common is 4-2-4, in which there are four backfield men, four forwards, and two linkmen. The purpose of this formation is to provide maximum flexibility, and what it means in practice is that at any given moment there are potentially six men on offense or on defense, with the remaining four men ready to help out. This fluid concept requires players who are in top-notch physical condition and skillful enough to play at any position.

Whenever you are watching a game, you can get a good idea of the team's strategic philosophy if you count the men in each field position. If there are more forwards than backfield men, the coach is interested in a vigorous, chancy, attacking game; the fewer forwards, the more defensive-minded he is.

OFFENSE

Soccer is usually very easy to follow by anyone who is already familiar with basketball or hockey, because many of the tactics and the basic strategy it uses are the same. The general idea of any team on offense is to get the ball into the opponents' penalty area, where it may be possible to take a shot at goal. The fastest way to do this is with a series of long passes, but this is also the most dangerous way, because a long pass gives the defense time to react and intercept the pass. Likewise, it is dangerous for a player to dribble the ball a long way down the field, because the longer he has the ball the more vulnerable he is to being tackled and having the ball taken away from him.

Therefore, teams usually move the ball by a combination of dribbling and shorter passing. The idea is always to get the ball to a man who is open, or relatively so. A corollary of this is for the men who do not have the ball to try to run toward an area where they will be free. By a series of feints and deceptive maneuvers such a player can elude the defender marking him long enough to receive and perhaps return a pass. This is known as "running off the ball" and is a cornerstone of good soccer offense.

When passing, a player learns to aim either directly at a teammate or for the spot he is running to. While it might seem that the easiest pass would be to a teammate who is running alongside (a "square pass"), this is considered a risky maneuver and is usually used only when a defender is about to tackle the passer. The majority of passes in pro soccer are aimed diagonally ahead or behind. When a team is running and passing well, the intricacy of passing can be breathtaking to watch.

With 20 men moving on the field, there is often a great deal of congestion. Getting through these traffic jams requires split-second timing, fine technique, and close cooperation of all teammates. A good example of this sort of play is the maneuver known as the "wall pass."

In performing the wall pass, a player with the ball who finds his path blocked by an opponent kicks the ball to a teammate, then accelerates quickly around the defender to receive a quick return pass from the teammate. In effect the teammate has acted as a "wall" off which the pass is deflected. This tactic is sometimes also known as "give and go."

Many other offensive plays in soccer develop from the talents of the particular men on a team. For example, a team that has a very fast winger will try to get the ball to him in an open area. The winger then races down the edge of the field, eluding all defenders, and quickly centers the ball to a striker who then heads it into the goal.

It is in the goal area, by the way, that heading is used most effectively both by offense and defense. A very high pass is often headed into the goal by a striker who takes a long leap upward at the ball, controlling it with his head before any defending man can reach it. It is for this reason that the tallest man on any team is usually one of the center fullbacks: His height may give him an edge in heading that ball away from the goal area before the striker is able to take his shot.

DEFENSE

There are two types of defense in soccer: man-to-man and zone. In a man-to-man defense, one man is responsible for marking a specific opponent on the opposite team (for example, center back against striker). In a zone defense, each man is responsible for a given area of the field, though the area shifts as the offensive team comes deeper into the defensive zone. In practice, most teams use a combination of man-to-man and zone, with players feeling free to move over if a teammate needs help. If an attacking player manages to evade the man marking him, it is common for the closest defender to immediately leave his own man and cover the escaped attacking man. The temporarily freed offensive man will be quickly picked up by someone else.

As with offensive play, then, players' responsibilities are constantly shifting as they respond to the changing conditions of the game. However, just as with offensive play, it is considered important for defenders to maintain position on the field. This means that left back, for example, must remain on the left side of the field toward the touchlines; a central man does not roam too far toward the edge of the field. This is important not only in covering zones, but also because all players must have a good idea where their teammates are at a given time. If a defender suddenly intercepts a pass but is about to be tackled, he needs to know that he can rely on a teammate to be in his own area and not somewhere clear across the field.

The best way for the defense to prevent the attackers from scoring is to take the ball away and start a counteroffensive. Interceptions and tackling are the most common ways of doing this. Sometimes the defense receives the ball by catching an attacking player in an "offside trap," which works like this: Since the man receiving the ball is not allowed to have fewer than two defenders between him and the goal at the time the pass is directed to him, the last backfield man can run past a potential receiver who will then be caught offside when the pass is delivered. An obvious drawback to this maneuver is the danger that something may go wrong, leaving the goalie alone to defend the goal.

Which brings us to the most important man on defense. The goalkeeper in soccer has a most difficult job. While there are usually teammates in the goal area to assist him, it is ultimately the goalie's responsiblity to stop the ball from going into the net. In performing this duty the goalkeeper is allowed to fall on the ball, head it, kick it, hold it, throw it, deflect it with his hands—in short, to stop it in any way possible. Watching a good goalkeeper at work is something like watching a gravity-defying acrobat. There will be times when a shot taken at goal seems almost certain to go in, then out of nowhere the goalkeeper arrives, diving, leaping, twisting his body in midair, and somehow managing to stop the ball. A great soccer save is one of the most thrilling sights in all of sports.

After you have been watching soccer for a while, you will realize that the goalkeeper also functions as an important member of the offense. Whenever he takes possession of the ball in his own penalty area, he decides how and where to put it back into play. Whether he employs a long goal kick or simply passes to a teammate to start the counterattack, the goalie functions as a sort of field general, directing his team's total play. Another way in which the goalkeeper assists the offensive men is by serving as a refuge. You will often see a soccer team start to mount an attack from their own penalty area, then suddenly return the ball to the goalie. This is usually done when the offense cannot get a good attack going for some reason and needs to retreat ("funnel back") before continuing on the attack.

Some of the plays we've been talking about won't be easy for you to see at your first game, especially if you are watching on television, but the overall flow of the game is so clear and easy to follow that you will immediately understand why soccer is the most popular sport in the world.

In the next chapter are tips on watching soccer and a look at why it has taken so long to become a major American sport.

CHAPTER 29 FOLLOWING THE GAME

READING ABOUT SOCCER

The biggest difficulty in reading about soccer is that until very recently there were few books about the sport and it received (and still receives) only minimal coverage in most American newspapers and sports magazines. Furthermore, because soccer is still so "new" to this country, there is often a confusion of terms in referring to player positions and field markings. (For example, "touchline" and "sideline" are used interchangeably. "Touchline" is of course the correct term, as used in international play, but "sideline" is more easily understood by new American soccer fans.) Still, if you understand soccer terminology, there should be little difficulty in following an account of a match: "The goal was scored on a quick kick to the winger Lopez for a fast break down the touchline, then a center was headed in by Gearry." What happened here was that the kickoff pass went to Lopez, a winger standing near the touchline; Lopez ran quickly down to the goal area and centered the ball with a pass to the striker Gearry, who put it into the goal with a head shot.

Keeping track of your team in soccer presents more of a problem because NASL teams are not ranked merely on the basis of the number of games won and lost, but rather on their total number of "points." This ranking system came about for two reasons. One of these is that traditionally (and this is still true in other parts of the world) soccer teams were ranked the same way hockey teams are; that is, a team was given two points for a win, one point for a tie, and no points for a loss. The points were added together and the teams then ranked in order. In the early days of the NASL, ties were eliminated (although the rival soccer league, the American, allows ties and uses the traditional method of ranking).

Once ties were eliminated it would seem that teams could easily be ranked according to their won-lost records, but the NASL promoters perceived yet another problem: soccer was becoming too defense-oriented. In an effort to reward higher scores, then, a system of ranking teams that provided an incentive for more scoring was made up, and this is how it works. A win in soccer counts as six points, while a loss counts for nothing. However, win or lose, each team in a match is eligible to receive up to three "bonus points" for goals scored. All teams are then ranked in order of total points, which are wins times six plus bonus points.

For example, suppose the Cosmos beat the Tampa Bay Rowdies by a score of 2-1. The Cosmos would receive eight points: six for the win plus two bonus points, while the Rowdies would receive one point. Likewise, if the score is 8-7, the Cosmos would receive nine points (the maximum allowed per game), while Tampa Bay gets three (the maximum number of bonus points).

Team statistics in soccer are broken down in the papers as follows: W—wins; L—loss; BP—number of bonus points given; Pts—total points (wins times six plus bonus points); GF—total number of goals scored by the team; GA—total number of goals scored against the team.

Players are likewise ranked in soccer, on the basis of goals scored, assists given, and total number of points. The goals scored figure goes to a player who scores a goal directly (kicks or heads the ball in); an assist is given to any player (a maximum of two players per goal) whose actions *indirectly* resulted in the goal—that is, who passed the ball or otherwise helped to set it up. In figuring a player's total points, double the number of goals and add his assists. Thus, a player who has scored 12 goals with 6 assists receives a point total of 30.

Goalkeeper statistics include the number of minutes played; the number of saves made (to be counted as a save, a shot must be taken directly at the goal); the number of goals scored against the goalie; and the number of his shutouts (games in which no goals were scored against him). The goalie's "average" is a three-figure decimal showing the average number of goals scored against him per game; anything under .200 is considered excellent.

SOCCER ON TV AND RADIO

The features of soccer that make it such an exciting and easy-to-follow sport are, unfortunately, responsible for limiting its coverage on television. While a virtually nonstop sport is thrilling for spectators, it is a good deal less than that for commercial television sponsors.

There are no convenient places in a soccer game to insert commercials, except between the halves. It has been suggested that commercials could be clustered before and after the game and at halftime, but such an idea would almost certainly be rejected by advertisers. In an article in *Sports Illustrated,* columnist Jack McCallum suggests with tongue in cheek the introduction of a "designated invalid" on each team who would fake a serious injury each time a commercial break was needed. In point of fact, something like this was tried during the 1967 season (before the formation of the NASL): the referee was equipped with a walkie-talkie that told him when to fake a delay of game or call an imaginary infraction so that a commercial could be inserted. Needless to say, this chicanery was stopped as soon as it became public knowledge.

Other possible solutions include such space-age concepts as playing a commercial in a corner of the screen while the action goes on, or even—and this must be viewed as a last resort—tampering with the laws of soccer and introducing regular time-outs.

Whatever is ultimately done to make soccer more attractive to sponsors, at present the commercials are simply shown during the game, *while it is going on.*

This is not done randomly, of course. As a rule commercials are inserted when there are real injuries, or during goal kicks, when a team has just begun on the attack and presumably will need some time to reach the opposition goal area. Nevertheless, a lot of action is missed this way, and—worse—goals are sometimes missed. It's true that since soccer is such a low-scoring game few goals score during commercials, but by the same token any goal is extremely important, because it is so infrequent. Furthermore, it's disorienting to suddenly cut away in the middle of the action and then return to a game where everything has changed and not really have any idea how it got that way.

In any case, in the next few years you will have more opportunities to watch soccer: in 1979 the NASL signed a limited contract with ABC to broadcast nine games live. Furthermore, European and South American matches are broadcast on public television in many parts of this country (without commercials).

Because of the limited TV coverage available and because of the interrupted nature of that coverage, for a real soccer fan her radio is her best friend. As with the other team sports, coverage on radio is far more detailed and expert than on TV. And, if you listen to the game on radio while you watch on TV, you'll be able to follow the action continuously or nearly so, because commercials on radio and TV don't usually coincide.

Because of the nature of soccer as a pattern game, with the interaction of team members generally more important than the precise details of what is happening to the ball, most fans prefer to sit near midfield, high up in the stands. This is also the best view for television, and is the TV perspective for the foreign soccer games that are made available in this country. While it's true that you can't always distinguish individual players (until you have become very familiar with their styles of play), the ball is quite visible from above, and the action that ranges over the entire field is relatively easy to follow.

Unfortunately, American TV directors seem to prefer to move in closer on the field, showing the individual players and following the ball. This cuts off most of the developments elsewhere on the field and makes it difficult to see what is happening except for one small part of the action. For this reason alone, it is better to go to soccer games in person if you possibly can. The final problem with watching soccer on television is again the confusion about terminology and names for player positions. Undoubtedly most of these problems will disappear as soccer grows more popular and the media become more accustomed to reporting it.

PLAY-OFFS

There are at present 24 teams in the American soccer league, but plans are to expand to as many as 40 within the next five years. The NASL is divided into two conferences, the National and the American, with each conference further subdivided into three divisions—East, Central, and West, containing four teams each. At the end of the season there is a series of play-offs culminating in the one-game "Soccer Bowl." One unfortunate aspect of the soccer play-offs and championship is that if a game is tied, it goes to a shoot-out, the artificial tie-breaking system used only in the NASL—hardly a satisfactory way to determine a champion. Or, as one radio announcer commented, "It's like the whole season comes down to five penalty kicks."

Since the American soccer season goes from March to August, with the play-offs extending into September, the players must often perform in weather that is less than ideal for such a strenuous sport. In one of the final games of the soccer play-offs in 1978, the two championship teams were forced to play in 87-degree heat with high humidity and pollution caused by a stagnant air mass. For days before the match, in fact, the air had been described as "unhealthy." This particular game went not only into the two overtime periods but also to two shoot-outs. In all the players were on the field for nearly two hours, and their fatigue became evident toward the end of the game, as they began noticeably to slow down and to pass inaccurately. Although the playing conditions were unavoidable, what the fans saw that night couldn't be classed as championship level soccer.

A main determining factor for scheduling the NASL season in hot weather is the fact that many of the top players in the NASL, particularly those from Great Britain, are only "borrowed" and must be able to return abroad where their soccer season begins in a more sensible month, September.

Which brings us to the heart of this discussion: the state of soccer in the United States.

THE AMERICANIZATION OF SOCCER

Because soccer is still largely an imported sport, the NASL has a rule that there must be a minimum of eight American citizens on the roster of 18 players for each team and, further, that there must be three Americans playing on the field at all times. (This number will be increased to four in 1982 and five in 1984.)

What this rule means is that the majority of players on a team may be foreign-born, and that eight out of the 11 active players during a match may also be foreign. Furthermore, since the NASL rule about American citizenship applies to Canadians and naturalized foreign citizens, it is possible to field an entire team that plays for an American city and is paid in American money without one American player on the team.

Almost all observers agree that if soccer is to truly catch on in this country, the number of native American players at the pro level must be increased as soon as possible. This is, in fact, the basis for one of two serious controversies that arise from soccer's international status, and that threaten the viability of pro soccer in this country.

The first controversy stems from the small number of American players in the NASL relative to the number of Europeans. The NASL coaches, most of whom are Europeans, reason that there simply aren't enough Americans of professional caliber. And this is because, even though Americans may be able to learn basic soccer skills, they do not have the years of training that makes it as instinctive for a European or South American player to kick and head the ball as it is for an American to catch and throw it with his hands.

According to American players, the difficulty is not so much that Americans are not good as that they are not given a chance to play by the European-trained coaches, who prefer to use their own countrymen. In an interview in *Sport* magazine, Dan Counce, an American-born forward, put the matter simply: "We're seldom judged as soccer players—only as *American* soccer players." And American soccer players, by the rest of the world's standards, simply aren't up to par. This judgment is in many ways reminiscent of the argument commonly expressed by some men that female athletes are not good, whether or not they have ever seen women play a sport.

Shep Messing, another American-born player who, with his flamboyant personality, is our first native superstar, feels that the very training of Americans may ultimately work for them: "Americans make great goalies in soccer because they have the hand-eye coordination since childhood," he told *Sport.* "Pelé saw that too. He told me that the first of the world-class Americans he expected to see would be 'keepers.' "

There is a kind of vicious circle at work here. Soccer writer Jack Feuer admits that American players are not as good as foreign players. But unless more Americans can get experience playing in professional games, they will not develop into top-notch players no matter how good their basic skills. And until they can perform on a top international level, their chances for playing time will be limited. The American Soccer League Player's Association, which by the way is *not* recognized by the NASL owners, and which is made up mostly of native-born players, recognizes this dilemma, and successfully petitioned the U.S. Labor Department to reduce the number of foreign players permitted to enter the United States in the 1979 season from 264 to 220. This was made possible by a law that prohibits the Labor Department from granting visas to foreign workers in any field if such a worker would affect jobs for Americans.

Because there are so few American superstar players, however, this visa restriction does not apply to such men as Franz Beckenbauer, formerly one of the German national team's greatest players and now with the Cosmos, who is allowed into the country on a special visa.

Well, so what? you might say. Why not play soccer with Americans, even if there aren't many superior players. Or why not continue to play with all-foreign teams? After all, aren't most hockey players Canadian?

This is a good point, except for two things. One is that the owners of the NASL teams have a lot of money invested in them. Mediocre teams of Americans will not attract large crowds the way exciting teams of foreign superstars will. More important, the true appeal of soccer in the United States or in any country, and the main reason that soccer could become our number-one sport, is that it is the only sport that is in fact international and that can be played on a wholly international level.

It is the international status of soccer that lies behind the second major controversy in the NASL, the one whose resolution will probably determine the fate of soccer in the United States.

NASL, FIFA, AND USSFA

It is obvious to anyone who has watched both games that soccer in the United States is not like soccer elsewhere. As Larry Merchant put it in his column in the *New York Times*, "Having seen major-league soccer abroad, with its raging color and emotion and tempo, I found [American soccer] to be weak, lukewarm tea."

Since there is no tradition of soccer in this country, American owners have tried to mold an unfamiliar sport into something more recognizable. Electronic scoreboards, scantily clad cheerleaders, and even deliberate changes in the rules of the game have all been introduced. If you watch world-class soccer, you will seldom see a player question an official decision. In NASL soccer, long, drawn-out arguments between players and referees are common—because they are common in the other American sports. While this may be American, to purists it is not soccer—or, as one exasperated announcer remarked in the 1978 season during a game that had been delayed repeatedly because of conflicts between the officials and the players, "This is ridiculous—it's like a basketball game."

The attempts to "Americanize" soccer would not really matter much once we develop top-caliber native players, except for one very important thing, and that is the existence of FIFA. This acronym stands for Federation Internationale de Football Association, the worldwide governing body for soccer, which has nearly 150 member nations, and which oversees all international competition culminating in the World Cup of Soccer every four years.

As the international governing body, FIFA makes all major decisions concerning the sport, and one of these decisions is that soccer rules must be the same in all member nations. It is here that the NASL is in potential trouble, because of the two rules changes it initiated to make soccer a higher scoring sport.

The first of these rules changes is the introduction of the tie-breaking shoot-out, though this doesn't really bother FIFA because it doesn't actually affect the structure of the game as played. What is really serious to FIFA is the NASL's offside rule, which states that a player is offside if he receives a pass with fewer than two defenders between him and the goal anywhere beyond the 35-yard "blue line" of his opponent. In international soccer, the offside rule applies to receiving a pass *anywhere* in the defenders' half of the field. The more restrictive international rule sharply limits the opportunities for offensive penetration into the penalty area, thus reducing scoring opportunities.

The 35-yard offside rule was originally instituted in 1973, with the permission of FIFA, strictly as an "experiment" to increase scoring. While the experiment worked out to the satisfaction of American fans and owners, apparently FIFA had second thoughts, and it has threatened serious action: in an ultimatum delivered in the early part of 1979, the governing body of FIFA has told the NASL that its teams must return to the original rules of the game. If they don't, the United States will be officially suspended from FIFA, which means that the United States will be ineligible to compete in World Cup competition, in Olympic competition, or in any other internationally sanctioned soccer.

This would be a disaster for soccer in the United States, because without the opportunity for U.S. teams to compete against very good players from other countries, our chances of ever developing to world-class caliber will be nil. The United States Soccer Football Association (USSFA), which sanctions the NASL, apparently has little to say in the matter: FIFA simply wants the NASL to buckle under. Possibly some sort of compromise can be worked out whereby NASL soccer will continue to be played under the present rules but all school and amateur soccer will be made to conform to strictest international standards. In any case, it is important to work something out, because, quite apart from the appeal of soccer itself as a sport, the ultimate goal of all Americans interested in the sport has to be participation in the World Cup.

THE WORLD CUP

Baseball's World Series is not, as so many detractors like to point out, a misnomer, because it usually does in fact come down to the two best baseball teams in the world playing against one another—it's just that both teams happen to be American because American-caliber baseball is not played anywhere else. Likewise, the football Super Bowl *is* super and is probably played by the two best football teams (American football, that is), simply because there aren't any teams of comparable quality anywhere else.

The World Cup of Soccer, however, is a true world championship, played between two of the best (there is always some dispute about whether the two *very* best always make the finals) teams chosen from countries all over the world. Each of the FIFA member nations stages competitions to pick the best national team; then there are regional championships among neighboring countries. At the end of the four-year selection process, which is followed fanatically by fans in soccer-playing countries, only 16 teams are left. And these are made up of the very best of the best soccer athletes in the world.

To most of the rest of the world, in fact, the World Cup is at least as important as—if not more so than—the Olympics as a test of national athletic prowess, because in a way it is a truer test. After all, the athletes are all playing the same game, and while one or two countries might predominate in the number of Olympic gold medals won, there is never any one overall victor at the Olympics, since such a variety of sports are played and since all countries don't enter all events or excel at all of them.

Even in non-World Cup years soccer seems to generate a kind of hysteria among fans that is unmatched by any other sport. The term "soccer riot" was coined to describe the occasional eruption of this hysteria into violence. In the worst such incident 318 people were killed in a riot that erupted at the end of a soccer match between the Peruvian and Argentinian Olympic teams. While World Cup play does not commonly lead to riots, there is no question that it stirs up nationalistic passions in a way unmatched by any other activity except war. In fact, Lowell Miller, writing in the *New York Times Magazine*, describes the World Cup as a kind of "world war, organized, transformed, sublimated."

Although the 1978 World Cup matches were not broadcast on American television (except for a few local stations, which carried some games on a feed direct from Argentina, where the finals were held), all finals matches were telecast on closed-circuit TV in large arenas all over the country. Almost all of these games, wherever they were held, were sold out, as transplanted fans from other countries jammed the theaters to see first-class soccer played—and to root for their own national teams. A Frenchman I know went to see his national team play a South American team on closed circuit at Madison Square Garden. As he explained later, he had to keep his pro-French cheers to himself, because all of the Latin Americans in New York had turned out to root for the South Americans.

The United States has remained relatively oblivious to the World Cup throughout its 48-year history, although we have fielded teams since the 1940s and even reached the finals in 1950. Since then our teams have not done particularly well, but the U.S. National Team is training with an eye toward making the 1982 World Cup finals—which is not beyond the realm of possibility if, as Jared

Lebow speculates in *All About Soccer,* FIFA allows 32 rather than 16 nations into the final round. It will undoubtedly be much longer before the United States can hope to produce a team that has a chance of actually winning the World Cup. There is one further way in which Americans could hope to compete in the finals for the World Cup, one which would assure soccer's future in America but which depends in part on the NASL and USSFA making peace with FIFA, and this would be to host the World Cup. The earliest that this could occur would be 1990, and it would ensure our participation in the matches because the previous winner and the host country are both automatically put into the finals.

Ultimately, then, the future of the NASL depends on the United States participating on an international level in the sporting passion that has dominated most of the world for most of this century. From all signs, the time for that participation has finally arrived.

AFTERWORD
Having Fun with Sports

ON BEING A FAN

One of the most traumatic evenings of my life occurred when I was seventeen years old and my high school basketball team was in the finals for the state championship. I had been following the team avidly, knew most of the players personally, and went to every single game. The week before the final game, however, I dislocated my jaw and my mouth was wired shut. Far worse than the pain or the inability to eat anything solid was the helpless feeling I experienced as I sat in the third row watching the close game, unable to cheer. To this day I'm convinced that my inability to urge my team on was at least partly responsible for its narrow defeat.

As it happens, I did not like my high school; most of my friends and all of the boys I dated were from other schools in the town. And yet I was a dedicated fan of that basketball team. It would no more have occurred to me to root for Tucson High than to attend biology lab there.

Much has been written about athletes as surrogates for the rest of us: They are our champions, our Davids going out after Goliaths, or our Goliaths taking on the brash young upstarts. I believe this is because sports appeal directly to our sense of community loyalty. I may not have liked Catalina High School, but it was *my* turf, and *my* basketball team was defending it against all challengers, just as the champions of a tribe of cavemen might, tens of thousands of years ago, have fought off invading Neanderthals.

It is this sense of almost tribal loyalty that marks a true fan. A fan identifies with a team and follows it through good times and bad. The game itself is important, of course, and many fans do become experts on sports, but the emphasis in fandom is above all on participation. Fans wear their team colors to a game; they collect baseball cards and game programs; they are ready to take on the followers of rival teams, defending the honor of their team verbally (and in some cases physically).

In international soccer fan loyalty is absolute, because teams are identified with towns, states, and ultimately nations. A referee who makes a call against the home team in some of the more rabid soccer countries is literally risking his life. In this country, fan loyalty is usually expressed in a less extreme way. Perhaps the ultimate baseball fan is Jonathan Schwartz, the writer and radio announcer, who admits that he has spent over fifteen thousand dollars on long-distance phone calls so that he can hear the Boston Red Sox play games from anywhere in the country or in the world.

Probably only a minority of sports-watchers at any given time are true fans in the sense I am talking about. There is no question, however, that you will enjoy almost any game more if you identify at least to some extent with one of the teams, and the more you know about that team, the more exciting the game will probably be, no matter how your chosen team is doing.

ROOTING FOR A TEAM

The easiest way to pick a team to root for is to go with your territorial instincts and start by watching a local college or pro team. (By local I don't necessarily mean from your own town, though that is probably easiest; a state team often draws the loyalties of everyone in the state.)

Lindsey Nelson, former announcer for the New York Mets, advises all new fans to "memorize the players' numbers and read everything you can about your favorite players." That way, when you see the team play it won't be a mob of faceless men but real people whom you already know something about. One of the most satisfying aspects of being a fan is being able to pick out your favorite players and note—or predict—what they do in a given situation. For example, if your baseball team is down by one run in the bottom of the ninth and Resnick is about to come up, it can add to the excitement of the moment if you know that this man is a good hitter in clutch situations and is likely to get the team out of trouble.

Of course you do not have to be an avid follower of one particular team to enjoy a sport, but it still helps to favor one over the other, especially during those times when everyone you know is glued to the tube and you decide you might as well join them. When I'm watching sports with friends or just to pass the time, I usually try to find some arbitrary way to make myself care about which team wins. The tried and true method is to root for the underdog, though I have a friend who perversely always roots for the favorite (and usually gloats a lot). If you've been reading the sports pages, maybe you know that a member of the team is from your hometown or college, and this can be just the edge that will keep you hoping his team will win. Now that I'm well into my thirties, I have a surefire method of picking which football team to watch. Since most sports figures are considered over the hill by their late twenties or early thirties, I always go with the team that has the oldest quarterback. The result of this is that for the last two years I've been something of a fan of the Dallas Cowboys (hated by many people because they have been so good for so many years) because their quarterback, Roger Staubach, is 37 years old. An added plus is that he was playing football for Navy during the years when I was in college.

When you're first becoming interested in a sport, much of the jargon and many of the names may be an unintelligible jumble. But you may find that with no effort on your part understanding will sneak up on you. Something of that sort happened to me, and it turned me literally overnight into a baseball fan. For years I had more or less ignored sports (after that bitterly disappointing loss in basketball), particularly and perversely baseball, because all my relatives were baseball fanatics. Then one week I took a long auto trip through New York State and couldn't get anything clearly on the radio but New York Mets' baseball games. Suddenly, everything clicked, and I actually understood all that jargon I'd been hearing all my life. The week after I arrived back in town I went to a game in person and was hooked. As any of my friends can tell you, I haven't been the same since.

Going to a game in person, particularly with a clued-in friend, is of course one of the best ways to get to know a team, and this is how many youngsters become experts on their favorite sports. After all, nobody is born knowing all about basketball, baseball, soccer. When you attend a game, not only will other nearby people be able to answer some of your questions, but you will get a sense of the totality of the game. You will also have a chance to get a close look at the players, seeing how they react even when they aren't in action.

Once you become devoted to a team or sport, you will want to read as much as you can about your team and about the sport itself. There are many nontechnical books on sports. Baseball seems to have the largest amount of pure literature devoted to it (as opposed to books strictly about the sport). The sports section in any library contains many biographies of sports heroes past and present, and there are in addition a number of interesting exposés of the sports world from the inside. My favorite is *Ball Four* by Jim Bouton, former Yankee pitcher, who writes with great humor and little tact about his life in the big leagues.

Novels with a sports setting have always been popular, and an increasing number of them are being made into movies. Baseball stories, again, predominate, from such classics as *You Know Me, Al* by Ring Lardner to modern works such as *The Natural* by Bernard Malamud and *The Great American Novel* by Philip Roth. *Bang the Drum Slowly*, by Mark Harris, was made into an excellent movie a number of years ago, and a series of movies about a children's baseball team, *The Bad News Bears*, continues in popularity. *The*

Year the Yankees Lost the Pennant, by Douglass Wallop, was transformed into a long-running Broadway musical, *Damn Yankees,* as well as a movie. (For more books on baseball, see Selected Bibliography.) Recent football novels that were made into movies include *Semi-Tough,* by Dan Jenkins, and *North Dallas Forty,* by Peter Gent.

The other sports have not received quite as much attention as settings for drama, but *Inside Moves,* a novel with a focus on basketball, by Todd Walton, has been highly acclaimed by critics, and the famous suspense writer Emma Lathen wrote a mystery with a hockey setting called *Murder Without Icing.* Reading such books and watching sports-oriented movies not only add to your understanding of a sport, but you will undoubtedly get much more out of the work itself if you know something about the sport to begin with. The first time I saw *Slap Shot* I walked out in the middle, mostly because I had no idea what was going on. The second time I saw it (on cable television) I had already become a hockey convert, and I laughed so hard I had trouble catching all the dialogue.

BETTING ON SPORTS

I must admit at the outset that I have some misgivings about discussing betting. I have a personal aversion to gambling in any form, and particularly any betting that involves large amounts of money, which much sports betting does. However, sports betting, both that which is legal (as at racetracks) and illegal (betting on all sports through "bookmakers" or "bookies," men who make a living processing bets), is a gigantic industry in this country, with profits reputedly over $40 billion a year. Some people make their living as professional sports bettors, while others bet simply to pick up a little spare cash or as a way of affirming their support for a team. I have mentioned earlier the "morning line," which is published in many newspapers, and which is simply a bettor's guide to all the major sports that are happening on a given day (see page 35). And, although I can't endorse them, there are published guides on all aspects of sports betting, from finding a bookie to making use of the line. For many people, however, making a small bet with a friend or taking part in an office pool are simply ways to heighten interest in a game. There are many different kinds of betting pools, each with variations. For example, just before the finals of a championship in basketball, you might enter a "team pool," which works as follows: You and a group of people (totaling the number of teams in the play-off) each put a small amount of money into the pool. Then each person draws a slip of paper with the name of one of the teams on it. Whoever holds the slip with the name of the team that ultimately wins the championship wins all the money.

In the baseball World Series you may be asked to join an "inning pool." For this to work best, you need nine people, each of whom, after putting money in the pool, draws a slip of paper with the number of one of the nine innings. The winner of the money is the person who holds the slip for the inning in which the winning run is scored. Similar stratagems can be worked out for the other sports, with the slips of paper corresponding to the segment of the game in which the winning goal is scored in soccer, hockey, or football.

You don't even need to bet on a particular game or team. Two men I know always have a ten-dollar bet at the beginning of the baseball season over which league will ultimately win the World Series six months later!

COLLECTING

Once you have become a fan, you may want to display your team loyalty visibly. The most obvious way to do this is to get a T-shirt or hat emblazoned with the name of your team and wear it to all games (even those you watch on television).

This can cause problems, of course. I happen to be a fan of the New York Islanders hockey team and the New York Mets baseball team, both of which are stationed in Long Island. They are generally scorned by my neighbors and friends in Manhattan, who are all die-hard Rangers (hockey) and Yankees (baseball) fans. After a great deal of searching I finally managed to buy an Islanders jersey, which I wore to a party one night, only to have friends refuse to speak to me unless I went home and changed. On the first day of spring in 1979 I wore my Mets T-shirt to go shopping and found myself involved in a number of discussions with perfect strangers, who wanted me to know that the Mets were going to be even worse this year than last (an opinion with which I was, sadly, in agreement), and that I ought to get wise and watch the Yankees. (One man, though, told me quietly that he too was a Mets fan, but would never admit it in public.)

Beyond wearable items, you may want to save programs of games, team yearbooks, buttons, or a number of other sports-oriented objects. The ins and outs of sports collecting and the potential value of many items are detailed in *The Sports Collectors Bible*, by Bert Randolph Sugar.

If you want to collect in a casual way, the easiest place to start is with sports cards, the best known and most widely distributed of which are baseball cards. These are nothing more than small cardboard photographs of players, with the man's history and statistics printed on the back. Sports cards are sold either in separate packets or sometimes as part of a package with bubble gum.

Baseball cards have been published for many years and are updated each year with all the current players. Cards from previous years are in some cases extremely rare, and some people collect them for their potential value. Most fans, however, collect them for fun. Probably the most avid card collectors are children, but a number of adults I know also collect them. The goal usually is to get a complete set of all the players on your team. Since the cards are packaged randomly, this is not easy to do without spending large amounts of money, so the best idea is to compare cards with friends and trade for the cards you need.

My friend Jack Shanahan told me about his experiences as a child "flipping" baseball cards, which is a kind of competition, something like playing marbles. First, you and a friend look at each other's collection and decide which cards you want. Now you take turns "flipping" your cards, or tossing them between thumb and forefinger toward a designated target (such as the edge of a wall or a line drawn on the ground). You take turns flipping one card at a time, and when each of you has flipped a card, the card that has arrived closest to the target is the winner. The successful flipper pockets both cards and the next round begins. It should be noted here that self-styled serious collectors never engage in this practice; they maintain that it damages and thus devalues the cards.

You needn't spend a cent to be a sports collector, of course. For example, I have a collection in my head of colorful names and nicknames of sports figures. I began this collection when a friend and I realized that there seem to be certain kinds of names that only go with certain sports. For example, while a person named Rejean Houle could only be a hockey player (because so many of them are French Canadian), there is something about the name Thurman Munson that immediately suggests baseball. (I was quite excited when the Mets brought up a rookie named Lee Mazzilli a few years ago, because it seemed to me that the name alone had superstar potential for baseball.) And what, for example, could men named Chris Hanburger or Jack Ham possible be except football linebackers (respectively for the Washington Redskins and Pittsburgh Steelers)?

Although all sports attract colorful nicknames, pro basketball seems to possess the most imagination in this respect, with fanciful, sometimes beautiful appellations that suggest the grace of the sport. My favorite nickname is that of a Harlem Globetrotter, a team that does not play in the NBA, but is professional in every other respect and gives exhibitions all over the world—Meadowlark Lemmon. Other appealing basketball nicknames include Marvin "The Human Eraser" Webster (who is so called because his defensive rebounds supposedly "erase" the opposing team's scoring chances), Earl "The Pearl" Monroe, and Fred "Downtown" Brown (who hits from "downtown," or far from the basket). In football, Robert Newhouse, a fullback for the Dallas Cowboys, is nicknamed "The Human Fireplug," but I have not been able to find out why.

So far I haven't collected many soccer names, perhaps because the sport is too new in this country, or because the nicknames are not easy to identify with. Franz Beckenbauer, the great Cosmos star, is nicknamed "The Kaiser," for example. The practice of some South American players to be known by one name only is appealing and may catch on here as more South Americans are imported to play on NASL teams. What, after all, could be a more perfect and recognizable name for the greatest soccer player of all time than the musical nickname "Pelé"?

Baseball, probably because it has been around so long, has a long history of great nicknames. In fact, the lyrics of a popular song in the sixties, "Van Lingle Mungo" by David Frischberg, consisted of nothing but names of baseball players, starting with the title. I have read through the baseball record books with fascination, imagining exciting games with the great players of the past, such as Oyster Burns, a slugger in the 1890s, and his contemporaries Candy LaChance, a catcher, and Stuffy McInnis, who played shortstop and first base. And how I wish I could have watched at least a few innings pitched by Lefty Grove in the thirties or Preacher Roe in the fifties. My personal favorite, though, pitched way back at the turn of the century. His lifetime ERA of 2.06 belies his nickname: Three Finger Brown.

I might add that some names are collectible because they are the opposite of apt. I was disappointed, for example, when the Yankees traded their infielder Mickey Klutts, and followed with interest the career of the pro basketball player Eugene Short. Of course I don't mean to make fun of any of these men or their name or nickname, but there is something about sports that seems to attract colorful, musical, or simply unusual names.

MAGIC

A true fan of sports is familiar with the wide variety of magic used in watching spectator sports. If you have ever followed a team, you may have used such magic without realizing that you did so. By magic I mean the attempt to influence the outcome of a game by your own personal actions. This may involve always wearing the same clothes to a game because the first time you did it your team won; or it may mean sitting in a certain position if the last time your team scored a touchdown you were sitting in that position.

My friend Nan and I found a form of magic that apparently ensured the Yankees' win over the Boston Red Sox during the one-game postseason play-off for the American League East championship in 1978. (As the Mets were long since out of the competition, I of course followed the remaining team from my city.) At a crucial point during the game we found that all went well as long as we took turns watching each pitch delivered by the Yankee reliever Rich ("Goose") Gossage: not only did this seem to help Gossage's control, but it spared each of us that few seconds of unbearable tension watching the drama unfold.

Jonathan Schwartz, who was rooting for Boston as feverishly as we were for the Yankees during that game, described the magic he used in an article in *Sports Illustrated:* "As . . . the first batter approached the plate I said out loud to no one, 'If Torrez gets Rivers right here, the Red Sox will win.'" Rivers got on base, and Schwartz continued, "'If Torrez gets out of this with only one run, the Red Sox have a shot.'"

And so it went for the entire game for the hapless Schwartz, whose magic was apparently not as strong as that used by Nan and me.

HOW TO STAY WITH A ROTTEN TEAM

Okay, you're a fan. You give your life's blood and sweat to this team that . . . never wins! Or that used to be great but has fallen from grace with little hope for a comeback. What do you do? Do you become a fair-weather fan, or do you stay with the team?

In my opinion, the answer to this question depends a great deal on *why* the team is not winning. Take the New York Mets, who were a special case to begin with. An expansion team, the Mets were the worst team in baseball during their first years, committing so many mistakes from such a profound lack of talent that fans went out to root for them precisely because they were so bad. And then, due to some good draft picks and their farm system, the Mets suddenly became a good team and won the World Series once and the National League East title twice. (Admittedly these wins were in large part due to the phenomenal success of their pitching staff, at that time the best in baseball.)

Unfortunately, the man who controlled the purse strings for the Mets didn't want to spend any money. Also, in the opinion of many fans, the owners didn't want any players who failed to conform to the Met "image," which was, apparently, humorless, conservative, and colorless. Over a period of a few years, then, the championship team was dismantled player by player until very little talent was left, and the team once again plunged to the depths of mediocrity.

This time, however, the ticket sales plunged with the team, because this was no longer a bunch of lovable klutzes but rather a formerly good team that had been destroyed by a seemingly uncaring management. I too deserted the team after the disastrous trade of the (then) best pitcher in baseball, Tom Seaver, who went to Cincinnati because of a salary dispute, and the simultaneous trade of the great slugger Dave Kingman, who always added excitement to a game. He would either hit three home runs or set another record for consecutive strikeouts each time he played. When these men were traded, I finally rebelled. I could no longer watch a team made up of a bunch of people I didn't know—because, after all, continuity is part of being a fan of a team. But I continue to follow all my former favorite players: reliever Tug McGraw (now with the Phillies); slugger Rusty Staub (now playing for the Montreal Expos); pitchers Seaver (Cincinnati Reds), Jon Matlack (Texas Rangers), and Jerry Koosman (Minnesota Twins); shortstop Tim Foli (Pittsburgh Pirates). . . . I could go on and on but I'm afraid I'll start crying. And I have to admit that I maintain my interest in the Mets—at least through the spring season, before they start playing just as badly as they did the year before.

Some teams are perversely followed by their fans even though they seem never to get anywhere. The Chicago White Sox, for example, have not won the World Series since 1917, and yet their fans are among the most loyal in all of baseball, claiming, as one fan did, "You have to really suffer to be a White Sox fan."

The Boston teams, particularly baseball and hockey, have in recent years picked up a reputation for "folding" or simply failing to live up to their potential in the closing games of a season. In fact, after Boston's loss to the Yankees in that one-game play-off in 1978, a joke made the rounds that the Red Sox had been bought by a Philippine consortium that was planning to rename the team the "Manila Folders."

Finally, though, if you're really a fan you stay with the team because it's *your* team, bringing us back to the sense of loyalty I discussed at the beginning of this chapter. A good example is the New York Giants football team, which has not had a winning season in many years and yet which continues to hold its many loyal followers. In the 1978 season, after a really disastrous year that started out with some promise, a number of season ticketholders staged a protest against the management of the team by publicly burning their tickets in the parking lot of Giants Stadium. And yet . . . Giant fans remain Giant fans. As an acquaintance I met during a game said sadly, "Watching the Giants is like watching a morality play. You know how it will end—with the Giants losing. The suspense is just that you don't know exactly *how* they will lose." Equally philosophical is my friend Diane, a Red Sox fan who, in spite of her team's many eleventh-hour defeats, describes her devotion thusly: "My family, right or wrong."

SELECTED
BIBLIOGRAPHY

The following books are the ones I have found to be most useful and accessible to fans of all levels.

SPORTS IN GENERAL

Bradley, Bill. *Life on the Run.* New York: Bantam, 1977. Paper, $1.95.
This thoughtful, well-written book describes the life of a pro athlete from the inside. Although Bradley played basketball, his book shows what it's like to be a pro in any sport—the training, life on the road, heartbreaks, and glory.

Gardner, Paul. *Nice Guys Finish Last.* New York: Universe Books, 1975. $8.95.
A survey of American sports from a British point of view. Fascinating, readable, and refreshingly inconoclastic.

Koppett, Leonard. *The New York Times Guide to Spectator Sports.* New York: Quadrangle, 1971. $7.95.
Excellent basic guide to all spectator sports.

Merchant, Larry. *Ringside Seat at the Circus.* New York: Holt, Rinehart & Winston, 1976. $7.95.
Terrific, witty essays on all aspects of sports.

Michener, James A. *Sports in America.* New York: Random House, 1976.
$12.50.
A good overview of the place of sports in American life.

Webster's Sport Dictionary. Springfield, Mass: G. & C. Merriam Company,
1976. $8.95.
This excellent book belongs in every sports lover's library. Not only
does it define concisely almost every term for any sport you can think of, but
it gives a mini-guide to the rules of most sports, including cricket, rugby,
and trapshooting, to name only three. Excellent illustrations.

BASEBALL

Koppett, Leonard. *All About Baseball.* New York: Quadrangle, 1973. $9.95.
This is by far the best guide to the ins and outs of baseball strategy.

Angell, Roger. *The Summer Game.* New York: Popular Library, 1972.
Paper, $1.50.
A series of beautifully written essays, which originally appeared in
The New Yorker, celebrating the fun, excitement, and drama of baseball.

Holst, Spencer. "The Institute for the Foul Ball" in *Spencer Holst Stories.*
New York: Berkley Windhover, 1977. Paper, $2.95.
This long short story cannot be described, but it's must reading for
anyone who loves baseball.

Kahn, Roger. *The Boys of Summer.* New York: New American Library,
1973. Paper, $1.75.
A nostalgic look back at the good old days of baseball, when the New
York teams were the Yankees, Giants, and Brooklyn Dodgers.

BASKETBALL

Sullivan, George. *This Is Pro Basketball.* New York: Dodd, Mead & Company, 1977. $6.50.
A clearly written, interesting guide to watching basketball.

Klein, Dave. *A Thinking Person's Guide to Pro Basketball.* New York: Grosset & Dunlap (Temp Books), 1978. Paper, $1.95.

Not quite as helpful as the other "Thinking" guides to sports, this book would be best for anyone who already knows and loves the sport.

FOOTBALL

Zimmerman, Paul. *A Thinking Man's Guide to Pro Football.* New York: Warner, 1972. Paper, $1.50.

A very thorough, well-written book that will tell you just about everything you need to know to appreciate pro football.

HOCKEY

Spencer, David and Barbara. *The Pocket Hockey Encyclopedia.* New York: Charles Scribner's Sons, 1976. Paper, $4.95.

This book is a must for any hockey fan. It not only defines all hockey terms, but includes mini-biographies of the great players, gives information on all teams past and present, lists all the rules of hockey, and as an added bonus includes fascinating bits of hockey lore under such entries as "Influenza epidemic 1919" and "Riots."

Eskenazi, Gerald. *A Thinking Man's Guide to Pro Hockey.* E.P. Dutton & Co., Inc., 1972. $6.95.

Excellent, readable guide for fans of all levels.

SOCCER

Kane, Basil. *How to Play Soccer.* New York: Grosset & Dunlap, 1975. Paper, $2.50.

This is an excellent basic guide to soccer, with concise explanations of the rules and skills needed to play.

Rote, Kyle, Jr., with Basil Kane. *Complete Book of Soccer.* New York: Simon & Schuster, 1978. $9.95.

For the soccer buff, this book has everything: rules, history, team statistics, and a good overview of international soccer.

PERIODICALS

Sport. Published monthly by MVP Sports, Inc. $1.00 per issue, $9.00 for a one-year subscription.

A very readable magazine with sometimes lengthy, uncensored, in-depth coverage of all aspects of pro and college sports. There is virtually no coverage of women's sports.

The Sporting News. Published weekly by The Sporting News, P.O. Box 56, St. Louis, MO 63166. $1.25 per issue, $20.95 for a one-year subscription.

For the hard-core fan, this tabloid gives in-depth details of all important games, endless stats, trivia, commentary, and profiles of sports figures. Virtually no coverage of women's sports.

The Sporting News also publishes a number of inexpensive booklets on the team sports, ranging from rule books to seasonal guides. For more information, write to the publisher at the above address.

Sports Illustrated. Published weekly by Time, Inc. $1.25 per issue, $25.00 for a one-year subscription.

Breathtaking photos and pithy, mostly short articles on all aspects of just about all sports. Occasional in-depth investigative reports of controversial issues in sports. Coverage of women's sports for the most part token, with heavy reliance on cheesecake-type photographs. Occasional fiction and true-life adventure stories.

In addition to the above, there are several periodicals, mostly seasonal, devoted to each major sport. Particularly good is *Soccer World,* published by World Publications, Inc.

INDEX